EAST–CENTRAL EUROPE AFTER THE COLD WAR

East-Central Europe after the Cold War

Poland, the Czech Republic, Slovakia and Hungary in Search of Security

Andrew Cottey
Lecturer, Department of Peace Studies
University of Bradford

First published in Great Britain 1995 by
MACMILLAN PRESS LTD
Houndmills, Basingstoke, Hampshire RG21 6XS
and London
Companies and representatives
throughout the world

A catalogue record for this book is available
from the British Library.

ISBN 0–333–63929–4

First published in the United States of America 1995 by
ST. MARTIN'S PRESS, INC.,
Scholarly and Reference Division,
175 Fifth Avenue,
New York, N.Y. 10010

ISBN 0–312–12701–4

Library of Congress Cataloging-in-Publication Data
Cottey, Andrew.
East-Central Europe after the Cold War : Poland, the Czech
Republic, Slovakia and Hungary in search of security / Andrew
Cottey.
p.   cm.
Includes bibliographical references and index.
ISBN 0–312–12701–4
1. Europe, Eastern—Politics and government—1989–   2. National
security—Europe, Eastern.   I. Title.
DJK51.C687   1995
355'.0033047—dc20   95–8652
                                                          CIP

10   9   8   7   6   5   4   3   2   1
04   03   02   01   00   99   98   97   96   95

Printed and bound in Great Britain by
Antony Rowe Ltd, Chippenham, Wiltshire

For my parents and Maeve

Contents

List of Maps and Tables

MAPS

TABLES

Preface

This book is based on PhD research undertaken in the Department of Peace Studies at the University of Bradford. I am grateful to the Economic and Social Research Council for providing financial support for that research. I am also grateful to the many people in East–Central Europe who gave generously of their time in allowing me to interview them. I would especially like to thank my colleagues and friends in the Department of Peace Studies for providing a friendly and stimulating working environment. In particular, I would like to thank Owen Greene, who acted as my PhD supervisor, for his support and encouragement. Finally, but most importantly, I wish to thank my parents and Maeve, who made the completion of this book possible.

ANDREW COTTEY

The author and publishers are grateful to the following for permission to reproduce copyright material: The International Institute for Strategic Studies for Tables 4.1, 4.3, 5.1, 5.3 and 6.2 and for the map on p. xi; Radio Free Europe/Radio Liberty, Inc. for Tables 3.1, 5.3 and 6.1; The Economist Intelligence Unit for Table 4.1; The Bulletin of the Atomic Scientists and The Natural Resources Defense Council for Table 4.1; The Stockholm International Peace Research Institute for Tables 4.2, 5.2 and 6.3; The Institute for Defense and Disarmament Studies for Table 5.3; The Guardian/Observer for Table 5.3; The Western European Union Institute for Security Studies for Map 6.1 p. 102 The Orion Publishing Group Ltd for Map 4.1 on p. 43. Every effort has been made to contact all the copyright-holders, but if any have been inadvertently omitted the publishers will be pleased to make the necessary arrangement at the earliest opportunity.

East–Central Europe

Source: J. Zielonka, *Security in Central Europe*, Adelphi Paper 272 (London: Brassey's for the International Institute of Strategic Studies, Autumn 1992) p. 2.

1 Introduction

Since the emergence of Germany and Russia as Europe's dominant powers in the eighteenth and nineteenth centuries, the countries of East–Central Europe – Poland, the Czech lands, Slovakia and Hungary – have been of central importance to the continent's balance of power.[1] In the eighteenth and nineteenth centuries the region was the focus of competition and cooperation between the Prussian, Austro-Hungarian and Russian empires. In the twentieth century it has played a key role in both of the two world wars and the Cold War. The fate of East–Central Europe, in short, has been closely intertwined with the peace and security of Europe as a whole.

In 1989, after forty years of Soviet domination, the peoples of East–Central Europe regained control of their countries. The revolutions of 1989 were rapidly followed by democratic elections, the formation of non-communist governments and the collapse of the post-war Soviet alliance system. For the first time since the late-1940s, the countries of East–Central Europe had the chance to pursue genuinely independent foreign and security policies. Given the region's geo-strategic importance and its potential as a focus of wider European conflict – particularly over spheres of influence, borders and national minorities – the security policy choices of the new East–Central European governments would have major implications for the post-Cold War European security order.

After the revolutions of 1989, Poland, Czechoslovakia and Hungary emerged as a distinct East–Central European group – the Visegrad group (named after the meeting of their leaders in the Hungarian town of Visegrad in February 1991). Domestically, they were the best placed of the East European states to make successful transitions to democratic politics and market economies. As a result, they were also the primary Eastern candidates for integration with Western political and economic institutions, particularly the European Community (EC). Internationally, they lay in the geo-strategically crucial region between the uniting Germany and the unstable Soviet Union. Reflecting their shared concerns, they gradually initiated a process of regional cooperation.

Since 1989, the countries of East–Central Europe have also faced broadly similar security concerns: the withdrawal of Soviet troops from their territory, the dismantlement of the Warsaw Pact, the implications of German unification, instability on their Eastern and Southern borders

1

as the Soviet Union and Yugoslavia disintegrated, restructuring their relations with the West, and the need to reform armed forces inherited from the Soviet era. This book examines how the countries of East–Central Europe responded to these challenges, from the revolutions of 1989 to the autumn of 1994. The book highlights the central national security policy choices made by the East–Central European states and analyses the forces which shaped those choices. The book primarily provides an analytical history of the East–Central European states' security policies since the end of the Cold War. It also, however, examines the overall dynamics of post-Cold War East–Central European security and assesses the position of the East–Central European states in the emerging European security order of the 1990s.

The book focuses on what may be described as political–military security, i.e., issues which relate to the prospects for armed conflict and for peace (in the sense of the absence of such conflict).[2] Central to the book, however, is a recognition that the prospects for armed conflict are not determined primarily by military factors.[3] The prospects for peace are fundamentally affected by a variety of non-military factors. The character of the governments in the countries of East–Central Europe and their neighbours, issues of ethnic minority rights, possible conflicts over borders, and disputes over economic and environmental issues are examined wherever they relate to the prospects for peace in the region or affect the security policy choices of the East–Central European governments.

The book focuses primarily on the national security policies of the East–Central European states, in the sense of examining the decisions and activities of their central governments.[4] While the countries of East–Central Europe face difficult domestic transitions, compared to their Balkan and former-Soviet neighbours they are internally relatively 'strong' states, where the control of national security policy remains largely in the hands of central governments and state structures.[5] Even in the case of the break-up of Czechoslovakia at the end of 1992, security policy and issues remained largely under the control first of the Czechoslovak government and then of the Czech and Slovak national governments, rather than becoming devolved to the sub-state level. The relative internal cohesion of the East–Central European states also means that, to a much greater extent than elsewhere in post-communist Europe, their primary security problems are external rather than internal. This book therefore focuses on external security issues and policies, rather than internal ones. The formulation of state policy, however, is a complex process, involving a wide variety of different groups, whose influence and role may change over time.[6] Where relevant, the impact of different branches of government, political parties, public opinion, the military and ethnic minorities on national security policy and issues is examined. Indeed, such factors have been central to the development of post-Cold War East–Central European security, since the process of democratization has played a pivotal role in the transformation of the East–Central European states' security policies.

In order to place the analysis in context, Chapter 2 examines the character of the post-Cold War European security environment, arguing that the dominant features are the existence of a security community – a 'zone of peace' where the likelihood of violent conflict is negligible – in Western Europe; a 'zone of instability' in Eastern Europe and the former-Soviet Union, where violent conflict is a real possibility; and a multi-institutional European security architecture comprised primarily of the European Union (EU), the North Atlantic Treaty Organizations (NATO) and the Conference on Security and Cooperation in Europe (CSCE). Chapter 2 concludes by noting that the central security predicament of the East–Central European states results from their position on the boundary between the Western zone of peace and the Eastern zone of instability. Chapter 3 explores the strategic security policy options open to the countries of East-Central Europe in the post-Cold War era, arguing that these were a reformed alliance with the Soviet Union or Russia, neutrality, regional security cooperation within Eastern European, pan-European security based on the CSCE, integration with the West, a return to a shifting realpolitik balance of power policy, or reliance on national defence.

Chapters 4, 5, and 6 examine in detail how Poland, the Czech Republic and Slovakia, and Hungary have reformed their national security policies since the end of the Cold War, exploring the strategic choices they have made and analyzing the way in which changing domestic and international circumstances have shaped those choices. Chapter 7 analyses the position of the East–Central European states in the European security order of the 1990s, highlighting the way in which they emerged as a distinct regional group with an informal special relationship with the West which makes them the primary Eastern candidates for membership of the EU and NATO. Chapter 8 concludes with an overall assessment of the evolution of East–Central European security since the end of the Cold War, exploring the factors which have shaped the radical transformation of East–Central European security which has occurred since 1989 and assessing the prospects for continued stability in the region.

2 The New Europe

The East European revolutions of 1989 radically altered Europe's security landscape. By early 1990, it was clear that the Soviet bloc was disintegrating. With the collapse of the German Democratic Republic (GDR), German unification became inevitable. The unexpected and rapid collapse of the bi-polar post-war order raised fundamental questions. Would the end of the Cold War herald a new era of peace and cooperation between East and West? Or might Europe return to its historic pattern of conflict and violence? What implications would German unification have? What were the prospects for democracy in Eastern Europe and the Soviet Union and what impact would developments within these countries have on European security? With the end of the Soviet bloc, was NATO redundant? If not, what role should the Atlantic Alliance play? Had the time come for the European Community (EC) to assume a greater security role? Alternatively, was the time ripe to implement the old idea of collective security, perhaps through the Conference on Security and Cooperation in Europe (CSCE)? This chapter reviews the main features of the new European security environment as they have emerged since 1989, highlighting the implications for the countries of East–Central Europe.

GERMAN UNIFICATION

By the spring of 1990, it was increasingly clear that German unification was inevitable.[1] The opening of the Berlin wall in November 1989 had triggered an exodus of people from East to West Germany, resulting in the collapse of the East German state. West German Chancellor Helmut Kohl proposed the development of confederal structures between the two states leading to eventual unification. In Ottawa, in February 1990, the 'two-plus-four' formula – the two Germanies plus the four wartime allies (the United States, the Soviet Union, Great Britain and France) – was agreed upon for negotiations on the future security status of Germany. The victory of the Alliance for Germany coalition in the GDR's March 1990 elections confirmed popular support for rapid unification. Within the Federal Republic, Chancellor Kohl's Christian Democrat-led government supported continued EC and NATO

4

membership. In April Chancellor Kohl and French President François Mitterrand, seeking to tie Germany closer to West European political structures, requested an EC inter-governmental conference on 'political union', including the framing of a common foreign and security policy. The proposal was endorsed by the EC's European Council at meetings in April and June 1990, with the conference to begin in December. German Foreign Minister Hans-Dietrich Genscher proposed a 'GDR in NATO, not NATO in GDR', whereby Soviet troops would remain in the GDR for a transitional period, with no allied NATO forces deployed in the former-GDR after this. The 'Genscher plan' rapidly gained the support of the West German government and the major Western powers. In order to reassure the Soviet Union, the West signalled its willingness to reform NATO and strengthen the CSCE.

Initially, the Soviet Union opposed the 'Genscher Plan', arguing that a united Germany should be neutral.[2] Meeting Chancellor Kohl at Zheleznovodsk in the Soviet Union in July 1990, however, Soviet President Mikhail Gorbachev accepted that a united Germany could be a member of NATO and that all Soviet troops be withdrawn by the end of 1994. In return, Kohl promised substantial aid, a Soviet–German friendship treaty and constraints on Germany's armed forces. After this, the 'two-plus-four' negotiations proceeded rapidly. On 12 September, in Moscow, the *Treaty on the Final Settlement with Respect to Germany* was signed. Under the treaty Germany rejected any territorial claims, confirmed its non-nuclear status, agreed to limit its future armed forces to 370,000 personnel and that only German forces be stationed on the territory of the former GDR, and was free to join any alliance.[3] On 3 October 1990 Germany was unified, with the six *lander* of the GDR joining the Federal Republic.

In terms of wider European security, the result of German unification was an informal grand bargain, fundamentally shaping the post-Cold War order.[4] The united Germany would remain a member of both the EC and NATO. The EC's members had committed themselves to establishing a political union, including a common foreign and security policy. NATO would remain intact, at least in the short-to-medium term, tying the United States into European security. At the same time, the CSCE would be given a strengthened security role. Although much remained uncertain, the central features of the new European security order were crystallizing.

THE WESTERN SECURITY COMMUNITY

One of the defining features of the new European security order is the existence of a 'security community' – a 'zone of peace', where war is inconceivable – amongst the states of Western Europe and North America.[5] A security community may be said to exist where 'there is a real assurance that the members of that community will not fight each other physically, but will settle their disputes in some other way'.[6] Such a situation has developed between the states of Western Europe and North America since the end of the Second World War. Countries, which for centuries have fought wars against each other, have now reached a state of relations where war between them is extremely unlikely, if not inconceivable.

A number of inter-related factors have underpinned the development of the Western security community. The emergence of the Soviet Union and the United States as dominant powers and the bi-polar division of the continent encouraged cooperation amongst the Western states. The 'Soviet threat' forced them to unite to balance Soviet power. The emergence of the United States as a hegemon within the West allowed it to act as an 'organizing power'.[7] The institutionalization of cooperation, through such bodies as NATO and the EC, reduced uncertainties about each others' behaviour and provided mechanisms for the peaceful resolution of disputes. Post-war cooperation facilitated the development of a pattern of 'complex interdependence', characterized by a multiplicity of cross-cutting ties betwen societies, reducing the primacy of military security issues and increasing the costs of the use of force.[8]

The development of relatively stable, prosperous, democratic states throughout the West also contributed to the emergence of the Western security community.[9] Internally stable states may be less prone both to intervention from other states and to attempt to resolve their internal problems through external aggression.[10] Moreover, there is empirical evidence that democratic states do not go to war with each other.[11] In democracies, 'national aspirations for power are fenced in by concepts of legitimacy, which act as powerful constraints on international behaviour', particularly the use of force.[12] Thus, amongst a group of established democracies, the emergence of the non-use of force as an established norm may be possible.[13] It may be argued that what has emerged in the West since the Second World War is an 'international society'[14] – a system of common rules and institutions for the conduct of relations – where the non-use of force and the peaceful resolution of conflicts are now the dominant norms.

With the demise of the Soviet threat, some analysts argued that the Western security community might fragment, making war once again a possibility within the West.[15] The Western security community, however, seems deeply rooted. The many factors which led to its emergence seem likely to sustain it in the post-Cold War era.[16] The existence of the Western security community, furthermore, alters the entire pattern and context of European security. For the first time in European history, the major Western powers are extremely unlikely to go to war with each other or to engage in competitive alliance formation elsewhere in Europe. The West's relative political stability, economic prosperity, military strength and cohesion also gives it very great influence over the future direction of European security. The existence of the Western security community, therefore, seems likely to preclude a return to the type of Europe-wide multipolar, balance of power system which existed before the Second World War and to make the West the continent's dominant political, economic and military force.[17]

INSTABILITY IN THE EAST

The second defining feature of the post-Cold War European security order has been the emergence of a 'zone of instability' in the East. By 1990, the international structures of the Soviet era were collapsing. What forms of relations might replace them was far from clear. The countries of the region had embarked on domestic transitions which seemed likely to produce instability for years to come.[18] Old disputes over borders and ethnic minorities were re-emerging. In these circumstances, war (both between and within the states) remained a real possibility – as the conflicts in Yugoslavia, Moldova, Georgia and Nagorno-Karabakh were to show.

By the summer of 1990 Poland, Czechoslovakia and Hungary had freely elected non-communist governments. The East–Central European states, however, found themselves in a vulnerable 'strategic limbo'.[19] They had large numbers of Soviet troops on their territory; remained members of the Warsaw Pact; depended on the Soviet Union for oil, trade and military hardware; and were tied to it by bilateral mutual assistance treaties and links between their armed forces. Although the re-imposition of Soviet control by force seemed unlikely, President Gorbachev was under growing pressure from hardliners arguing that the Soviet Union should retain a sphere of influence in Eastern Europe. By the winter of 1990–91 the Soviet Union was taking a tough stance in talks on troops withdrawals, the dismantling of the Warsaw Pact and new bilateral treaties. Intervention by the Soviet armed forces to suppress secession moves in Lithuania in January 1991 intensified East–Central European concerns. The struggle between reformers and hardliners within the Soviet Union came to a head with the August 1991 coup. The failure of the coup was followed by a softening of the Soviet position towards Eastern Europe, resulting in agreements on troops withdrawals and new bilateral treaties.

The break-up of the Soviet Union at the end of 1991, however, posed new problems for the East–Central European states. Suddenly, they had to develop relations with a series of new and unstable neighbours with whom they had potential disputes over borders and ethnic minorities. In Russia, political struggle between reformers and conservatives continued. In October 1993 President Boris Yeltin's dissolution of the parliament prompted an unsuccessful attempt by conservatives to overthrow his government. A large vote for Vladimir Zhirinovsky's neo-fascist Liberal Democratic Party in the December 1993 parliamentary elections indicated growing support for conservative forces. Russia also increasingly sought to re-establish influence in the former-Soviet Union – the 'near abroad' – and assert a right of veto over East–Central European security. In Belarus, national and reform movements proved relatively weak and the country moved increasingly close to Russia. Ukraine remained divided between Western oriented reformers and Eastern oriented conservatives, whilst worsening economic conditions raised fears of social collapse or civil war. Tensions with Russia over nuclear weapons, control of the Black Sea Fleet, and the Russian-dominated province of Crimea raised fears of possible Russo-Ukrainian conflict. In the Baltic states, the position of the Russian minorities created tensions and potential conflict with Russia.

The East–Central European states faced an equally unstable situation on their Southern borders. In the summer of 1991, tensions over the future of the Yugoslav federation escalated to war between Serbia and Slovenia and Croatia. By the spring of 1992 the war had spread to neighbouring Bosnia. Elsewhere in the Balkans nationalism, authoritarianism economic crises and tensions over borders and ethnic minorities made violent conflict a real possibility.[20] Conflict in the Balkans might spill over into East–Central Europe, particularly Hungary, which had large Hungarian minorities in Serbia and Romania and potential border disputes with both states.

NEW SECURITY 'ARCHITECTURE'

As was noted above, one of the results of German unification was an informal grand bargain, involving the development of the EC into a European political union, including a common foreign and security policy; the reform of NATO; and a strengthened security role for the CSCE. Developments since German unification have confirmed this framework of multiple, overlapping institutions as one of the main features of the new European security landscape.

The European Union

The European Council's June 1990 agreement to convene an Inter-governmental Conference (IGC) on political union resulted in a major debate on the Common Foreign and Security Policy (CFSP) which was to be part of that union.[21] The Maastricht negotiations, which opened in December 1990, polarised between those (led by Britain) wishing NATO to remain the dominant security institution and those (led by France) wishing to give Western Europe a greater security role. Not surprisingly, the Treaty on European Union, agreed in December 1991 and signed in February 1992, was a compromise between the two views. The Treaty, which came into effect, formally creating the European Union (EU), towards the end of 1993, includes a CFSP 'covering all areas of foreign and security policy'.[22] The CFSP, however, remains an inter-governmental process, with key decisions made by consensus. The CFSP also involves 'the eventual framing of a common defence policy, which might in time lead to a common defence'. The Western European Union (WEU) is requested 'to elaborate and implement decisions and actions of the Union which have defence implications'.[23] Since then, the WEU has established a planning cell and made some progress in defining military units available to it.[24] Differences within the EU over the Yugoslav conflict have, however, highlighted the practical problems of implementing the CFSP.[25]

At the same time as 'deepening' their integration, the EC/EU and the WEU also took steps to 'widen'. By early 1995 Austria, Sweden and Finland had joined the EU. More significantly for the countries of East–Central Europe, EC leaders agreed in June 1990 to negotiate association agreements with the East European states. Negotiations with Poland, Czechoslovakia and Hungary opened in December 1990 and the agreements were signed in December 1991. Similarly, the WEU proposed in June 1991 to explore the possibilities for ad hoc ministerial meetings with East European states and in November 1991 invited East European foreign and defence ministers to develop more institutionalized ties with it.[26]

NATO

The end of the Cold War also led to reforms of NATO. This process was begun in the summer of 1990 when NATO leaders, meeting in London, agreed to develop an enhanced political role for the Alliance and a new military strategy.[27] By November 1991 they had agreed on a new 'strategic concept', defining a role for the Alliance in developing dialogue and cooperation with its Eastern neighbours and in preventive diplomacy and crisis management outside the NATO area.[28] The coming to power of the Clinton administration in the United States saw further steps to reform NATO, culminating in the Alliance's January 1994 Brussels summit. The Brussels summit gave 'full support' to the development of a European Security and Defence identity, agreed to make NATO forces available for WEU operations, and endorsed the idea of Combined Joint Task Forces available to both NATO and the WEU.[29]

Most significantly for the countries of East–Central Europe, NATO also began to expand its ties with its Eastern neighbours. At their London summit in June 1990, NATO leaders offered 'the hand of friendship' to Eastern Europe and the Soviet Union through expanded diplomatic liaison and military contacts.[30] In November 1991 NATO went further, creating the North Atlantic Cooperation Council (NACC) as a forum for a 'more institutional relationship of consultation and cooperation'.[31] At the January 1994 Brussels summit, NATO leaders initiated the Partnership for Peace programme (involving expanded participation in NATO activities, consultation if a partner state feels threatened, and joint military planning and exercises) and confirmed that the Alliance remained 'open to membership of other European states'.[32] Despite these developments, however, the future of the Alliance remained uncertain. Doubts persisted about the US commitment to European security. The Yugoslav conflict had provoked deep rifts within the Alliance. Whether, and in what circumstances, NATO membership might be expanded remained unclear.

The CSCE

By early 1990 there was general acceptance that the CSCE should be strengthened.[33] Some, such as German Foreign Minister Hans-Dietrich

Genscher, argued that it should have a 'security council' and military forces at its disposal. The major Western powers, particularly the United States and Britain, however, doubted that the CSCE could be effective and feared that a strong CSCE might undermine NATO. The November 1990 summit, therefore, agreed to the institutionalization of the CSCE, but left it a relatively weak body. Heads of state or government would meet every two years; a Council of Foreign Ministers would meet at least once a year; a Committee of Senior Officials (CSO) would prepare the meetings of the Council and implement its decisions; and a Secretariat, a Conflict Prevention Centre and an office of Free Elections would be established.[34] Decisions, however, continued to be made by consensus.

Meeting in Helsinki in July 1992 CSCE leaders mandated the further development of the body, agreeing on regular consultations in the CSO to provide early warning of conflicts; mechanisms for bringing situations to the CSO's attention; the right of the CSO to recommend measures in relation to conflicts and to authorize peacekeeping operations; and, the creation of a High Commissioner on National Minorities, to provide early warning and action in relation to minority conflicts.[35] In December 1992 CSCE Foreign Ministers agreed to appoint a CSCE secretary-general and to a 'consensus minus two' principle whereby the CSO could impose conciliation on the parties to a conflict.[36] Despite these developments, however, the CSCE's inability to deal with the Yugoslav conflict emphazised the fact that it remained a relatively weak organization.

CONCLUSION: IMPLICATIONS FOR EAST–CENTRAL EUROPE

In order to place the security policy choices open to the new, democratic East–Central European governments in context, this chapter has reviewed the central features of the new European security environment. With the end of the Cold War, the countries of East–Central Europe found themselves on the boundary between the Western security community and the zone of instability to their East and South. Although they were primary candidates for integration with the West, they were not yet part of the Western security community, nor did they have the formal security guarantees embodied in NATO membership or the less formal assurance of EC membership. They remained vulnerable to the unstable situation to their East and South and their prospects for integration with the Western security community were unclear.

In this context, the new East–Central European governments were faced not with any immediate military threats to their national security, but with a diverse and amorphous range of risks and uncertainties. The unification of Germany raised fears of its re-emergence as an independent great power. The unstable situation to the their East and South, however, was their greatest concern. The growing strength of hardliners in the Soviet Union raised fears about how far they might go in attempting to maintain a sphere of influence in Eastern Europe. With the disintegration of the Soviet Union and the onset of the war in the former-Yugoslavia, the East–Central European states faced potential disputes over borders and ethnic minorities with their Eastern and Southern neighbours. Even if they were not directly involved, armed conflicts to their East and South might spill over into East–Central Europe. At the same time, the West's uncertain response to their security predicament raised fears that it might abandon the East–Central European states or subordinate their interests to its relations with Russia.

The new European security environment also had major implications for the security policy options open to the countries of East–Central Europe. The existence of a security community amongst the major Western powers ensured that rather than facing a multipolar European balance of power (as they had done before the Second World War), they faced a situation in which the West as a whole was the continent's dominant force. This largely precluded the development of bilateral alliances with West European states and made the issue of how to align with the West as a whole a central security question. At the same time, the emergence of a complex and evolving multi-institutional European security architecture raised both new opportunities and new uncertainties. Could the East–Central Europeans' emerging relationship with the EU and its CFSP contribute to their security? How might ties with NATO contribute to their security? In what circumstances might they join the Alliance? How far could a strengthened CSCE contribute to their security? In short, the countries of East–Central Europe faced a new, highly uncertain and rapidly changing security environment.

3 Strategic Options for East–Central Europe

When the new, democratic governments came to power in Poland, Czechoslovakia and Hungary in 1989 and 1990, they faced a wide range of security policy options.[1] The primary alternatives open to them were:

- a reformed alliance with the Soviet Union
- neutrality or non-alignment
- regional security cooperation within Eastern Europe
- integration with the West
- pan-European collective or common security through the CSCE
- a realpolitik balance of power policy
- reliance on national defence.

Although not entirely mutually exclusive, these policies represented distinct stragetic directions. Which of these strategic directions the countries of East–Central Europe would pursue remained an open question. This chapter examines these differing options, assessing their possible advantages and disadvantages for the countries of East–Central Europe and exploring the dilemmas and problems involved in each.

A REFORMED SOVIET ALLIANCE

When the new East–Central European governments came to power in 1989 and 1990 the most immediate security policy option open to them was to retain a reformed alliance with the Soviet Union. Such a strategy had at least one central advantage: it would avoid antagonizing the Soviet Union. Given the experience of Hungary in 1956 and Czechoslovakia in 1968, Soviet intervention remained a primary security concern. In the worst case, a precipitate attempt to break Soviet alliance ties might provoke military intervention. Short of this, East–Central Europe's high level of economic dependence on the Soviet Union, the continued presence of Soviet troops in the region and ties between Soviet and East–Central European internal security forces and intelligence services meant that the Soviet Union retained significant leverage.

If provoked, it might use that leverage to undermine the East–Central European state's democratic transitions by cutting crucial economic ties (such as deliveries of oil or gas) or using intelligence and security links to foment political instability.

From mid-1990, conservative forces within the Soviet Union, advocating a continued Soviet sphere of influence in Eastern Europe, gained increasing political power.[2] By the autumn of 1990, the Soviet Union was refusing to reform or dissolve the Warsaw Pact, resulting in the cancellation of the alliance's planned summit.[3] In January 1991 the International Department of the Soviet Communist Party's Central Committee called for the 'neutralization' of 'anti-Soviet tendencies' in Eastern Europe and the use of the region's dependence on Soviet oil and gas 'as an important instrument of our strategy'.[4] In the spring of 1991, the Soviet Union began to press for new bilateral treaties with the states of Eastern Europe, which would include 'security clauses' limiting their foreign and security policy independence. In April Romania became the first East European state to accept the Soviet-proposed treaty (see Table 3.1).

In this context, the possibility of maintaining a reformed alliance with the Soviet Union might be seen as a classical strategy of accommodation with major power interests by small or medium states which cannot compete with larger neighbours in terms of power. Such a strategy might be particularly attractive if it involved accepting Soviet security interests in return for a Soviet commitment not to interfere in the East–Central European states' internal affairs. Such a strategy might also be more attractive if mutual defence commitments were maintained but the character of the alliance was significantly reformed (for example, through the withdrawal of Soviet forces and greater East–Central European military independence). A continued alliance with the Soviet Union might also contribute to East–Central European security by providing guarantees or diplomatic leverage in relation to other security threats or concerns. For Poland and Czechoslovakia, who in 1989–90 still faced potential German claims on their territory, a continued alliance with the Soviet Union might be seen as providing guarantees against such claims or diplomatic leverage in relation to German unification.

Balanced against these factors, however, were strong arguments in favour of breaking Cold War alliance ties with the Soviet Union. The Soviet alliance system involved a complex web of ties, subordinating the East–Central European states' foreign and security policies to Soviet interests: the Warsaw Pact, bilateral mutual assistance treaties, Soviet troops in East–Central Europe, integration of armed forces and close

Table 3.1 *'Security Clauses' under the April 1991 Soviet–Romanian Treaty*

- To 'consider each other . . . in any situation, as friendly states'.
- Not to participate in any circumstances in alliances against each other.
- Not to allow third parties to use their territory (or make communications or infrastructures available to third parties) for aggression against each other.
- Consultations 'without delay' if either party considered a situation threatened its security.
- Regular consultations on international and bilateral security issues.
- Development of cooperation and exchanges in the military field.
- Cooperation in European security and arms control structures.

Source: V. Socor, 'The Romanian–Soviet Friendship Treaty and Its Regional Implications', *Report on Eastern Europe*, 2 (3 May 1991), pp. 26–7. Copyright © 1991 by RFE/RL, Inc.

ties between internal security forces.[5] These ties might be used to attempt to reassert Soviet influence over the region. Even a reformed alliance with the Soviet Union might tie the East–Central European states to the Soviet Union for the 1990s and beyond, severely limiting their foreign policy independence. Given its unstable internal situation, the Soviet Union was as likely to be a threat to East–Central European security as a guarantor of it. A continued alliance might also preclude or retard the development of political and economic ties with the West, since the West might well be reluctant to develop ties with a country which remained allied to the Soviet Union. Given the East–Central European states, need for economic aid from the West and their desire for expanded ties with and eventual membership of the EC, this might be a significant consideration. In short, therefore, the alliance with the Soviet Union was both the means and the symbol of forty years of Soviet domination and dismantling it was widely viewed as central to securing the East–Central European states' newfound independence.

NEUTRALITY

After the East European revolutions of 1989 the most widely canvassed alternative to a continued alliance with the Soviet Union was some form of neutrality.[6] Formally, neutrality is non-participation by a state in a war involving other states.[7] The Central element of neutrality as a security strategy, however, is an attempt to mitigate the 'security dilemma'.⁸ The security dilemma arises when actions taken to enhance a states' security (such as joining an alliance or improving its armed forces) may threaten other states and thereby risk provoking similar responses from those states and undermining the first states' security. The dilemma is that if the state does not take action to enhance its security it may remain vulnerable, yet if it takes action it may undermine its security. Neutrality attempts to resolve this dilemma by developing security strategies which do not threaten the security of other states (e.g., rejecting membership of alliances, avoiding being drawn into other states' conflicts, developing armed forces structured to defend only ones national territory) and are therefore unlikely to provoke a negative reaction.⁹ From this perspective, the main advantage of neutrality for the countries of East–Central Europe was that it might mitigate the security dilemma in their relations with their major power neighbours, providing for their security and independence, whilst threatening neither the Soviet Union nor the West.

The existing European neutral states provided possible models.¹⁰ A Finnish model might involve bilateral agreements with the Soviet Union/Russia, entailing East–Central European commitments not to join alliances against the Soviet Union/Russia in return for Soviet/Russian commitments to respect their political independence and territorial integrity. An Austrian model might involve multilateral agreements with the Soviet Union/Russia and the West, under which the East–Central European states would agree not to join alliances or allow their territory to be used by the armed forces of other states in return for a commitment from the major powers not to intervene in the region.¹¹ Sweden and Switzerland illustrated the option of 'armed neutrality' – an independent, nationally declared policy of non-involvement in international political–military alliances. All four states offered models of territorial defence designed to support neutrality.¹²

Neutrality, however, faced a number of serious drawbacks. Neutrality relies on the respect of external powers for one's neutral status, the ability to avoid being drawn into conflicts or the ability to defend one's national territory. The highly unstable situation in the Soviet Union/Russia raised doubts about whether it could be relied upon to respect East–Central European neutrality. The East–Central European states' historical experience also gave them little confidence that major power neighbours could be relied on to respect their territorial integrity or political independence. There remained a widespread fear in East–Central Europe of 'another Yalta', with the major powers consigning the region to a Soviet/Russian sphere of influence. At the same time, the

East–Central European states were in a geo-strategically important region, lying largely on vulnerable plains. They had inherited armed forces whose political loyalty was open to doubt, whose command and control was linked to the Soviet/Russian military, which were structured to participate in Warsaw Pact (rather than national) military operations, and which were deployed almost wholly in the West of their countries. Their ability, therefore, to sustain credible policies of 'armed neutrality' was questionable.

With the end of the Cold War, further, it was no longer clear what neutrality meant or how it related to the security problems of the 1990s. Austria, Sweden and Finland were in the process of re-defining their security policies, including negotiating to join the EU and develop of new relations with NATO and the WEU.[13] Neutrality seemed of little relevance to the ethnic and national conflicts which appeared to be the primary threat to East–Central European security in the new environment. Perhaps most significantly, however, a policy of neutrality might limit or even preclude political and economic integration with the West, particularly the EU. With the EU developing its CFSP and a defence role through the WEU, strict neutrality might well prevent the expansion of ties with and eventual membership of the EU. More generally, the East–Central European states wished to become fully integrated with the West, not to gain a neutral status distinct from it.

REGIONAL SECURITY COOPERATION

Another strategic security policy option open to the countries of East–Central Europe was to develop regional security cooperation within Eastern Europe.[14] One possibility was the formation of a neutral bloc, acting as a buffer zone between the Soviet Union/Russia and the West. Another similar possibility was the formation of a loose diplomatic or political coalition, coordinating policies in relations with the West and the Soviet Union/Russia. Alternatively, more formal multilateral or bilateral East European alliances might be formed, committing signatories to provide military support to each other if attacked. Such alliances might be designed to counter-balance the Soviet Union/Russia or Germany or to provide security against other East European states (similar to the inter-war Czechoslovak–Romanian–Yugoslav 'Little Entente' against Hungary). A further alternative was the establishment of bilateral or multilateral frameworks for developing cooperative security relations within Eastern Europe. The East–Central European states, sharing similar security concerns, might develop cooperation alone. Alternatively cooperation might be expanded to include some or all of the Balkan states and perhaps also the Baltic states, Belarus and Ukraine. Regional security cooperation, therefore, might involve a number of overlapping multilateral and bilateral forms, offering a spectrum of possible security relationships within Eastern Europe.

Regional cooperation might contribute to East–Central European security in a number of ways. Loose cooperation might provide the East–Central European states with diplomatic leverage in relation to shared security concerns or enable them to support each other in reforming national security policies. Negotiations on issues such as German unification, Soviet troop withdrawals or relations with the EU and NATO might be coordinated in order to present common positions. Information on reforming civil–military relations and developing new military doctrines might be exchanged or common armaments procurement projects established. The establishment of formal alliances might contribute to East–Central European security by providing security guarantees and more concrete forms of military assistance in relation to specific threats. Alternatively, security cooperation might contribute to East–Central European security by helping to prevent the re-emergence of old conflicts over borders and ethnic minorities through agreements on mutual recognition of borders, ethnic minority rights, confidence-building measures and arms control.

East European security cooperation, however, faced a number of serious problems. Before the First World War and in the inter-war period, the East European states had failed to cooperate, forming alliances against and coming into conflict with one another.[15] With old disputes from these periods re-emerging, the omens for cooperation seemed poor. Regional security cooperation, particularly the formation of formal alliances, might also risk exacerbating the security dilemma outlined earlier by provoking a negative reaction from states not involved. The Soviet Union/Russia might well view East European security cooperation as a threat to its interests. Limited East–Central European security cooperation or alliances might risk provoking counter responses from those East European states not involved. Regional security cooperation, therefore, might risk provoking antagonistic relations with major power neighbours, the re-emergence of historic disputes over borders and ethnic minorities, the formation of counter-alliances or new regional arms races.

The credibility of East European security cooperation was also open to serious doubts. The re-emergence of historical disputes, combined with the region's unstable political and economic situation, suggested that cooperation might be difficult to achieve and weak once established. These factors, combined with the limited political, economic and military resources of the East–Central European states and their neighbours, suggested that any formal alliance would have little credibility in terms of political will and military power. The unstable situation in the region would make the development of common principles and norms in areas such as respect for borders, human and minority rights and military transparency difficult.

Regional security cooperation might also risk delaying or preventing integration with the West. Although the two were not necessarily mutually exclusive, East European security cooperation might be viewed as an alternative to integration with the West. Given Western fears of the economic costs of integrating the East–Central European states, of importing instability into Western institutions and of antagonising the Soviet Union/Russia, the West might see a loose Eastern bloc as a desirable alternative to Eastward expansion of the EU and NATO.

INTEGRATION WITH THE WEST

The end of the Cold War created new possibilities in terms of association with the EU, bilateral ties with Western states, new forms of relations with NATO and the WEU, and possible future membership of the EU, WEU and NATO. One of the main security options open to the countries of East–Central Europe, therefore, was to seek integration with the West. As a security strategy for the East–Central European states, integration with the West had many advantages. The West's combined political, economic and military power clearly gave it the ability to buttress the East–Central European states security, whether through political support, economic aid, military assistance, or formal security guarantees. Short of explicit security guarantees, the development of close ties with the West might place the East–Central European states informally under a Western 'security umbrella', increase their chances of receiving Western support in a crisis and make them strong candidates for full membership of Western institutions in the longer term. EU membership would obviously strengthen perceptions of being under an informal Western security umbrella. Thus, the East–Central European states' situation might be somewhat similar to that of the European neutral states during the Cold War, who were sometimes described as 'free riders' benefiting from the existence of NATO and ties with the Alliance but not being members. Beyond this, joining NATO and the WEU would give the East–Central European states formal security guarantees and commitments from the West to provide them with military support. The West might also give them more practical material support in terms of economic aid, military hardware and advice on developing new security and defence policies.

Integration with the West also had less tangible, but perhaps equally significant, advantages. With the East–Central European states seeking to establish Western-style democracies and market economies, the West represented a community of common values which they were seeking to join. The development of close ties with the West would be a signal that they were on the road to full membership of that community, reinforcing domestic and foreign policy reforms. Integration with the West also raised the possibility of joining the Western security community, in the sense of becoming part of the 'zone of peace' where war had become inconceivable. Should this occur, it would be a major contribution to the East–Central European states' security, effectively removing the possibility of war with the West, particularly Germany, and within East–Central Europe itself.

A strategy of integration with the West, however, also had potentially significant disadvantages. It faced the security dilemma outlined earlier, in that it might risk provoking counter-actions from the Soviet Union/Russia (and perhaps also other former-Soviet and Balkan states) which could undermine East–Central European security. In particular, there was a risk that the Soviet Union/Russia might perceive the development of close ties between East–Central Europe and the West as threatening its interests, leading it to use its residual political, economic and military influence to undermine East–Central European security. In the worst case, this might lead to the establishment of a new military confrontation along the East–Central European states' Eastern borders or even provoke armed conflict.

There were also doubts as to how far the West would be willing to deepen its ties with the East–Central European states, as it was wary of the possible economic and political costs of expanding the EU, of importing instability into Western organizations, and of provoking the Soviet Union/Russia. In particular, it was far from clear that the West would be willing to extend EU membership and especially the formal security guarantees of NATO and WEU membership. Integration with the West would almost certainly also be dependent on the East–Central European states progress in establishing democracies and market economies, which was not guaranteed.

PAN-EUROPEAN SECURITY

One way for the East–Central European states to mitigate the security dilemma involved in alliances and limited regional groupings, was to support the development of a pan-European security system. Here, one option was the development of a collective security system, involving formal commitments from its members to come to each others defence if attacked by another member of the system (as distinct from an alliance involving commitments to come to its members defence against attack by states outside the alliance).[16] A second alternative was a concert system, involving cooperation amongst the major powers to manage conflicts and maintain peace, similar to the nineteenth century Concert of Europe.[17] A third alternative was the development of a common or cooperative security regime, based on norms for states behaviour in such areas as arms control, confidence-building measures, conflict prevention and management, and human and minority rights.[18] To varying degrees, these differing models might be combined to produce hybrid systems (for example, by combining collective security commitments with cooperative security). Given that it already included all European states, the CSCE was the most likely vehicle for some form of pan-European security system.

The central advantage of all of these models was their potential to mitigate the security dilemma. By being pan-European in character they could, in theory, provide for the security of the East–Central European states without threatening other states and thereby avoid the danger of provoking responses which might undermine East–Central European security. A collective security system would provide security guarantees for the countries of East–Central Europe. Unlike a Western alliance, however, it would also provide security guarantees for the Soviet Union/Russia, rather than being directed against it. A concert system would facilitate the cooperative management of security problems amongst the major powers, rather than competition or conflict amongst them. A cooperative security system would provide for cooperation amongst all European states, avoiding the danger that cooperation amongst more limited groups might be perceived to be directed against those states not involved.

The various possible models of pan-European security had different advantages. The most obvious advantage of a collective security system was that it would provide the countries of East–Central Europe with formal security guarantees, which ought to deter aggression against them and provide them with material support if attacked. A concert system, while probably not providing formal security guarantees, might reduce the chances of East–Central Europe becoming the focus of conflict or competition between the major powers. A cooperative security system would constrain possible threats (through arms control or the defensive restructuring of armed forces) and promote the resolution of conflicts (through agreed mechanisms for resolving disputes).

These various options, however, also had significant drawbacks.[19] The historical record of all-inclusive security systems was poor and the credibility of the various proposed models was open to doubt as they might be vulnerable to rogue states failing to abide by the 'rules' of the system. The primary historical example of a collective security system, the League of Nations, had collapsed when its members had failed to meet commitments to oppose aggression. Both history and theory suggested that defining an act of aggression and determining whether and how to respond would be difficult. Moreover, the credibility of a collective security system would, in the end, depend on whether its members (especially the major powers) would meet their commitments, even in situations where their national interests were not immediately involved. In short, whether the countries of East–Central Europe could rely upon the generalized guarantees of a collective security system was questionable.

For small and medium states, such as the countries of East–Central Europe, the central strength of a concert system – cooperative great power management of security issues – was also its main weakness. By definition, in a concert system key security issues are determined by the major powers and the operation of the system depends on cooperation amongst them. Small and medium states are largely excluded from decision-making and remain vulnerable to having their security interests ignored or over-ridden – as occurred with both the Concert of Europe and the United Nations. The eventual break-down of the Concert of Europe and the sidelining of the United Nations during the Cold War illustrated the vulnerability of concert systems to changes in great power relations. Similarly, a successful cooperative security system depends on the willingness of its members to abide by the norms of the system (such as commitments to the non-use of force, to respect existing borders, and to limit national armed forces). Given the unstable situation in Eastern Europe and the former-Soviet Union, whether the states of the region could be relied upon to abide by such norms was questionable. Should cooperation break-down, moreover, a cooperative security system would provide no guarantee of a response to an actual or potential threat.

BALANCE OF POWER REALPOLITIK

An alternative to the idealism embodied in the various proposals for pan-European security systems was to pursue a traditional realpolitik balance of power policy. This would involve the countries of East–Central Europe shifting their security policies in response to changing international events, forming and breaking alliances and international allegiances as the European balance of power changed. Such a policy would reflect a 'realist' or 'neo-realist' view, assuming international relations to be characterized by an on-going and inevitable competition for power amongst states, creating constant insecurity and a permanent risk of war.[20] For realists and neo-realists, a state's security depends on its ability to respond to the constant evolution of the international balance of power. States achieve security by balancing against threats and potential hegemons, through forming alliances or expanding their armed forces.[21] In short, a realpolitik balance of power policy would reflect the nineteenth century British Foreign Secretary Lord Palmerston's dictum that states have no eternal allies or perpetual enemies, only interests – above all an interest in their own security.[22]

The central advantage of such a strategy would be its focus on maximizing flexibility and freedom of manoeuvre and responding to specific threats. Rather than making permanent commitments, such a strategy would allow the countries of East–Central Europe to alter their security policies in response to changes in the European balance of power, forming alliances or changing their military doctrines as differing threats arose. If German unification appeared to be threatening, they might align with the Soviet Union/Russia. If the Soviet Union/Russia appeared threatening, they might align with Germany or the West. If threats emerged within Eastern Europe, sub-regional alliances might be formed (as Czechoslovakia, Romania and Yugoslavia had done against Hungary in the 1920s and 1930s).

A realpolitik balance of power strategy, however, also had disadvantages. The most obvious was that it would exacerbate the security dilemma the East–Central European states faced in their relations with their neighbours. By constantly seeking to balance against potential threats from their neighbours, the East–Central European states would almost certainly provoke similar reactions from those neighbours. A likely consequence of such a policy would be the formation of counter-alliances and the adoption of military strategies directed against the countries of East–Central Europe. Indeed, a realpolitik balance of power policy might become self-fulfilling, perpetuating and intensifying the international competition for power and state of constant insecurity which it purported to be a response to. In an already unstable situation in Eastern Europe, such a policy might further undermine regional stability by provoking new alliance confrontations and arms races. In the worst case, it might even provoke war, since by assuming an environment of constant insecurity and threats and by focussing on balancing against those threats it would increase tensions and contribute to the development of conflictual relations.

Further, if – as was argued in Chapter 2 – the existence of a security community amongst the major Western powers was one of the dominant features of the European landscape, there might also be broader doubts as to the appropriateness of a realpolitik balance of power strategy. A policy which viewed the Western security community as a source of stability and sought to join it might be more appropriate. In contrast, a realpolitik balance of power policy might risk alienating the West by creating a perception that the countries of East–Central Europe were unreliable states, pursuing provocative security policies which undermined regional stability. Such a policy might thereby also seriously undermine the East–Central European states' prospects for integration with Western political and economic institutions.

NATIONAL DEFENCE

A further option open to the countries of East–Central Europe was to rely on national defence for security. In theory, they might choose from a wide range of defence policies. One extreme option might be to develop nuclear weapons. Here, the smaller nuclear powers – Britain, France and Israel – might offer a model, with nuclear weapons acting as a 'great equalizer' allowing the countries of East–Central Europe to deter their more powerful neighbours.[23] Short of developing nuclear weapons, they might develop conventional defence strategies based on mobile armoured warfare and offensive airpower, aiming to deter attack by threatening any aggressor with costly conventional retaliation.[24]

Alternatively, the countries of East–Central Europe might adopt more defensive military strategies, aiming to deter attack by making any invasion difficult and costly, rather than by threatening retaliation. This might involve maintaining armoured forces and strike airpower, but limiting their offensive potential by dispersing their deployment and constraining their logistic capabilities – a strategy of 'defensive defence'.[25] Alternatively, it might involve relying on the ability to mobilize large territorial forces in the event of an attack (a strategy similar to those practiced by Sweden and Switzerland).[26] Further options might include guerilla or civilian resistance, aiming to make invasion costly and deny an aggressor the 'fruits of victory'.[27]

The central advantage of relying on national armed forces for security is self-reliance. All the other security policy options open to the countries of East–Central Europe involved some degree of reliance on other states. In contrast, a strategy of relying on national defence offered the possibility of deterring attack and defending one's territory without depending on other states. Whilst attractive in theory, however, such a strategy faced major problems in practice. Forty years of Soviet domination had created armed forces whose political loyalty was questionable, which were deployed almost entirely in the West of their countries, and whose force structures, weapons, doctrines and training reflected Soviet Cold War concerns. The development of new defence policies, therefore, would be difficult.[28]

The first task in developing new defence policies was to ensure the loyalty of the armed forces to the new democratic, civilian authorities. De-politicizing the military, however, might be difficult. Forty years of Soviet control had created a system under which the primary loyalty of senior commanders and officers was to the communist regime and the Soviet Union.[29] Rapid and widespread purges of the armed forces might risk provoking the military to intervene in politics or oppose reforms of national defence policies. Since the training of a new generation of personnel would take some years, however, the new East–Central European governments needed the support of the military if they were to implement new defence policies – suggesting a need for caution in reforming civil-military relations.

Developing new military strategies and force structures would be equally difficult. The redeployment of forces from West to East would be expensive, involving transporting large amounts of equipment and building new bases and infrastructure. The maintenance of largely conscript forces would require regular training for large numbers of personnel. Developing fully professional armed forces would, however, involve even greater expense. The East–Central European states also had outdated equipment and depended on the Soviet Union for supplies and spare parts, while the procurement of more modern equipment would be expensive.[30] In particular, the East–Central European states would need to develop entirely new national air defence structures, since air defences had previously been fully integrated with those of the Soviet Union.[31] Further, all this took place in context of difficult economic transitions which were likely to severely limit the resources available for defence reforms.

Relying on national defence as the main element of their security policies also risked exacerbating the security dilemma the East–Central European states faced in their relations with their neighbours. By strengthening their armed forces, they might undermine the security of their neighbours, leading their neighbours to respond by strengthening their own armed forces. This dilemma would be most extreme if one of the East–Central European states decided to develop nuclear weapons, since this would probably trigger other states in the region to 'go nuclear'.[32] More generally, however, they faced the dilemma of how to deploy their armed forces. Maintaining the deployment of the majority of their armed forces in the West of their countries, for example, might risk antagonizing the West, especially Germany. Redeploying forces to the East or South, however, might be seen as provocative by their Eastern or Southern neighbours. In the worst case, this dynamic might trigger new arms races or create militarized border confrontations, increasing incentives to mobilize or strike pre-emptively in crises. The development of a defence *à tout azimuths*, defensive military doctrines and arms control regimes, in contrast, might mitigate these dangers. How successful such policies would be in practice, however, was less clear.

CONCLUSION

This chapter has examined the differing security policy options open to the countries of East–Central Europe after the Cold War. Whilst it has highlighted the main strategic alternatives open to the East–Central European states, it has also noted that the various security policy options open to them were not mutually exclusive and might be combined in various different ways. What is clear from this analysis, however, is that none of these options (or combinations of options) was entirely cost-free – each had possible advantages, but each also had potentially significant disadvantages. Thus, East–Central Europe's new, democratic governments faced a range of dilemmas. The following chapters explore how they responded to this multiplicity of dilemmas.

4 Poland

Since the collapse of the Polish-Lithuanian commonwealth in the eighteenth century, Poland's central security problem has been its geo-strategic position between Europe's two dominant powers, Prussia/Germany and Russia. After 1795, Poland was partitioned between Prussia, Russia and Austria, with an independent Polish state only re-emerging in 1918. During the inter-war period Poland followed the 'two enemies' policy, viewing conflictual relations with both Germany and Russia as inevitable and seeking security through guarantees from the West (Britain, France and the United States). This policy collapsed in 1939 when the Western powers failed Poland, and Germany and Russia collaborated once more in its dismemberment.

In 1945 Poland was, in effect, moved Westward, gaining territories East of the Oder and Neisse rivers from Germany and losing territory to the Soviet Union in the East. The country was occupied by the Soviet army and, in 1948, a compliant pro-Soviet communist regime was established. Under pressure from Moscow and fearing that Germany might question the new Oder–Neisse border, the Polish government accepted an alliance with the Soviet Union, including a mutual assistance treaty and over 40,000 Soviet troops on Polish territory. This policy, which guaranteed Poland's territorial integrity but denied its political independence, provided the bed-rock of Polish security until 1989.

In August–September 1989, after the overwhelming election victory of Solidarity, Poland became the first East European country with a non-communist government since 1948. The election of Solidarity leader Lech Walesa as President in December 1990 removed residual communist control of the presidency and the Ministries of Defence and Interior. The parliamentary elections of October 1991, however, produced a fragmented parliament. Throughout the first half of 1992 a prolonged battle for political power ensued between the government of Prime Minister Jan Olszewski and President Walesa. The collapse of the Olszewski government in June 1992, led to a period of relative stability, with cooperation between President Walesa and the new government of Prime Minister Hanna Suchocka. The Suchocka government was, however, defeated in a parliamentary no-confidence vote in May 1993. The resulting September 1993 elections saw the return of a 'post-communist' government composed of the political successors of the former communist party, under Prime Minister Waldemar Pawlak. This chapter examines how Poland's governments have reformed their country's national security policy since 1989.

THE 'ROUND-TABLE' AND THE REFORM OF THE SOVIET ALLIANCE

When the Polish 'round-table' negotiations on the transition to democracy opened in February 1989, both the Polish Communist Party (PZPR) and the Solidarity opposition movement accepted that the alliance with the Soviet Union must be maintained in order to avoid provoking Poland's superpower neighbour:

> It was understood informally that (PZPR leader General Wojciech) Jaruzelski was to occupy the newly established post of President of the Republic; he would maintain communist control over the armed forces and reassure allies.[1]

Solidarity's overwhelming victory in the June 1989 elections, however, raised new questions. Would the Soviet Union accept a Solidarity government? Would Jaruzelski remain President? Who would control the Ministries of Foreign Affairs, Defence and Interior? Solidarity leader Lech Walesa emerged as the key figure, brokering an agreement between the various political forces in Poland. With Walesa's endorsement, Jaruzelski was elected President by the parliament in July, ensuring that the PZPR retained control of the military. Walesa, however, proposed that Solidarity form a government without the PZPR. The Soviet Foreign Ministry warned that this might damage Poland's 'allied obligations'.[2] Walesa, whose advisers were in regular contact with the Soviet ambassador in Warsaw, accepted that the PZPR be included in a Solidarity-led coalition, reassuring the Soviets that such a government would not threaten 'the functioning of the Warsaw Pact'.[3]

The formation of the Solidarity-led government under Prime Minister Tadeusz Mazowiecki in September 1989 resulted in a compromise under which the Ministries of Defence and Interior remained under the nominal control of the PZPR, but President Jaruzelski (presenting himself as a national leader above political divisions) was given ultimate authority in defence and foreign policy. Krzysztof Skubiszewksi, a political neutral, became Foreign Minister, affirming his support for Poland's membership of the Warsaw Pact.[4] In his inaugural address to the Sejm on 12 September 1989 Prime Minister Mazowiecki confirmed that his government wished to 'maintain allied relations with the Soviet Union'.[5] The new government, however, argued that 'spheres of security' should not 'mean spheres of influence': alliances should be geared to ensuring their members external security, not their domestic political orientation.[6] President Gorbachev was willing to accept this formula and an October 1989 Polish–Soviet communiqué stressed the importance of 'non-interference in internal affairs'.[7]

The strategic situation was altered by the revolutions of November and December 1989 in East Germany, Czechoslovakia and Romania. Until then, Mazowiecki had assumed that a cautious approach was necessary in order to avoid provoking the Soviet Union. By mid-January 1990, however, the Czechoslovak and Hungarian governments had demanded the withdrawal of all Soviet forces from their territory. Popular pressure emerged within Poland for a similar withdrawal, with protests against the Soviet presence in January and February.[8] Lech Walesa told the Soviet ambassador to Poland that the Soviet forces should be withdrawn by the end of 1990.[9] The Mazowiecki government, however, maintained its cautious approach. Despite a Soviet offer to open negotiations on the complete withdrawal of the troops, Mazowiecki argued that his government did not want an immediate withdrawal because of 'the Germany problem'.[10] The Soviet Union did, indeed, provide Poland with diplomatic support in relation to German unification, insisting at the February 1990 Ottawa summit that the mandate for the 'two-plus-four' negotiations on German unification include a commitment to discuss 'security of neighbouring states'. In April 1990 Presidents Gorbachev and Jaruzelski issued a joint statement confirming the Soviet Union's support for Poland's 'sovereignty and territorial integrity'.[11]

The Mazowiecki government, however, viewed the Soviet military presence as temporary. In April 1990 Foreign Minister Skubiszewski told the Sejm that the government intended to initiate talks on a complete withdrawal of Soviet troops from Poland.[12] By mid-June, according to a Polish official, the basic structure of a transitional agreement had emerged, whereby 10,000 Soviet logistics/support personnel would remain in Poland so long as Soviet troops remained in Germany.[13] Janusz Onyszkiewicz, Deputy Defence Minister at the time, later revealed that:

> the Soviet side constantly assured us that we could count on their understanding whenever the Polish government expressed its expectations with regard to the withdrawal of Soviet troops and the timing of the withdrawal. These explanations reassured us.[14]

Statements by Onyszkiewicz and other officials suggest that the Mazowiecki government believed that the Soviet forces in Poland could prove a useful 'bargaining chip' in relation to German unification, while their withdrawal could be achieved quickly and easily when Poland desired it. The Mazowiecki government, therefore, appears to have had little interest in maintaining the post-war alliance with the Soviet Union as a long-term policy. By the summer of 1990 the Polish Foreign Ministry was arguing that a new bilateral treaty with the Soviet Union should not include the alliance commitments involved in the existing mutual assistance treaty and Foreign Minister Skubiszewski was expressing scepticism about the future of the Warsaw Pact.[15]

GERMAN UNIFICATION

The opening of the Berlin wall in November 1989 brought to the fore longstanding Polish fears of Germany:

> As (German Chancellor) Mr. (Helmut) Kohl was telling cheering East and West Berliners that 'we are and will remain one nation', the government in Warsaw said Poland expected 'guarantees that a new united Germany, no doubt a powerful state, will not threaten security and cooperation in Europe'.[16]

Although both East and West Germany had recognized the Oder-Neisse border in post-war treaties with Poland, the West German constitution still referred to Germany within its 1937 borders, including the territories lost to Poland in 1945. Right-wing groups within Germany also demanded the return of these territories. The fact that Chancellor Kohl's November 1989 plan for inner-German relations 'made no reference to German borders and thus created the impression that unification would reopen the territorial issue', therefore, provoked Polish fears.[17] The Polish government insisted that the two Germanies commit themselves absolutely to their current borders.[18] Kohl argued that a united Germany could only reaffirm its borders after unification.[19]

At the Ottawa summit in February 1990, when the 'two-plus-four' negotiating framework for German unification was agreed, Foreign Minister Skubiszewski came out decisively in favour of a united Germany remaining a member of NATO: 'through neutrality . . . you might create a situation where Germany tries to become a power or a super-power on the European stage'. Acceptance of the Oder–Neisse border, however, was not 'being said clearly by the German government'.[20]

Poland wanted a decisive commitment to the Oder–Neisse border prior to unification and the right to participate in the 'two-plus-four' talks.[21] To press for these objectives, the Polish government pursued an intensive diplomatic campaign, with Prime Minister Mazowiecki telephoning President Gorbachev, meeting the United States and French ambassadors in Warsaw, and writing to the United States, the Soviet Union, Britain and France.[22]

Chancellor Kohl came under increasing pressure, both domestically and internationally, to accept the Polish demands. Kohl accepted that a resolution be issued by the German parliament recognizing the Oder–Neisse border. However, he rejected the Polish proposal that a border treaty be drawn up and initialled then (to be signed after German unification) and stipulated that any border treaty also guarantee the rights of the German minority in Poland.[23] The Polish government rejected Kohl's attempt to link the issues.[24] After further domestic and international pressure Kohl agreed to ask the Bundestag to declare that a united Germany would unconditionally guarantee the Oder–Neisse border and dropped his demand for linkage to German minority rights.[25] On 8 March 1990 the Bundestag passed a resolution accepting the existing border. At the first sub-ministerial meeting of the 'two-plus-four' talks later in March, West Germany agreed that Poland join the talks when border issues were discussed.[26]

At the first full session of the 'two-plus-four' talks in Bonn in May it was agreed that Poland be invited to attend the third session in Paris in July to discuss the border question, participate in preparatory meetings and be able to raise issues not directly related to the border question (such as the implications of Soviet troop withdrawals from Germany for Poland).[27] Progress was confirmed in June when the West and East German parliaments passed matching resolutions recognizing the Oder–Neisse border. Poland responded by dropping its insistence that both Germanies initial a treaty prior to unification.[28] Tensions continued into July, however, with the Germans refusing to discuss a border treaty before unification.[29]

The issue was finally resolved at the 17 July 1990 meeting of the 'two-plus-four' talks in Paris. The two German states committed themselves to sign a border treaty with Poland 'as soon as possible after unification', abandon 'territorial ambitions toward any other country', amend the German constitution accordingly, and conclude a friendship and cooperation treaty with Poland. Foreign Minister Skubiszewksi declared all sides 'totally satisfied'.[30] These commitments were reflected in the *Treaty on the Final Settlement With Respect to Germany*, signed at the last meeting of the 'two-plus-four' talks in Moscow on 12 September 1990: the territory of the united Germany would cover only the territory of the former East and West Germany, the united Germany and Poland would confirm their border in an international treaty, the united Germany would have no territorial claims, and the German constitution would be altered to reflect these commitments.[31] The unification treaty was approved by the two German parliaments on 20 September, paving the way for the unification of the two German states on 3 October 1990.

Tensions re-emerged shortly after unification, however. German expellee groups demanded a Polish renunciation of the post-war expulsion of Germans and the right for expellees to return to Poland. Chancellor Kohl suggested that there should be only one treaty covering all bilateral relations and that the treaty might be delayed until the spring of 1991 (after the German elections). After further Polish pressure, however, agreement was reached on the border treaty in early October.[32] The treaty, signed on 14 October 1990, states that the Oder–Neisse border is and will remain inviolable and binds the two states not to make any territorial claims against each other.[33]

Two features of Poland's approach to German unification were particularly notable. First, the Polish government clearly viewed unification as a possible danger, but also as an opportunity to definitively settle the issue of Poland's border with Germany. The diplomatic negotiations surrounding German unification provided Poland with an opportunity to tie future German governments to a binding commitment to the Oder-Neisse border. According to Foreign Minister Skubiszewski:

> The moment of unification is also a moment for definitely removing any doubts or uncertainties which were and are being raised by West Germany with regard to the frontier. The frontier issue ... should not re-emerge at the moment of and after German unification. ... After unification, it is legitimate for us to expect that there would be no more talk of Germany existing in the frontiers of 1937 and the Oder–Neisse territory being German, both in international and domestic law.[34]

Second, Poland's support for Germany's continued membership of NATO indicated a major shift in Polish security thinking. The Mazowiecki government clearly believed that a Germany contained within the EC and particularly NATO was preferable to the potential 'loose cannon' of a neutral Germany. For the new Polish government NATO was an important stabilizing force, not a threat.

DISMANTLING THE SOVIET ALLIANCE

With its immediate concerns over German unification satisfied, Poland began to dismantle its post-war alliance with the Soviet Union. After the July 1990 meeting of the 'two-plus-four' talks had agreed that the united Germany would commit itself to the Oder–Neisse border, Foreign Minister Skubiszewski said that Poland would not work to keep the Warsaw Pact 'artificially alive'.[35] By the autumn of 1990, however, pressure was growing within Poland for a more rapid break with the Soviet Union. In September the Polish Senate passed a resolution calling for an early withdrawal of Soviet forces, withdrawal from the Warsaw Pact's military structures, and the development of direct ties with Lithuania, Belarus, Ukraine and Russia.[36] According to the chairman of the Senate Foreign Affairs Commission, with the two German states' recognition of the Oder–Neisse border the Soviet Union was no longer the sole guarantor of Poland's Western border and Poland had entered the Western sphere of influence.[37]

Foreign Minister Skubiszewski argued that the government was now pursuing a policy of equal proximity between the Soviet Union and Germany. On 7 September 1990 the Soviet ambassador to Poland was informed that negotiations on a complete withdrawal of Soviet forces should begin as soon as possible.[38] Skubiszewski visited Moscow in mid-October, where it was agreed that talks on the withdrawal would begin before the end of 1990 and the existing mutual assistance treaty between the two states would be replaced by a friendship and cooperation treaty.[39] By mid-November 1990 Poland's new Defence Minister Admiral Piotr Kolodziejczyk was declaring that his country followed a policy of *de facto* neutrality.[40] With both Presidential and Parliamentary elections due in the next few months, however, the government was criticized for having allowed concerns over German unification to overshadow the need to dismantle the alliance with the Soviet Union.[41] In response to growing public demands for the Soviet forces to be withdrawn, the government set up a special ministerial commission to deal with the issue.[42] At the first round of negotiations in Moscow in mid-November Poland demanded a complete withdrawal by the end of 1991.[43]

By late 1990, however, the crisis within the Soviet Union had begun to spill over into relations with Poland. Disputes emerged over the future of the Warsaw Pact, resulting in the postponement of a planned Pact summit.[44] In January 1991 the Soviet intervention against the independence movements in the Baltic republics posed serious dilemmas for the new Polish government of Prime Minister Jan Krzysztof Bielecki. The new government expressed its support for the Lithuanian people and supported calls for a CSCE meeting to discuss the crisis.[45] President Walesa went further, warning of:

> A dark possibility that Poland is under a deadly threat and that Lithuania was only a rehearsal of an attempt by the Soviet empire to make up for the loss of East Germany and others . . . we had some signals that it was possible, that there would be provocations.[46]

Walesa's warning, however, was probably exaggerated and driven by domestic pressure to take a stronger line. Foreign Minister Skubiszewski argued that the situation in Poland had progressed beyond one where the Soviet Union might intervene militarily.[47]

Poland remained vulnerable, however, over the troop withdrawal issue. The timing of the withdrawal remained unresolved. Poland insisted that the withdrawal be agreed and begun before any Soviet troops transit across Poland from Germany.[48] The Supreme Soviet of the USSR argued that the withdrawal could not occur before the transit of Soviet forces from Germany.[49] Poland responded by halting a Soviet military train from Germany and announcing that it would block any further transits.[50] The Polish government had begun to fear that the Soviet Union wanted to maintain a military presence in Poland as part of an air defence and electronic intelligence network.[51] However, as one adviser to President Walesa observed, 'we don't have the means to exert pressure on the Soviet Union'.[52] Poland, therefore, needed to avoid provoking the Soviet Union over the Lithuanian crisis. Foreign Minister Skubiszewski noted that, while 'we are interested in the best possible relations with Lithuania . . . our relations with the USSR are of primary strategic importance'.[53] The Polish government resisted domestic pressure to recognize Lithuania's independence. President Walesa pulled out of a proposed summit of the three East–Central European countries' leaders at which withdrawal from the Warsaw Pact was to have been discussed, arguing that 'if there is no need, it's better not to bluff "the Bear"'.[54]

When Skubiszewski met his Czechoslovak and Hungarian counterparts later in January to discuss the crisis he rejected a Czechoslovak proposal that the three countries accelerate their withdrawal from the Warsaw Pact, instead agreeing that the delayed Pact summit must be held no later than mid-March, that the Pact's military structures must be dissolved by the end of June, and that the Pact itself must be dissolved by March 1992.[55] Against a background of statements that the three East–Central European countries might withdraw from the Pact *en bloc* if their demands were rejected, President Gorbachev agreed that the Pact's military structures be abolished by 1 April 1991. The Pact itself was formally terminated at a meeting in Prague on 1 July 1991. However, as was seen in the last chapter, the Soviet Union began to press the East European states to accept restrictive 'security clauses' in new bilateral treaties. Poland joined Czechoslovakia, Hungary and Bulgaria in rejecting the clauses. By May 1991 the Polish–Soviet treaty negotiations were deadlocked.[56] The Soviet Union also continued to insist that the withdrawal of its forces from Poland could not be completed until mid-1994, when the Soviet forces would complete their withdrawal from Germany. Poland continued to oppose this, refusing to allow any further transit of Soviet troops from Germany until agreement was reached on the withdrawal from Poland.[57] In March 1991 Soviet Chief of Staff General Mikhail Moiseyev broke the logjam, announcing that the Soviet Union would unilaterally begin the withdrawal from Poland and the transit of forces from Germany, to be completed by the end of 1993. Poland accepted that some transit from Germany could occur once the withdrawal from Poland had begun. On 9 April 1991 the first Soviet forces began to leave Poland.[58] Negotiations on the troop withdrawal and the cooperation treaty continued throughout the early summer of 1991, however, without significant progress. The Polish government accused the Soviet side of intentionally delaying the talks and a summit between Presidents Walesa and Gorbachev was postponed.[59]

The coup in the Soviet Union on 19 August 1991 intensified Polish concerns. Fearing a hardening of the Soviet position on the troop withdrawal, the Polish government's reaction was cautious. Skubiszewski met with the Soviet ambassador to Poland, receiving a pledge that all scheduled Polish–Soviet talks would go ahead as planned. Soviet troop withdrawals remained on schedule, while there was no unusual activity from Soviet troops and transport and communication links with the Soviet Union remained normal.[60] Poland's armed forces, however, were put on alert and preparations made for the mobilization of other units, indicating that the Polish government was perhaps more concerned than it publicly revealed.[61] Illustrating the extent to which Poland had already broken its ties with the Soviet Union and saw the West as central to its security, officials from NATO's headquarters and the United States visited Warsaw during the coup for consultations.[62] Although the contents of these talks have not been made public, according to one Polish Foreign Ministry official the fact that the talks took place indicated that the countries of East-Central Europe were 'not left alone in the face of a threat from the East'[63] – implying an informal Western commitment to support them if they faced Soviet pressure.

Ironically, progress was made on the troop withdrawal issue during the coup, with the Soviets agreeing to remove all combat troops by October 1992 and support troops by the end of 1993.[64] After the failure of the coup, the Soviet Union also dropped its insistence on the 'security clauses' in its bilateral treaty with Poland.[65] The treaty on the withdrawal of Soviet forces was initialled in Moscow on 26 October 1991. All Soviet combat forces were to be withdrawn by 15 November 1992, with 6,000 non-combat troops (to be reduced to 2,000 in the last quarter of 1993) remaining to support the transit of forces from Germany until the end of 1993.[66] On 10 December 1991 the treaty on friendship and cooperation and an agreement on the transit of Soviet forces from Germany were initialled.[67] With the break-up of the Soviet Union, the obligations negotiated with the Soviet Union were taken on by Russia in January 1992.[68] President's Walesa and Yeltsin signed the withdrawal agreement in Moscow in May 1992. The withdrawal proceeded on schedule and on 28 October 1992 the last Russian combat troops left Poland.[69]

POLAND'S SHIFT TOWARDS THE WEST

The Polish government's support for the united Germany's membership of the EC and NATO indicated its changing attitude towards the West in general and NATO in particular. Thus, it responded positively to NATO's July 1990 proposal for the Warsaw Pact countries to establish permanent diplomatic liaison and expand political and military contacts with the Alliance, receiving NATO Secretary-General Manfred Woerner in Warsaw in September 1990.[70] However, when one Polish analyst proposed in June 1990 that NATO forces be stationed in Poland, a presidential spokesperson stated that the idea ran 'counter to the philosophy and practice' of Polish foreign policy.[71]

From late 1990 onwards, however, the Polish government made integration with the West, particularly NATO, the central element of its security policy. This clearly reflected a view that NATO played a central role in integrating Germany into the West, tying the United States into Europe and deterring aggression. The election in December 1990 of President Walesa, who had criticized the Mazowiecki government for being too slow in breaking the alliance with the Soviet Union and developing ties with the West, accelerated the shift in policy.[72] By January 1991 Foreign Minister Skubiszewski was arguing that NATO could not 'be indifferent to a threat to, or breach of, security in whatever corner of the continent it might occur'.[73] A Foreign Ministry spokesman reiterated that while Poland did not want to join NATO, the Atlantic Alliance could not 'remain indifferent if international security is breached in any part of Europe'.[74] In effect, Poland was seeking an informal Western commitment to guarantee its security. This policy shift was reflected in increased diplomatic activity. President Walesa visited Washington, Brussels, Paris and London in March and April 1991, making clear Poland's intention to press for full membership of the EC.[75] Friendship treaties were signed with France and Britain.[76] Meeting NATO Secretary-General Manfred Worner in May 1991, Defence Minister Kolodziejczyk announced that military contacts with NATO would be expanded.[77] In July 1991 President Walesa visited NATO's headquarters, welcoming the Alliance's June 1991 statement of its interest in the security of all European states. NATO was 'the principal pillar of the European security system' and Poland wanted 'partnership' with it:

> For us, of primary importance is the wording that the security of the states of the Alliance is inseparably linked to the security of all other states in Europe and that of direct concern to the states of the Alliance is the consolidation and preservation throughout the continent of democratic societies and their freedom from any form of coercion or intimidation.[78]

After the coup in the Soviet Union, Poland intensified its diplomatic activity towards the West. In late August 1991 President Walesa joined with Czechoslovak President Vaclav Havel and Hungarian Prime Minister Jozsef Antall in pressing for faster integration of their countries with the EC.[79] In early October, when NATO was discussing the formation of the North Atlantic Cooperation Council (NACC), Poland joined with Czechoslovakia and Hungary in calling for a 'close and institutionalized' association with NATO and 'direct involvement' in its activities. By now, Skubiszewski was arguing that Poland wanted any form of association with NATO, including 'joining the Alliance itself'.[80] Jerzy Milewski, the newly appointed head of the Presidential National Security Bureau stated that Poland wanted, in the relatively near future, to become a full member of NATO.[81] NATO's November 1991 decision to form the NACC, therefore, was a disappointment, since it failed to give the East-Central European states security guarantees or differentiate them from the disintegrating Soviet Union. As one Polish diplomat put it: 'Russia is mainly an Asian country. Are you saying that the West would go to defend it in the event of war with China? We are good Europeans'.[82]

Despite the struggle for political power between the Olszewski government and President Walesa in the first half of 1992, both it and the subsequent Suchocka government made integration with the West and membership of NATO their central national security goals. The Olszewski and Suchocka governments took further steps to develop security relations with the West: active participation in the NACC, the development of bilateral political and military contacts with Western countries, and the restructuring of Poland's military to make it more compatible with NATO forces. Bilateral military cooperation agreements were concluded with France and Greece in June and November 1992. Negotiations for similar agreements were begun with Germany, the United States, Britain and other West European countries.[83] The Polish government also hoped to develop close military cooperation with NATO. One analyst noted that 'the new system of air defence foresees tight cooperation between Poland and NATO countries . . . Poland will be part of the NATO air defence system, without being a member of NATO'.[84]

By late 1992 Prime Minister Suchocka was calling for 'increasingly substantial commitments leading to integration with the Atlantic security system'.[85] The Polish government argued that NATO should 'differentiate' the countries of East–Central Europe from their Eastern and Southern neighbours, providing them with a special relationship.[86] Visiting the United States in November, Defence Minister Onyszkiewicz argued that Western countries should make a material commitment to Poland's security through joint use of Soviet bases in Poland for training of international peacekeeping forces and 'lend-lease' agreements allowing Poland to borrow Western equipment if tensions emerged on its Eastern border.[87] According to one Ministry of Defence official the aim was to prepare 'future cooperative instruments for the time of crisis'.[88] The United States, however, was not ready to make such commitments.

Poland also sought to develop security relations with the EC and the WEU. With the conclusion of their association agreements with the EC in December 1991, the countries of East–Central Europe argued that they should be given a similar special relationship with the WEU.[89] The WEU's willingness to differentiate was confirmed in June 1992 when the first meeting of its new consultation forum involved the three East–Central European states plus Romania, Bulgaria and the

Baltic states but not Russia and the other post-Soviet states. Poland, however, wanted 'the same stages of relations with the WEU as exist between Poland and the European Community under our association agreement. . . . we should be granted on a selective basis participation in the European Political Cooperation' (the EC's foreign policy-making process).[90]

Parallel to the central policy of integration with the West, Poland was also an active supporter of a strengthened CSCE. Reflecting this, the November 1990 Paris CSCE summit decided that the CSCE's Office of Free Elections – later to become the Office for Democratic Institutions and Human Rights (ODIHR) – would be based in Warsaw. Poland also supported the development of the CSCE's conflict prevention and peacekeeping role. In September 1991, President Walesa joined with President Havel in calling for a permanent CSCE peacekeeping force.[91] By late 1992 Polish officials were arguing that the CSCE should 'have at its disposal European peacekeeping forces or cooperate with NATO in peacekeeping . . . peacekeeping is the main avenue for the CSCE in the years to come'.[92] Poland also strongly supported CSCE arms control agreements, particularly the implementation of the CFE (Conventional Armed Forces in Europe) Treaty by the states of the former-Soviet Union and possible further agreements with its new Eastern neighbours.[93]

Poland also actively promoted cooperation with the other East–Central European states in the Visegrad group, viewing this as a way of signalling to the West that they were stable and ready for integration with the EC and NATO, of giving them greater diplomatic leverage in negotiations with the Soviet Union and the West, and of preventing the re-emergence of conflicts within East–Central Europe.[94]

The central features of Poland's new security policy were confirmed in November 1992 with the adoption by the National Defence Committee of a formal national security doctrine, under which 'the strategic objective of Poland for the 1990s is to obtain membership in NATO and the Western European Union'.[95] While emphazising the central role of NATO and a continued US military presence in Europe, the doctrine also confirmed the other elements of Polish policy: integration with Western Europe, including membership in the EC; the development of the CSCE; and cooperation with Germany, with Poland's Eastern neighbours and within the Visegrad group. By late 1992, further, there was a broad political consensus within Poland on national security policy. According to one Polish observer there was 'no debate about the joining of NATO as a future strategic option . . . there is no alternative to joining the Western security and military structures'.[96]

The victory of the former-communist Democratic Left Alliance (SLD) and its allies the Polish Peasant Party (PSL) and the Union of Labour in the September 1993 elections raised doubts about Poland's Western orientation.[97] By early October, however, foreign policy experts from the three parties were reaffirming 'Poland's will to join NATO as quickly as possible'.[98] The new Foreign Minister Andrzej Olechowski stated that he would 'continue the strategic direction of the hitherto foreign policy'.[99] The new Defence Minister Piotr Kolodziejczyk stated that there was 'no other alternative' to NATO.[100] The October 1993 coup attempt in Russia and the success of Vladimir Zhirinovsky's Liberal Democratic Party in the December 1993 elections only strengthened the new Polish government's desire to join NATO. While endorsing NATO's January 1994 Partnership for Peace (PFP) proposal, it described it as 'an insufficient step in the right direction'. Foreign Minister Olechowski, however, noted that 'now we are in the waiting room – before there wasn't even talk of NATO membership'.[101]

Despite the initial uncertainties raised by the emergence of the SLD-dominated government, by 1993–94 Poland was perhaps the most active of the East European states in developing security ties with the West. Military cooperation agreements were signed with the US, Canada, Germany, the Netherlands, Belgium, and Denmark.[102] In June 1993 Poland took part in naval exercises with NATO in the Baltic Sea.[103] In March 1994 Defence Minister Kolodziejczyk suggested that Poland might join the West European Eurocorps.[104] In May reports suggested that in order to move towards NATO membership Poland had offered to make English mandatory for all officers; to integrate its command, control, communications and intelligence structures with NATO; to hold a wide range of military exercises with NATO countries in Poland (including parachute and fighter training, infantry manoeuvres and extensive naval exercises); and to bring its ports and airbases up to NATO standards.[105] Visiting Poland in July President Clinton stated that 'when NATO does expand, as it will, a democratic Poland will have placed itself among those ready and able to join'.[106] In September 1994 Poland hosted the first multilateral exercises in Eastern Europe under NATO's PFP programme.[107]

A POLISH–GERMAN SPECIAL RELATIONSHIP

With its immediate concerns over German unification addressed, Poland sought to develop a Polish–German 'community of interests', modelled on post-war Franco-German relations.[108] A treaty on 'friendship and good-neighbourliness' – the basis of the new relationship – was signed by Prime Minister Bielecki and Chancellor Kohl in Bonn on 17 June 1991. The treaty included recognition of the inviolability of the existing Polish–German border; pledges to abstain from the use of force against each others, territorial integrity and political independence; agreements on regular governmental and parliamentary consultations; a German commitment to develop the same relationship with Poland as it had with France and to support Polish membership of the EC; and, Polish recognition of its German minority and guarantees of their rights consistent with general international norms.[109] According to Bielecki, 'never in their long history have Poles and Germans been so close and so confident about the future'.[110] Germany was 'Poland's most important partner in all areas'.[111] Both countries parliaments voted overwhelmingly in favour of the treaty in October 1991.[112] The emerging Polish–German special relationship was confirmed in March–April 1992, when President Walesa became the first Polish head of state to visit Germany since 1918, stating that 'my dream is that in the year 2000 you will not notice the border between Poland and Germany. I think this dream will come true'.[113]

The new Polish–German relationship paved the way for increasingly close security cooperation. Germany emerged as a key advocate of developing EU and NATO ties with Poland and eventual Polish membership of both organizations.[114] By November 1993 the German Secretary of State for Defence was arguing that Polish membership of NATO was not a question of if, but of when and how.[115] Close military cooperation also developed. In November 1991 Poland's Defence Minister Piotr Kolodziejczyk visited Germany to discuss military cooperation. In March 1992 German Defence Minister Gerhard Stoltenberg visited Poland, agreeing to strengthen military ties and that joint military action might be discussed in a crisis.[116] By late 1992 discussions had been held on a wide range of military issues and German navy vessels were refuelling at Polish military ports.[117] As a result of exchanges between units, Polish soldiers were seeing 'Germans in German uniform on our soil and they think about them as friends'.[118] By January 1993 a defence cooperation agreement covering training, arms reduction, and environmental protection had been reached.[119] In September 1993 German Defence Minister Volker Ruhe went further, proposing joint army manoeuvres.[120]

Poland's emerging special relationship with Germany was symbolized by the 'Weimar Triangle' Franco-German-Polish cooperation process.

From August 1991 the three countries' foreign ministers met annually, supporting Poland's membership of the EU and Poland's desire to gain 'associate' membership of the WEU.[121] In March 1994 the three countries defence ministries met for the first time, agreeing to meet annually.[122] By July they had agreed to stage joint military manoeuvres in France later in the year and to establish a joint commission on arms technology.[123]

Although attacks on Poles in Germany, tensions with the German minority in Poland, and cross-border economic ties have caused problems, these have not seriously undermined Polish–German relations. Unless major domestic political changes in either country re-open the border or minority rights issues, increasingly close cooperation between Poland and Germany, particularly in the security sphere, seems likely. As Poland's national security doctrine notes, 'cooperation with Germany is one of the main routes leading Poland towards the integrated Western Europe'.[124]

A NEW EASTERN POLICY

With the collapse of the Soviet Union at the end of 1991, Poland faced the challenge of developing a policy towards its new Eastern neighbours: Russia, Ukraine, Belarus, Lithuania, and Kaliningrad (part of the Russian federation, but located on the Baltic coast between Poland and Lithuania). The military legacy of the Soviet Union left Russia, Ukraine and Belarus with nuclear weapons on their soil and conventional armed forces far larger than Poland's (see Table 4.1). The unstable situation in the post-Soviet states made developing good, long-term relations with them problematic. There was also a danger that historic disputes over borders and ethnic minorities might re-emerge (see Map 4.1). Lithuania, Belarus and Ukraine's incorporation in the pre-eighteenth century Polish-Lithuanian commonwealth and the inter-war Polish state has left them with significant Polish minorities and a fear of Polish domination and territorial claims. Historic Polish–Russian conflict over the lands lying between them has left a legacy of mistrust and antagonism between the two states, with Poland being particularly sensitive to possible Russian neo-imperialism.

Poland moved rapidly to develop relations with its new neighbours, formally recognizing Lithuania in September 1991 and Ukraine, Belarus and Russia in December. According to the new national security doctrine, 'it is in Poland's interest to develop friendly relations and cooperation . . . with our neighbours to the East'.[125] Poland's post-1989

Table 4.1   Poland and its Eastern Neighbours (1991–2)

	Population (Based on 1989 census)	Area (sq. km.)	Nuclear Warheads	Main Battle Tanks	Armoured Personnel Carriers	Artillery Pieces	Combat Aircraft	Attack Helicopters
Poland	38,000,000	313,000	n/a	2,850	2,319	2,300	506	29
Russia	148,000,000	17,075,000	19,000	21,500	33,500	15,500	2,750	1,215
Ukraine	51,800,000	604,000	4,000	6,404	6,394	3,052	2,431	285
Belarus	10,300,000	208,000	1,250	5,100	5,000	2,500	650	84
Lithuania	3,700,000	65,000	n/a	184	1,591	253	46	0

Sources: The Economist Intelligence Unit, *Commonwealth of Independent States Country Report*, 1 (London: EIU, 1992) p. 9, reproduced by permission of the Economist Intelligence Unit; The International Institute for Strategic Studies, *The Military Balance 1991–1992* (London: Brassey's for the IISS, 1991); 'Where the Weapons Are', Nuclear Notebook, *Bulletin of the Atomic Scientists*, 47 (November 1991) pp. 48–9, Copyright © 1994 by the Educational Foundation for Nuclear Science, 6042 South Kimback, Chicago, IL 60637, USA; and 'Spoils of Peace', *The Economist* (21 March 1992) p. 63.

Map 4.1   Poland since 1945

Source: A. Palmer, *The Lands Between: A History of East-Central Europe since the Congress of Vienna* (London: Weidenfeld and Nicolson, 1970) p. 307.

governments have consistently rejected any territorial claims and the national security doctrine states that Poland 'considers its borders immutable and has no territorial claims against its neighbours'.[126] At the same time, Poland has pressed for guarantees of the rights of the Polish minorities in Ukraine, Belarus and particularly Lithuania (creating some tensions, given residual fears of Polish interference or territorial claims). Underlying Poland's Eastern policy, however, has been a dilemma. The new national security doctrine states that Poland 'desires close cooperation with all its neighbours and does not intend to enter into military agreements with one neighbour against another'.[127] According to a member of President Walesa's National Security Bureau staff, however:

> our relations with Ukraine and Belarus are a priority of our Eastern diplomacy . . . this is a consequence of accepting the main strategic goal of preserving those countries, of helping them in maintaining their independent existence. It is better to exist with two relatively weaker neighbours than having borders with this 'great bear' . . . this is one of the main dilemmas of our foreign policy: how to maintain very good relations with Ukraine and Belarus and maintain as good as possible relations with Russia.[128]

Russia

The apparent triumph of democratic forces within Russia after the August 1991 Soviet coup appeared to offer a new opportunity to develop cooperative Polish–Russian relations. Russia rapidly accepted the Soviet commitment to withdraw its forces from Poland by the end of 1992. The negotiation of a Friendship and Cooperation Treaty proved uncomplicated. Under the treaty, signed by Presidents Walesa and Yeltsin in Moscow in May 1992, Poland and Russia recognize each other's territorial sovereignty; reject the use of force in their relations; agree to resolve disputes by peaceful means; pledge not to interfere in each other's internal affairs; agree to hold political consultations and expand economic and cultural cooperation; and undertake to respect the rights of ethnic minorities.[129] The new relationship seemed confirmed in October 1992 when the last Russian combat forces left Poland and Russia released documents accepting Soviet responsibility for the massacre of over 20,000 Polish servicemen at Katyn in 1940.[130]

By late 1992, however, the expansion of Poland's ties with Lithuania, Ukraine and Belarus was leading Russia to accuse it of trying to court these states behind its back.[131] Although there appeared to be no prospect of a Polish military alliance with any of these states, Poland clearly had an interest in sustaining them as strong, independent states forming a *de facto* buffer zone between it and Russia. Balancing relations with Russia and the other post-Soviet states, therefore, seemed likely to remain a serious dilemma.

More serious differences emerged over the issue of Polish membership of NATO. Visiting Poland in August 1993 President Yeltsin appeared to accept Polish membership of the Alliance. A joint declaration with President Walesa stated that 'such a decision would not be in contradiction with the interests of other countries, including Russia'.[132] Under domestic pressure, however, Yeltsin rapidly 're-interpreted' the declaration. In September the Russian ambassador to Poland stated that Yeltsin had not 'agreed' to Polish membership of NATO. Russian Foreign Minister Andrei Kozyrev warned that expansion of NATO might 'cause tension in Europe'.[133] President Yeltsin wrote to Western leaders, proposing joint Western–Russian security guarantees for East–Central Europe, rather than expansion of NATO.[134] The Polish government rejected the proposal.[135] Although the Alliance's January 1994 summit endorsed the possibility of new member's joining NATO and Poland joined the PFP programme, the Polish government remained concerned that Russian pressure might delay or preclude Polish membership.[136]

The unstable situation within Russia and the reassertion of Russian influence in the former-Soviet Union exacerbated Polish fears of Russian neo-imperialism. Polish concerns were intensified by the October 1993 coup attempt in Russia. The Polish government formed a crisis team to monitor developments. Defence Minister Janusz Onszkiewicz stated that it had 'prepared various options for our actions'.[137] The success of Vladimir Zhirinovsky's Liberal Democratic Party in Russia's December 1993 parliamentary elections further exacerbated Polish concerns, especially given statements by Zhirinovsky that Poland should be repartitioned between Germany and Russia.[138] Appearing to recognize the dangers involved in poor relations with Russia, however, by the summer of 1994 the Polish government was seeking to expand diplomatic contacts and conceding that it would 'have to accept a certain special status for Russia within the Partnership for Peace programme'.[139] The unstable situation within Russia and differences over Polish NATO membership, however, suggested that Polish–Russian relations might remain difficult.

Ukraine

The need to prevent the re-emergence of historic conflicts with Ukraine, combined with the important role a stable Ukraine might play as a buffer against Russia, made Ukraine particularly important in Poland's new Eastern policy. The Polish national security doctrine states that 'cooperation between Poland and Ukraine, in particular, should become a factor for stabilizing the situation in our region'.[140] In October 1990, long before Ukraine's independence, Poland concluded a declaration of friendship and good-neighbourly relations with it, confirming their mutual border; rejecting the use of force in their relations; and, pledging to respect international law, not to interfere in each others affairs and to respect minority rights.[141] Reflecting the special importance it attached to Ukraine, Poland became the first state to formally recognize its independence in December 1991.[142] A friendship and cooperation treaty, signed by President Walesa and Ukrainian President Leonid Kravchuk in May 1992, confirmed the inviolability of the border between the two states and their renunciation of territorial claims against each other.[143] Meeting in May 1993 the two Presidents signed further agreements on economic cooperation and established a bilateral Presidents Committee on Polish-Ukrainian relations designed to promote policy coordination and the further development of relations.[144]

Military cooperation also developed quickly. In mid-January 1992 Ukrainian Defence Minister General Konstantin Morozov visited Poland, assuring Polish officials that Ukraine would not maintain its own nuclear weapons, had no territorial claims on other countries, rejected force as an instrument of international politics, and would adhere to the CFE Treaty. Poland's then Defence Minister Jan Parys responded that once these declarations were implemented Poland would 'not be in danger from the Ukrainian armed forces'. The two ministers agreed to set up joint working groups on military education, defence industries and military preparedness.[145] Under the May 1992 cooperation treaty, the two countries also agreed to consult each other on issues of mutual interest, including defence and security.[146] In February 1993 Polish Defence Minister Janusz Onyskiewicz visited Kiev, signing an agreement to share military training facilities and organize military exchanges and ensuring that Poland would continue to be able to service its military aircraft in Ukraine and purchase spare parts.[147]

Polish–Ukrainian relations, however, remain potentially problematic. Ukraine's formal security policy remains one of neutrality. President

Kravchuk also proposed in 1993 a regional security zone encompassing Eastern European, Ukraine, Belarus and the Baltic states. With its central goal of integration with the West and membership of NATO, Poland is unlikely to show interest in either option – as indicated by President Walesa's cool response to Kravchuk's 1993 proposal.[148] Poland also remains sensitive to provoking worsening relations with Russia by developing an overly close relationship with Ukraine. The likelihood that Ukraine may pursue closer relations with Russia or face Russian economic pressure to accept closer relations could intensify Polish concerns over Russian neo-imperialism and limit the prospects for Polish–Ukrainian cooperation. The unstable situation within Ukraine and the tensions in Ukrainian–Russian relations also remain a source of concern for Poland: 'the collapse of a very delicate political equilibrium in Ukraine . . . instability in Russia, instability in Ukraine, some problems between those two countries . . . then we can expect a spill-over affect or some incident'.[149] Whilst Poland's central goal of integration with the West is likely to lead it to attempt to insulate itself from any conflict in Ukraine (rather than intervening), whether such a policy would succeed is less clear.

Belarus

The relative weakness of the national movement within Belarus and its development of close political, economic and security ties with Russia has created concerns in Poland that a close Belarus–Russian relationship might effectively extend a new Russian empire to Poland's Eastern border. The outlines of these tensions existed even before the break-up of the Soviet Union. In October 1990 the Belarusian government rejected Poland's offer to sign a declaration of friendship and good-neighbourliness, arguing that the declaration included a reference to the 1945 Polish–Soviet border treaty (which Belarus had not been party to) and that the Belarusian minority in Poland was being discriminated against. Polish observers, however, suggested that the real reason for the refusal to conclude the agreement was a reluctance to take steps independently of the central Soviet authorities.[150]

Belarus's progress towards independence in the autumn of 1991, paved the way for improved relations. In October 1991 the two states signed a Declaration on Good-neighbourliness, Mutual Understanding and Cooperation, renouncing territorial claims against each other and agreeing to respect ethnic minority rights.[151] After Poland recognized Belarus's independence in December 1991, progress on a formal cooperation treaty was rapid. The Treaty on Good-neighbourly Relations and Friendly Cooperation, signed by President's Walesa and Stanislau Shushkevich in Warsaw in June 1992, reaffirmed the two states renunciation of any border claims and commitments to respect ethnic minority rights, and established guidelines for economic, political and security cooperation.[152] Belarus, like Ukraine, also committed itself to become a non-nuclear state and to abide by the CFE Treaty, addressing Polish concerns about its military potential. In December 1992 the Polish and Belarusian defence ministers concluded a 'statement on establishing cooperation', providing for the establishment of contacts and the expansion of cooperation in the future.[153]

Although formal relations between the two states remain good, however, Polish concerns over Belarus's relationship with Russia continue. When Prime Minister Suchocka visited Minsk in November 1992, she expressed concern at Belarus's growing economic dependence on Russia.[154] At the same time, military contacts between the two remain limited, while most Polish security analysts believe that 'to some extent we should treat the armed forces of Belarus as *de facto* Russian troops'.[155] Polish concerns seemed confirmed when Belarus joined the Commonwealth of Independent States (CIS) collective security system in 1993. Given Poland's historic fears of Russia, the close Belarus–Russian relationship seems likely to remain a concern for Polish security planners.

Lithuania

As a result of its incorporation in the pre-eighteenth century Polish-Lithuanian commonwealth present-day Lithuania still has a 260,000 strong Polish minority (seven per cent of its total population and a majority in the regions surrounding Vilnius) and Lithuanians still fear Polish domination of their country.[156] The emergence of the Lithuanian independence movement in the late-1980s sparked tensions with the Polish minority. In September 1989, after the Lithuanian government refused to grant Polish equal status as an official state language, Polish-dominated local authorities declared their regions autonomous, raising fears of possible secession. The Polish government stated that it would not interfere in Lithuania's internal affairs and confirmed the inviolability of the existing border, but argued that Lithuanian Poles should be free to maintain links with Poland and develop their own language and culture.[157] The dispute continued into 1990, with Foreign Minister Skubiszewski accusing Lithuania of doing 'nothing . . . to improve the situation'.[158] Tensions worsened in October 1990 when delegates from Polish regions proclaimed a Polish National Territorial District. The Lithuanian government responded by suspending self-government in these regions.[159] Despite Poland's recognition of Lithuania's independence in September 1991, the dispute worsened. The Lithuanian government, accusing Polish minority leaders of supporting the August coup in Moscow, dissolved local governments in the Polish regions and imposed direct rule by central authorities. Foreign Minister Skubiszewski stated that the Polish government would have 'to defend the rights of the Polish minority'.[160]

By January 1992, however, the Lithuanian government had agreed to compromise and a declaration of friendship and good-neighbourly relations was signed, guaranteeing the border between the two states and the right of Poles in Lithuania to education in Polish, to write their names in Polish and to receive Lithuanian citizenship.[161] In September 1992 Lithuania's new Prime Minister Aleksandras Abisala visited Warsaw, meeting President Walesa and Prime Minister Suchocka. Suchocka concluded that there was 'hope for the development of good, even very good, Polish–Lithuanian relations in the future'.[162] From this point onwards, progress was made on the cooperation treaty, with both sides agreeing to drop controversial historical questions. By February 1994 the treaty had been successfully completed.[163]

Despite the tensions over the Polish minority, relations with Lithuania are not viewed as a significant security problem in Poland. Lithuania's size and small armed forced preclude it posing any military threat to Poland. Conflict is only likely if the minority issue escalates. Poland's post-communist governments, however, have consistently committed themselves to the existing Polish–Lithuanian border and rejected any interference in Lithuania. Polish government officials, further, view the minority issue as one that can be successfully managed. According to the Deputy Director of the European Department of the Polish Foreign Ministry, there is 'nothing alarming between Poland and Lithuania'.[164] Against this background, Poland has begun to develop military and security cooperation with Lithuania. In September 1992 Defence Minister Onyszkiewicz met with his Lithuanian counterpart Audrius Butkevicius, discussing the formation of joint working groups and greater mutual cooperation.[165] In June 1993 a military cooperation agreement was signed, covering the expansion of contacts, periodic consultations and exchanges, and control of the airspace over the Baltic sea.[166] Symbolising the improved relationship, in July 1993 Poland donated armoured transport vehicles and other military equipment to Lithuania.[167] With both states concerned about Russia and seeking to integrate themselves with the West, particularly NATO, they seem likely to maintain good security relations.

Kaliningrad

Poland also faced the question of the future of Kaliningrad – an *oblast* (region) of Russia, located between Poland and Lithuania on the Baltic coast. Before 1945 Kaliningrad (then Konigsberg) was part of German East Prussia. In 1945 the region became part of the Soviet Union. With the break-up of the Soviet Union, Kaliningrad became an enclave, isolated from the rest of Russia, with its future political and military status unclear. From 1991, the Russian military presence in the region grew, as forces withdrawn from Eastern Europe and the Baltic states were re-deployed there. In 1991–92, the scale of the Russian military presence was a matter of some debate. The International Institute for Strategic Studies suggested a force of two tank divisions, two motorized rifle divisions and one artillery division comprising 50,000 men, plus a coastal defence division.[168] Another western source suggested a further motorized rifle division and a force of 80,000 troops.[169] The Polish press suggested there might be 200–300,000 troops, implying that the Russian forces in the Kaliningrad region alone were larger than Poland's entire armed forces. In the spring of 1992, the Olszewski government argued that the Russian military presence was a 'potential threat', warning of a 'steady growth of offensive military forces'.[170] These warnings, however, appeared to be part of an exaggerated perception of a threat on Poland's Eastern border. Jerzy Milewski, the head of the Presidential National Security Bureau, argued that the troop build-up was not a hostile act since it resulted from the problem of housing forces withdrawn from Eastern Europe.[171] Recognizing that Russia faces problems in withdrawing forces and the Russian military view the region as an important base, Poland has pressed for reductions in Russian forces, rather than a complete withdrawal.[172] Polish officials also argue for 'the establishment of a regional table' covering Kaliningrad and Poland's other Eastern neighbours within the CSCE security forum,[173] which might focus on 'state of readiness, perhaps deployments, structure of forces . . . constraints on border area deployments and activities'.[174]

Poland has also been concerned about the possible re-emergence of German influence in Kaliningrad, fearing a repeat of the inter-war situation when Poland was squeezed between Germany proper and East Prussia. In 1990 the German government – fearing that nearly two million Volga Germans (ethnic Germans transferred to Central Asia by Stalin) might emigrate to Germany – suggested that the Volga Germans be resettled in 'an ethnic German territory or republic' in Kaliningrad. The Polish government insisted that Kaliningrad remain part of Russia (with its population unchanged), informing the Soviet government that the resettlement of the Volga Germans in Kaliningrad would be viewed as a direct threat to Poland's security and demanding that the plan be abandoned.[175] The plan was dropped and in April 1992 Russia and Germany agreed to establish a German 'Volga Republic' in Central Asia.[176]

The long term future of Kaliningrad, however, remains unclear. Although there appear to be no immediate problems, a number of possible sources of tension remain. German firms are developing economic links with the region. Former-East Prussians within Germany have advocated a 'condominium status' for the region, under joint authority, perhaps of Russia, Poland, Lithuania and Germany.[177] The Russian inhabitants of the region are re-discovering its German past and seeking closer political, economic and cultural links with Germany, the Nordic countries and the West in general, hoping to establish it as a de-militarized, autonomous free-trade zone (a 'Hong Kong on the Baltic').[178] Disputes between Lithuania and Russia also remain possible. Although Lithuania agreed to respect the territorial status quo and to permit transit to the region, in February 1992 Lithuania's then President Vytautas Landsbergis called for Russia to withdraw its armed forces from Kaliningrad.[179] Given the existence of a Lithuanian minority in the region, Lithuanian territorial claims cannot be absolutely ruled out.[180] Should relations with Russia worsen, Lithuania might also be tempted to use its control of access to Kaliningrad as a form of leverage over Russia.

Against this background, Poland has consistently supported the territorial and political status quo. According to a Polish Foreign Ministry official, Kaliningrad 'should stay Russian. It would be very unwise to try to deprive Russia of this entry to the Baltic sea. We are against any special German status in the Kaliningrad area. We have no territorial claims and we will reject any proposals for divisions of this area between Poland and Lithuania. The status quo is the best solution for the Kaliningrad area'.[181] Thus, under the May 1992 Polish–Russian treaty, Poland committed itself to respect Russia's present international boundaries. Poland has also tried to expand its economic links with the region, viewing this as the best way to counter German economic influence.[182] Russia, Germany and Lithuania have also committed themselves to support existing boundaries in the region. In the short-to-medium term, therefore, major changes in Kaliningrad's status seem unlikely. How far its current anomalous status is sustainable in the longer term is less clear.

DEFENCE POLICY

De-politicizing the Military

Since the late 1940s, the armed forces had played a central role in upholding communist power in Poland, suppressing popular unrest in 1956 and 1970, and imposing martial law in 1981. When Solidarity came to power in September 1989, therefore, whether they would remain loyal to a non-communist government and accept national security reforms was unclear. Sensitivity towards the Soviet Union and the armed forces led Solidarity to accept that the communist party retain control of defence policy through the Presidency.[183] Prime Minister Mazowiecki argued that:

> The Communist Party in opposition would be a negative thing – a trap both for us and for Poland. It would be difficult to imagine an opposition that controls the army and the police ... these people have a heightened sense of danger and insecurity at the moment. I don't want to foster this.[184]

Despite his previous record, President Jaruzelski initiated reforms, replacing some senior commanders and ending political education within the armed forces.[185] After the revolutions elsewhere in Eastern Europe at the end of 1989, reforms were accelerated. Political activity and membership of political parties were banned in the armed forces.[186] In April 1990 two Solidarity civilians, Bronislaw Komorowski and Janusz Onyszkiewicz, were appointed as Deputy Defence Ministers.[187] Admiral Piotr Kolodziejczyk, a former communist but considered supportive of reform, replaced General Florian Siwicki as Defence Minister in July 1990.[188] In November Kolodziejczyk announced the formation of a civilian Ministry of Defence (with the general staff concentrating on commanding the armed forces), the abolition of political officers, and the establishment of links with Western armies (including the training of officers in the West).[189] The election of President Walesa at the end of 1990 transferred ultimate control of the military to a democratically elected civilian. The first fully democratic parliamentary elections in October 1991 further accelerated reforms, with Jan Parys named as

Poland's first civilian Defence Minister in December 1991.[190] Indicating the extent of the changes, the Defence Ministry announced that in the past two years over 10,000 officers and seventy-eight generals had been retired and that all top commanders and commanders of military districts had been replaced.[191] Thus, by the end of 1991, Poland had made significant progress in dismantling the structures of communist control of the military and establishing a system of democratic civilian control.

Some, however, feared that the military might remain unwilling to introduce radical changes in defence policy or might intervene in domestic politics. The right-wing Olszewski government, in particular Defence Minister Parys, was committed to rapid 'de-communization' – involving controversial, large-scale purges of the armed forces. President Walesa, however, argued that the military had accepted Poland's democratic transition and experienced personnel were needed to implement defence reforms. Control of defence policy became the focus of the wider struggle for political power between the Olszewski government and President Walesa.[192] Parys rapidly took steps to de-communize the military and assert control of defence policy, unexpectedly announcing the retirement of his predecessor Admiral Kolodziejczyk, dismissing senior military commanders, and replacing the civilian Deputy Defence Ministers of the Mazowiecki government with controversial figures whom he deemed more politically reliable. Parys also argued that some within the military were unwilling to implement the new pro-NATO policy and should be dismissed.[193] There appeared, however, to be little evidence for his accusations.

In April 1992 Parys caused a major political controversy, accusing 'certain politicians' of 'entertaining officers and promising them promotions in return for the army's support in political intrigues' and warning of 'attempts to destroy democracy'. In short, Parys was suggesting that Poland faced a possible Presidential coup and that Walesa was seeking the support of the military.[194] Eventually, it became clear that Jerzy Milewski, the head of President Walesa's National Security Bureau, had met with the military to discuss plans for martial law in the event of a crisis.[195] Parys supporters argued that Walesa's staff were seeking to gain the military's support for an expansion of presidential powers, blocking the de-communization of the armed forces and opposing a pro-Western security policy.[196] In May, however, a Sejm commission concluded that Parys charges were 'groundless and damaging to the national interest' and that no attempt had been made to overthrow democracy or involve the armed forces in politics. Parys was forced to resign.[197]

The formation of the Suchocka government in July 1992 saw a return to relative stability, with the new government accepting a central role for the President in defence policy. Onyszkiewicz was appointed Defence Minister with the support of the Sejm and the President. Agreement was reached between the government and the President on a military reform package.[198] The adoption of the temporary 'little constitution' by the Sejm in August 1992 confirmed the situation, giving the President overall supervision of defence policy; the right to consultation over the choice of Foreign, Defence and Internal Affairs Ministers; and the power to appoint the chief of the General Staff.[199] Rapid progress was made on a new formal defence doctrine, which was unanimously agreed by the National Defence Committee at the beginning of November. Under the doctrine, the President 'coordinates the drawing up of the national defence strategy', 'determines the main directions' of the armed forces development and has direct control of the Commander-in-Chief in time of war.[200]

The election of the left-of-centre Pawlak coalition government in September 1993, however, re-opened the question.[201] The Pawlak government initially accepted that the President should play a central role in shaping defence policy, resulting in the re-appointment of Kolodziejczyk as Defence Minister with Walesa's support. In the summer of 1994, however, disputes re-emerged when the government proposed subordinating the chief of the General Staff to the Defence Minister, rather than the President.[202] The dispute prevented the establishment of a National Security Council to replace the existing National Defence Committee, since its operation would be shaped by the constitutional question.[203] The President then attempted to assert direct Presidential control of the General Staff and to gain the military's support for such a move, calling for Defence Minister Kolodziejczyk to resign. In October the Parliament responded by passing (with overwhelming support) a motion of censure accusing Walesa of creating a state crisis and threatening Polish democracy.[204] In November, however, Prime Minister Pawlak (who had previously supported Kolodziejczyk) unexpectedly sacked his Defence Minister, accusing him of failing 'to bring normality to the Defence Ministry'.[205] Fears of military intervention in politics, however, remained limited. As in 1992, the central struggle was between the government and the President for control of the military. The situation was further complicated, however, by growing divisions within the coalition government and the forthcoming 1995 Presidential election. By late 1994, the issue remained unresolved.

It appears that Poland's post-1989 governments have been largely successful in de-politicizing the military. Much of this success may be due to the shallowness of the armed forces apparent loyalty to the communist system. As President Walesa commented in 1991, 'in the past the army was like a radish – it was only red on the outside'.[206] The armed forces accepted with relatively little opposition both their subordination to civilian, democratic control and the reforming of Polish security policy. Despite Parys' accusations, they appear to have little interest in becoming involved in domestic politics. The more problematic issue is whether they should be under the control of the President or the government. This is only likely to be resolved by a permanent new constitution clearly defining the powers of the President and government. Although the parliament was due to discuss the new constitution in 1994–95, whether this debate would resolve the issue before the 1995 Presidential elections was less clear. In the meantime, should serious political instability emerge, there may remain a residual risk that the military will be dragged into politics.

Defense Strategy

In February 1990, shortly after the Mazowiecki government came to power, the National Defence Committee (which at this point remained dominated by communists) prepared a new military doctrine, asserting national control of the Polish armed forces in wartime and restricting operations to the defence of Polish territory.[207] The threat, however, remained to Poland's West and the Warsaw Pact remained central to Poland's defence. *Gazeta Wyborcza* described the doctrine as 'spiritually bound to the past'.[208] According to one Polish analyst, it 'failed to correspond from the very beginning to the then politico-military situation . . . a dead letter for it saw threats to the security of the country as originating solely in the West, the West which after all will become Poland's mainstay also in the area of security'.[209]

The extent to which the February 1990 military doctrine was a dead letter was confirmed in November 1990 when Defence Minister Kolodziejczyk announced new plans for the 'Army Of The 1990s'. The armed forces would be reduced by 50–70,000 personnel over five years, leading to a total size of under 250,000. Equipment would be cut significantly to bring Poland into line with the CFE agreement. More defensive (anti-tank, engineer and anti-aircraft) equipment would be purchased. New defensive tactics would be introduced, with no exercises at divisional level or above. Most significantly, two new military districts would be created in Eastern Poland (replacing the one existing district) and forces redeployed from the West to provide 'equal defence' of all borders.[210]

Defence strategy, however, became one of the foci of the conflict between President Walesa and the Olszewski government in 1992. The Presidential National Security Bureau was developing plans for further cuts in the armed forces and an 'all-round' defence. The Olszewski government, led by Defence Minister Parys, rejected further cuts and wanted to focus Poland's armed forces on its Eastern border.[211] At a February 1992 meeting of the National Defence Committee, the National Security Bureau proposed further reductions of 50,000 to a force of 200,000, but the government rejected the proposal.[212] Shortly after this, the National Security Bureau published its proposed new military doctrine, which suggested reducing the armed forces from 250,000 to 180,000; moving in the direction of a smaller, more professional army, with the capability to mobilize to a force of about 700,000 in the event of war; replacing the existing twelve divisions with seven military corps, each with some units at full operational readiness and others mobilizable at short notice; and adopting a strictly 'defensive doctrine'.[213] Parys refused to implement the plan.[214]

The consensus between the Suchocka government and President Walesa, however, allowed progress on a new strategy. The formal military doctrine, agreed in November 1992, stated that:

> In the event of a war which goes beyond a local conflict, Poland's strategy will be the longest possible resistance in order to repel invasion by inflicting the largest possible casualties on the aggressor, demonstrating the determination to continue our defence, and gaining time for reaction by other countries and international organizations. In the event of a conflict of lesser intensity, military actions will be conducted in order to assure that the invading force will be contained, halted, and destroyed in the shortest possible time.[215]

The new strategy aims to move towards a force which is 60–70 per cent professional, with some forces available for immediate action, mobilizable reserves and a combination of operational and territorial forces:

> The operational forces are prepared to fulfil the main tasks during wartime. The territorial defence units support and secure the actions of the operational forces and independently carry out defensive and protective activity in their assigned areas of operation.[216]

Although the doctrine does not define the detailed structure and size of the armed forces, the Suchocka government and President Walesa agreed to return to earlier plans involving reductions to a force of 180–200,000 and redeploying forces so that thirty per cent would be stationed in the East, thirty per cent in the centre and forty per cent in the West.[217] Ministry of Defence officials, however, conceded that 'we still are not certain about the structures of the forces, how they should look, how big will be the mobile corps operational forces, how big will be the territorial forces . . . this is a long process'.[218] As with other areas of security policy, the Pawlak government committed itself to continuity in defence policy, supporting the basic strategic direction established by the Suchocka government.

Implementing the new strategy, however, will take some years. Since the late 1980s, Polish defence spending has been cut drastically (see Table 4.2). According to official Polish data, in real terms the defence budget in 1993 was only 38 per cent of its level in 1986.[219] The Polish armed forces have been significantly reduced in size (see Table 4.3), with total active forces falling by over 100,000 since the late 1980s. By the time the CFE Treaty is fully implemented in 1996, Poland will have reduced its main ground armaments to roughly half the levels of the mid-1980s. With defence spending falling, the proportion spent on personnel costs has increased significantly; operational readiness has fallen significantly; exercises and training have been cancelled; conscripts have been returned home early; and logistics and procurement have been cut significantly.[220]

The military view the situation as 'a death struggle' and 'all-out destruction' of the armed forces.[221] Although these views may be somewhat exaggerated, it is clear that those elements of restructuring which involve substantial expenditure are likely to take many years to implement.

Table 4.2   Polish Defence Expenditure

	1986	1987	1988	1989	1990	1991
bn. zloty[1]	466	576	889	2,154	14,637	23,275
mn. US $[2]	5,945	5,863	5,657	3,904	3,869	3,612
% GDP	3.6	3.4	3.0	2.0	2.9	—

Note: 1. Current price figures.
2. 1988 prices and exchanges rates.

Source: S. Deger, E. Loose-Weintraub and S. Sen, 'Tables of world military expenditure', Appendix 7A, in Stockholm International Peace Research Institute, *SIPRI Yearbook 1992: World Armaments and Disarmament* (Oxford: Oxford University Press, 1992), pp. 254–64.

Table 4.3   Poland's Armed Forces in Transition

	1989	1990	1991	1992	1993	1994	CFE
Active	412,000	312,000	305,000	296,500	287,500	283,600	234,000
Reserves	505,000	505,000	507,000	435,200	465,500	465,500	—
Army	217,000	206,600	199,500	194,200	188,500	185,900	—
Airforce	105,000	86,200	86,000	83,000	79,800	78,700	—
Navy	25,000	20,000	19,500	19,300	19,200	19,000	—
Main Battle Tanks	3,300	2,900	2,850	2,850	2,545	2,110	1,730
Armoured Fighting Vehicles	3,950	3,250	2,319	2,161	2,051	1,536	1,807
Artillery	2,090	2,359	2,300	2,316	2,321	1,880	1,610
Combat Aircraft	565	516	506	423	468	398	460
Attack Helicopters	30	40	29	31	30	30	130

Source: The International Institute for Strategic Studies, *The Military Balance* (London: Brassey's for the IISS, annually, 1989 to 1994).

According to one analyst, even in late 1992 'practically, our military posture under our membership of the Warsaw Treaty remains (unchanged) until now'.[222] The commander of the Warsaw military district argued that the re-deployment of troops to Poland's Eastern border and the creation of the new Cracow military district would take five to seven years.[223] By late 1992, Polish Ministry of Defence Officials were admitting that the re-deployment had been 'retarded, actually frozen, because of the budgetary squeeze'.[224] Similar problems will be involved in procuring new equipment, increasing the proportion of professional soldiers, developing new operational plans and maintaining links with Western militaries. According to one Polish analyst, due to the 'lack of sufficient finances ... it is very difficult to imagine the creation of very mobile, rapid deployment forces' which Poland will need to cope with the types of threat it is most likely to meet in the 1990s.[225] In the absence of a clear military threat, however, significant increases in defence spending seem unlikely.

CONCLUSION

Since 1989 Poland has radically restructured its national security policy. Initially, concerns over securing the country's democratic transition, not antagonizing the Soviet Union and the Oder–Neisse border led the Mazowiecki government to pursue a cautious policy. Since then, Poland has made integration with the West, particularly membership of NATO, the central element of its security policy – reflecting a clear perception that the primary threats to Polish security lie in the unstable situation on its Eastern border. Parallel to this, Poland has supported a strengthened CSCE, cooperation with the other East–Central European states in the Visegrad group, bilateral security cooperation with Germany and its Eastern neighbours and the development of a defensive military strategy of 'all-round' defence.

Poland's new security policy has achieved significant successes. By 1993–94 Western officials were increasingly suggesting that Polish membership of the EU and NATO was a question of when rather than whether. Even short of NATO membership, Defence Minister Kolodziejczyk suggested that 'to a certain degree NATO also guarantees the security of our country today. Although there has been no declaration to this effect, there are, however, certain facts'.[226] The impressive progress in Polish–German relations is a major step in addressing one of Poland's main historic security problems. Although tensions exist with Poland's Eastern neighbours, none of these seem likely to lead to conflict in the short-to-medium term.

Despite Poland's fragmented political scene, further, a large degree of consensus has developed over foreign and security policy. By the autumn of 1994 no significant political forces were questioning the central objective of integration with the West, particularly membership of NATO. The main issue of contention was not the content of security policy, but rather the on-going question of whether the President or the government should play the central role in formulating that policy. While fundamental domestic political change leading to changes in foreign and security policy (such as some form of nationalist policy) could not be entirely ruled out, such a development did not seem likely.

5 Czechoslovakia and After

Historically, the central security problem of the Czech and Slovak lands has been that of domination by their neighbours – the former by Prussia/ Germany, the latter by Hungary. The creation of Czechoslovakia in 1918 failed to resolve this problem. The incorporation of the Sudetenland and part of Hungary into Czechoslovakia created a German minority of three and a half million and a Hungarian minority of one million, leaving the new state vulnerable to territorial claims from its neighbours and pressure for secession from the minorities within. Czechoslovak security policy in the inter-war period aimed to deter revisionist claims from Germany, Hungary and Poland through alliances with France, the Soviet Union, and Romania and Yugoslavia (the 'Little Entente'). The collapse of these alliances in 1938–39 resulted in the incorporation of the Czech lands into the German Reich, the loss of territories to Hungary and Poland, and Slovakia's emergence as an independent state under German tutelage.

The failure of the inter-war policy led the re-established, post-war Czechoslovak state (under the leadership of President Eduard Beneš) to seek security through a closer alliance with the Soviet Union, combined with friendly relations with the West. The Communist coup of 1948, however, resulted in the breaking of ties with the West and the subordination of Czechoslovak policy to that of the Soviet Union. The 1968 intervention to suppress the 'Prague spring' only confirmed Soviet unwillingness to see a genuinely independent Czechoslovak state.

The 'velvet revolution' of November 1989 radically transformed the domestic context of Czechoslovak security policy. Within the space of a few weeks a government dominated by non-communists was in power, with the communist party discredited and Vaclav Havel elected President. Security policy decision-making came under the control of a new elite comprised of President Havel, the new Foreign Minister Jiri Dienstbier and a small group of former opposition activists. With the Czech and Slovak opposition coalitions Civic Forum and Public Against Violence winning the June 1990 elections, this group played the central role in shaping Czechoslovakia's new security policy. The divergence of the Czech Republic and Slovakia's political paths after the June 1992 elections, however, resulted in the break-up of the Czechoslovak federation at the end of 1992 and the emergence of indepen-

60

dent Czech and Slovak states. This chapter examines the evolution of Czechoslovak security policy after the 'velvet revolution' of November 1989, the security implication of the break-up of Czechoslovakia and the emerging security policies of the two new states.

DISMANTLING THE SOVIET ALLIANCE

The most immediate security issue facing Czechoslovakia's new noncommunist leadership when it emerged in early December 1989 was how far to question their country's post-war alliance with the Soviet Union. The unexpected and rapid nature of Czechoslovakia's 'velvet revolution', combined with the absence of any formal negotiated transition, made this dilemma particularly sharp. Vaclav Havel's adviser Michal Kocab met with Soviet embassy officials in Prague at the end of November 1989, informing them that Civic Forum wanted the withdrawal of Soviet forces from Czechoslovakia, but would respect Soviet security interests.[1] At the government's first press conference in mid-December the new Foreign Minister Jiri Dienstbier announced that discussions had begun with the Soviet Union on the withdrawal of its forces from Czechoslovakia.[2] According to the Chancellor of President Havel's office, the withdrawal of the Soviet forces was the new government's primary security objective because they 'foresaw that developments in the Soviet Union might be difficult and one never knows what the (Soviet) army might have done'.[3] By early January 1990 Czechoslovak and Soviet diplomats had reached agreement on the principle of a complete withdrawal 'in the very near future'.[4] The Czechoslovak government stated that it expected the majority of Soviet troops to leave by the end of May 1990 and a complete withdrawal by the end of the year.

After further negotiations and a letter from President Gorbachev to President Havel, however, the Czechoslovak leadership accepted that the Soviet Union faced significant problems in implementing a rapid withdrawal and agreed to a somewhat slower timetable.[5] Meeting in Moscow on 26 February 1990 President Havel and Gorbachev signed the troop withdrawal agreement and a declaration on bilateral relations. The majority of the Soviet forces were to leave by 31 May 1990, with the withdrawal to be completed by 1 July 1991. Bilateral relations would be based on 'equality and complete mutual respect for each other's state sovereignty'.[6] President Havel stated that the existing mutual assistance treaty between the two states, which was to expire in the summer of 1990, should not be renewed, as it reflected their old relationship[7] – implicitly rejecting a continued alliance with the Soviet Union.

The new Czechoslovak government, however, took a cautious approach towards the Warsaw Pact. Civic Forum's political programme, developed during the November 1989 revolution, accepted Czechoslovakia's 'international and legal obligations' under the Warsaw Pact.[8] This view was reiterated by President Havel and Foreign Minister Dienstbier in December 1989 and January 1990.[9] Czechoslovak policy was clarified at a meeting of Warsaw Pact foreign ministers in March 1990. Dienstbier proposed a 'European agreement on collective security' based on the CSCE process. While both NATO and the Warsaw Pact 'would go on existing for some time', they would gradually be replaced by the new body.[10] In April, however, Dienstbier confirmed that Czechoslovakia was not considering leaving the Pact.[11]

As the Soviet Union became increasingly reluctant to discuss the reform of the Warsaw Pact, Czechoslovak policy shifted. In July 1990 Prime Minister Marian Calfa threatened to pull Czechoslovakia out of the alliance unless reforms were instituted.[12] Czechoslovakia proposed, with Hungary, a calendar for reform involving the transformation of the Pact into a political body by November 1990 and the dissolution of its military structures by the end of 1991.[13] In September Czechoslovakia announced that it would no longer participate in Warsaw Pact exercises.[14] By October President Havel was arguing that the Pact had 'outlived its day'.[15] Concern began to be expressed about the nearly 20,000 Soviet troops remaining of Czechoslovak soil, dependence on Soviet oil supplies and the possibility of an influx of refugees.[16]

The Soviet military crack-down in Lithuania in January 1991 intensified Czechoslovak fears, leading the government to press for a more rapid dismantling of the Warsaw Pact. The Czechoslovak government condemned the violence and announced that it would consider withdrawing from the Pact.[17] While the Foreign Ministry stated that there was no military threat to Czechoslovakia, Civic Forum leader Jan Urban suggested that the Soviet action in the Baltic states might be extended to Eastern Europe, arguing that 'democracy in Eastern Europe can still lose'. Interior Minister Jan Langos also suggested that Czechoslovakia could face a military threat from the Soviet Union.[18] Foreign Minister Dienstbier warned that the increasing influence of conservative forces in the Soviet Union might have serious implications for Czechoslovakia's security.[19]

The Federal Assembly requested Foreign Minister Dienstbier 'to consult

Poland and Hungary about a joint response, including consideration of a speedy withdrawal from the Warsaw Pact'.[20] As was seen in the previous chapter, Poland, facing problems in its negotiations over the Soviet troop withdrawal, opposed a joint withdrawal. Thus, when Dienstbier met his Polish and Hungarian counterparts in Budapest later in January they instead proposed that the Pact's military structure be abolished by 1 July 1991 and its political structures abolished by the end of 1991 or March 1992 at the latest, effectively forcing the Soviet leadership to accept the Pact's demise.[21] The Czechoslovak government's willingness to take a stand against the Soviet Union was further confirmed when it joined Poland and Hungary in opposing the Soviet demands for 'security clauses' in new bilateral treaties with the countries of Eastern Europe. According to President Havel the 'security clauses' were unacceptable because they restricted Czechoslovakia's sovereignty; contravened CSCE principles, which upheld the right of any member to join alliances; and might prevent Czechoslovakia joining the EC.[22]

The August 1991 coup in the Soviet Union brought the tensions in Czechoslovakia's relations with its Eastern neighbour to a head. The Czechoslovak government argued – at least publicly – that the coup did not, in itself, represent a threat to the country's security. With the last Soviet troops withdrawn at the end of June and the Warsaw Pact dismantled, concerns focussed on the maintenance of Soviet oil supplies and the fear of an influx of refugees. Havel expressed concern, but suggested that Czechoslovakia was 'not directly endangered'. The Foreign Ministry, in discussions with the Soviet Ambassador to Prague, insisted that the Soviet Union maintain energy deliveries and observe all other international agreements. Six thousand soldiers were deployed to the country's Eastern border to help border guard units deal with a possible refugee influx.[23] The Soviet coup intensified Czechoslovak security concerns, leading the government to press for faster integration with Western institutions, particularly NATO. Defence Minister Lubos Dobrovsky warned of the possibility of a threat to Czechoslovakia from the Soviet Union and the Soviet troops in Germany, while the army's mobile rapid deployment force was placed on a higher state of readiness and intelligence cooperation was undertaken with NATO.[24] During the coup a Foreign Ministry official stated that, 'we hope that we would be under the wing of the North Atlantic Treaty Organization, especially during a crisis like this'.[25] Foreign Minister Dienstbier said that Czechoslovakia would seek full membership of NATO if it felt threatened pending the establishment of a new European security system.[26]

GERMAN UNIFICATION

The second short-term security issue facing the new Czechoslovak government was the prospect of German unification. The issue was a less serious concern for Czechoslovakia than for Poland. The Sudetenland (returned to Czechoslovakia in 1945) had only been part of Germany after the Munich agreement of 1938. Both East and West Germany had accepted their post-war frontiers in treaties with Czechoslovakia. The West German constitution only laid claim to Germany's 1937 territories (not including the Sudetenland). Post-war expulsions and emigration had reduced Czechoslovakia's three million German minority to about 50,000 people.[27] Despite this, many Czechs were concerned by the prospect of German unification. The communist regime had stoked fears of Germany. Demands by German expellee groups for compensation for Sudeten Germans expelled in 1945 (including the right to return to previously-owned property) and special rights for the remaining German minority were provocative for most Czechs. German claims to the Sudetenland, though unlikely, could not be absolutely ruled out.

The new Czechoslovak leadership, however, did not see German unification as a threat. President Havel argued that:

> If Germany is reunified as a democratic entity I would not be afraid even if it had 100 million people. But if it is a country of a totalitarian nature, I would be afraid even if it had only two million people.[28]

The end of communism in Czechoslovakia and German unification were seen by the new leadership as opportunities to re-build relations with Germany on a cooperative basis, in order to forestall possible conflicts. Early in January 1990, at a time when the prospect of German unification was a sensitive issue in Czechoslovakia and abroad, Havel chose to go to both East and West Germany on his first foreign visit as President, publicly endorsing the right of the two German states to unite. Havel argued, however, that unification must be conditional on a commitment to Germany's existing borders and should take place within a framework of European unification.[29] Foreign Minister Dienstbier similarly argued that the best guarantee against a re-birth of 'traditional German expansionism would be the political, economic, and social integration of a united Germany into Europe'.[30] In the first few months of 1990 the Czechoslovak government, like its Polish counterpart, came out strongly in favour of a united Germany's continued membership of the EC and NATO.[31] According to the Chancellor of President Havel's

office, the 'paramount question' was to 'have Germany involved as far as possible in the European security conference and to have Germany fixed in NATO ... so that Germany would be fixed in European structures'.[32] While it supported Poland's request for inclusion in the 'two-plus-four' talks, the Czechoslovak government did not press for participation itself, arguing that its interests would not be directly affected.[33] According to Foreign Minister Dienstbier 'our border with Germany is not contested but Poland's frontier is under question'.[34]

The eventual outcome of the 'two-plus-four' negotiations – a united Germany's continued membership of NATO and guarantees of its existing borders – saw Germany unified along lines which the Czechoslovak government had advocated from the beginning of 1990. Reflecting the government's positive view, President Havel expressed joy at Germany's unification on 3 October 1990, arguing that as democratic states Germany and Czechoslovakia were bound to become good neighbours.[35] Popular concern about German power and influence, however, remained.

SECURITY POLICY: FROM CSCE TO NATO

The new Czechoslovak government very rapidly developed two core elements to its new security strategy: the strengthening of the CSCE to create a pan-European collective security system and collaboration with Poland and Hungary in pursuing integration with the West. The new policy was enunciated by President Havel during official visits to Poland and Hungary in January 1990. Poland, Czechoslovakia and Hungary 'should not mutually compete' to join West European institutions, but should rather coordinate their 'return to Europe', aiming to 'fill with something meaningful the great political vacuum that arose in central Europe after the break-up of the Habsburg Empire'. Havel invited Polish and Hungarian government representatives to Bratislava to discuss what 'institutional forms' cooperation might take.[36] The Presidents, Prime Ministers and senior officials of the three East–Central European states met in Bratislava in April 1990. The meeting, however, lacked a specific agenda and was marred by disputes over the Hungarian minority in Slovakia. It ended in failure, with the Poles and Hungarians rejecting a joint declaration proposed by the Czechoslovaks.[37] Despite this, Havel's proposals should be seen as one of the antecedents of what was to become the Visegrad group.

During his January 1990 visits to Poland and Hungary, Havel also outlined the key aim of Czechoslovak security policy:

Europe as a friendly comity of independent nations and democratic states, a Europe that is stabilized, not divided into blocs and pacts, a Europe that does not need the protection of superpowers, because it is capable of defending itself, that is of building its own security system.[38]

The basis for the new security system should be a strengthened CSCE, eventually resulting in the dissolution of NATO and the Warsaw Pact. Havel reaffirmed Czechoslovakia's new policy during a visit to the United States in February 1990, calling for 'a new pan-European structure which could decide about its own security system, based on a legal guarantee of existing borders and commitments to human rights, political pluralism and free elections'.[39] Although Havel suggested that NATO might be dissolved and US troops withdrawn from Europe, the Bush administration appears to have persuaded him that NATO and the US military presence in Europe were stabilizing factors.[40]

The origins of the new Czechoslovak leadership's support for a pan-European security system based on the CSCE can be traced to their time as opposition activists. During this period, key members of the new elite, in particular Havel and Dienstbier, had been active in pan-European peace and human rights movements, such as European Nuclear Disarmament. High on the agenda of these groups was the diffusing of the East–West confrontation through the withdrawal of US and Soviet troops from Central Europe and the dissolution of the Warsaw Pact and NATO.[41] According to Dienstbier, his colleagues and he had had:

> time to think about . . . the kind of Europe that we would want to have one day . . . a 'political and military security system' for Europe . . . a collective system. Now, when we can influence foreign policy, we want to try to build something like that.[42]

By March 1990 the Czechoslovak leadership had developed more specific ideas. Foreign Minister Dienstbier proposed an Agreement on Collective European Security based on the CSCE, including commitments to peaceful settlement of disputes and 'mutual assistance, including military assistance'; and an executive European Security Commission; and, eventually, an Organization of European States based on the EC and the Council of Europe.[43] These ideas were formally presented in a memorandum to all CSCE states in April 1990, calling for a 'new Europe-wide structure of peace, stability and confidence'. A European Security Commission, involving all CSCE states, operating on the basis of consensus and with a Military Committee subordinated to it, would hold regular high-level meetings. The Commission would consider the international situation in Europe and propose appropriate measures; forestall threats to peace and security and recommend means of settling disputes; and support and propose arms control, disarmament and confident-building measures. This would in due time be followed by the establishment of an 'Organization of European States' and eventually a European confederation.[44] These proposals formed the basis of Czechoslovak security policy for much of the rest of 1990. Although not included in the memorandum, Dienstbier argued that the new security system must 'guarantee that no one can ever attack anyone else and, should there be an attack nevertheless, to provide for reasonable, adequate defence guaranteed by all'. 'Completely lacking' in the CSCE as then constituted were 'tangible security guarantees'. A collective security treaty involving 'an explicit contractual obligation to give assistance, including military assistance, to a participant in the system that has been attacked' was needed.[45] President Havel also called for an 'obligation to provide mutual assistance in the case of an attack'.[46]

Czechoslovakia's proposals for a strengthened CSCE met with considerable success. The institutionalization of the CSCE agreed in the November 1990 *Charter of Paris for a New Europe* reflected many of the Czechoslovak ideas: regular meetings at various levels and the creation of the Committee of Senior Officials, a Conflict Prevention Centre and a Secretariat (based in Prague). Czechoslovak Deputy Foreign Minister Zdenek Matejka noted that 'a number of our suggestions have been used in drafting the documents of the preparatory committee for the Paris summit'.[47] The institutionalization of the CSCE which emerged from the Paris summit, however, did not live up to early Czechoslovak hopes, failing to provide the formal security guarantees which Havel and Dienstbier had advocated. At the Paris summit, Havel implicitly recognized that, in the absence of CSCE security guarantees, the countries of East–Central Europe might be forced to seek closer relations with NATO. NATO had 'proved itself to be a guarantee of freedom and democracy' and 'could conclude certain association agreements with other European countries'.[48]

Disappointment with the way in which the CSCE was developing as a security institution, combined with growing concern at the direction of developments within the Soviet Union, led to a significant re-think of national security policy. Czechoslovakia again pushed for greater cooperation with Poland and Hungary. As has been seen, it was at Czechoslovak instigation that the foreign ministers of the three countries met during the Baltic crisis in January 1991, resulting in an intensification of cooperation. More significantly, recognition of the limitations of the CSCE appears to have convinced the Czechoslovak government that the expansion of ties with the West, particulary NATO, should play a central role in Czechoslovakia's security – a significant strategic re-direction of security policy. When a NATO delegation visited Czechoslovakia early in February 1991, Havel and Dienstbier agreed to increase information exchanges, exchanges of military observers and diplomatic contacts, arguing that the situation in the USSR meant that Europe could not do without NATO.[49] Later that month Dienstbier visited NATO's headquarters in Brussels, meeting NATO Secretary-General Manfred Woerner and stating that European security was impossible without NATO[50] – reflecting how far Czechoslovak security policy had evolved from earlier suggestions that NATO be dissolved.

The shift in policy was made clear in March 1991 when President Havel became the first East European leader to visit NATO's headquarters. A formal declaration by the Czechoslovak government stated that NATO constituted 'an important security factor for Central and Eastern Europe'. Czechoslovakia was determined 'to build new partnerships with the North Atlantic Alliance, to deepen their dialogue on security matters, to develop broader and more active exchanges and cooperation'.[51] Havel warned that the countries of East–Central Europe were 'sliding into a . . . security vacuum'. While Czechoslovakia could not yet join NATO, 'an alliance of countries united by the ideals of freedom and democracy should not be forever closed to neighbouring countries that are pursuing the same goals'. Havel called for a 'lasting system' of 'cooperation and exchange' with NATO and intensified 'dialogue on security matters'. The forthcoming association agreement with the EC should enable Czechoslovakia to take part in its 'security and defence aspects'. 'Increasingly intensive cooperation' would ensure that Czechoslovakia, 'even in the event of a threat, will not feel alone and forgotten by the democratic community'.[52]

While NATO leaders made clear that Czechoslovakia could not join the Alliance, Havel's plea was followed by an expansion of contacts. In April 1991 NATO and Czechoslovakia jointly sponsored a conference on European security in Prague. NATO Secretary-General Manfred Woerner, while rejecting formal NATO links with East–Central Europe, offered a web of close relations.[53] Foreign Minister Dienstbier concluded that NATO's 'interest' in East–Central Europe was 'one of the important guarantees' of Czechoslovakia's incorporation into the West.[54] The chairman of NATO's Military Committee, General Vigleik Eide, visited Czechoslovakia, meeting Defence Minister Dobrovsky.[55] In June 1991, General John Galvin, NATO's Supreme Allied Commander Europe, visited Prague, meeting Foreign Minister Dienstbier and President Havel, and stating that NATO considered itself responsible for Central and Eastern Europe.[56] Deputy Foreign Minister Martin Palous summarized the new policy in June 1991:

> When the outcome of the revolution in this region was so uncertain, we wanted to get rid of the bipolar system that divided Europe. That meant getting rid of NATO and the Warsaw Pact. Now our priority is to find some stability, and NATO is the only structure that still works in a pan-European context.[57]

According to one Czechoslovak Foreign Ministry official, 'we had to get integrated into existing European security mechanisms. So, in effect, we were trying to get as close to NATO as possible'.[58]

The August 1991 coup in the Soviet Union prompted the Czechoslovak government to intensify demands for a special relationship with NATO. Although Foreign Ministry officials noted that Czechoslovakia had not formally applied for membership,[59] in October 1991 President Havel suggested to US President George Bush that NATO offer associate membership to the countries of East–Central Europe. Bush rejected Havel's suggestion, instead supporting the US–German proposal for a liaison relationship through what was to become the North Atlantic Cooperation Council (NACC).[60] Indicating Czechoslovakia's support for the NACC idea, Foreign Minister Dienstbier argued that NATO was the only European security institution which had 'proved its effectiveness and viability . . . this is why we consider this alliance so important'.[61] One Czechoslovak Foreign Ministry official later argued that 'we were at least partially successful because we contributed to the creation of the NACC . . . that at least gives us the possibilities and the chances to have regular and systematic political contact with NATO countries'.[62] However, according to a member of the Foreign Affairs Committee of the Czechoslovak federal parliament, 'we were slightly disappointed by the results of the (November 1991 NATO) Rome meeting (where the NACC was agreed). . . . we really need some guarantees from the West concerning our security'.[63] Prime Minister Marian Calfa argued that the collapse of the Soviet Union might create new security problems and Czechoslovakia wanted NATO to fill the security gap left.[64] In this context, Foreign Ministry officials noted that their country was particularly active, as Chairman-in-Office of the CSCE from January 1990 to December 1992, in 'trying to get NATO involved, as much as it was practical and feasible, in the CSCE activities, in order to facilitate for NATO . . . some new missions' outside the NATO area.[65]

RELATIONS WITH THE NEW GERMANY

With the immediate issues relating to German unification settled, the Czechoslovak government hoped to build cooperative relations between the two states. The immediate focus became the negotiation of a bilateral cooperation treaty. In November 1990, shortly after unification, German Foreign Minister Hans-Dietrich Genscher, under domestic pressure to secure guarantees of compensation (including the right to return) for Germans expelled from Czechoslovakia and special rights for the German minority in Czechoslovakia, raised these issues during a visit to Prague.[66] Almost the whole political spectrum in Czechoslovakia, however, rejected the German claims for reparations and special minority rights. President Havel argued for a 'zero solution,' whereby wartime reparations claims would be dropped by both sides.[67]

Reflecting the sensitivity of the issue for both sides, the negotiations were 'held behind closed doors' and proved to be 'unusually protracted', with little information about their contents revealed.[68] By mid-1991, however, the Czechoslovak government had become frustrated at the slow pace of the negotiations and continuing German demands for compensation and settlement rights. In August and September the Czechoslovak ambassador to Germany accused the Germans of delaying the treaty out of excessive concern for Sudeten Germans and urged the German government to show 'real political courage' by signing the treaty that autumn.[69] Later in September a compromise was reached. The treaty would be signed but the issue of property lost by Germans expelled at the end of war would be addressed separately.[70] According to a Czechoslovak Foreign Ministry spokesman, this was 'a disappointment. We would have preferred a treaty which closed the whole past once and for all. But we concluded even without such a clause it would be worthwhile to have a treaty'.[71]

The Czechoslovak–German Treaty of Friendship and Cooperation, initialled by Foreign Ministers Dienstbier and Genscher in October 1991, included commitments to base relations on the principles of international law, the UN Charter and CSCE documents; resolve disputes by peaceful means; guarantee minority rights for Czechs and Slovaks in Germany and Germans in Czechoslovakia; and regular meetings at Prime Minister and Foreign Minister level. It also included a rejection of any territorial claims; agreement on mutual respect for the principle of national self-determination; and German support for Czechoslovak membership of the EC.

The failure of the treaty to address the reparations issue, however, created problems. In January 1992 German Chancellor Helmut Kohl, under domestic pressure, postponed the signing of the treaty. Within Czechoslovakia, critics of the government argued that the treaty conceded too much to Germany and failed to settle the border and compensation questions. Later in January Dienstbier met Genscher and the two, fearing that the treaty might be postponed until after the June 1992 Czechoslovak elections, agreed that it must be signed soon to prevent it becoming a controversial issue in the election campaign. Kohl eventually agreed and the treaty was signed in February.[72] Despite further debate within Czechoslovakia, the treaty was ratified by the Federal Assembly in April and the German parliament in May–June.[73]

Czechoslovakia's support for German unification and the convergence of the two countries' security policies paved the way for security cooperation, with Germany emerging as a strong advocate of expanding EC and NATO ties with Czechoslovakia. The convergence of the two states' security policies was confirmed in April 1991 when Foreign Ministers Dienstbier and Genscher reached agreement on the 'Prague Theses' on European security, which stressed the importance of a continuing 'trans-Atlantic dimension' to European security and the right of the countries of East–Central Europe to join the EC.[74] The two countries also began to explore possible military cooperation.[75]

Tensions, however, remained. The failure of the cooperation treaty to address the issues of compensation for German expellees, compensation for Czechoslovak victims of Nazism, and (due to legal complexities) the annulment the 1938 Munich agreement, suggested that these problems would re-emerge.[76] Fears of German economic domination also remained. In February 1992 the Czechoslovak intelligence service controversially warned that Germany was seeking political domination of Czechoslovakia through a 'massive economic offensive' and might use its economic power to pressure Czechoslovakia to accept the right of German expellees to return to property lost in 1945.[77] Although the government rejected this analysis, Prime Minister Calfa argued that the government should seek investment from other Western countries to balance that of Germany (which according to the Czechoslovak foreign trade office accounted for three quarters of foreign investment).[78] With no significant political forces in Germany questioning the border and the position of the remaining German minority in Czechoslovakia relatively good, however, these issues seemed unlikely to lead to security problems, at least in the short-to-medium term.

RELATIONS WITH THE POST-SOVIET STATES

Russia

While relations with Russia remained important for Czechoslovakia because of Russia's continuing role as a major regional power, there were no major sources of conflict between the two states. With the withdrawal of Soviet forces already completed, no direct border between the two states, and no border or minority disputes, Russia appeared unlikely to pose any immediate security problems for Czechoslovakia. Negotiations for a bilateral cooperation treaty proved uncomplicated.[79] The treaty, signed by Presidents Havel and Yeltsin on 1 April 1992 in Moscow, included commitments to base relations on international law, the UN Charter and CSCE principles; not to allow the use of either states territory for aggression against the other or to support any other state in such aggression; to regular inter-governmental meetings; and a condemnation of the 1968 Soviet-led intervention.[80] The absence of any major problems in relations was confirmed in July 1992 by the symbolic release from the Russian archives of the 1968 letter from Czechoslovakia's communist leaders 'inviting' the Soviet Union to intervene and in October 1992 by the approval of an agreement allowing former-Soviet forces withdrawing from Germany to transit through Czechoslovakia.[81]

Ukraine

Czechoslovakia's relations with Ukraine were complicated by a potential territorial dispute over the Transcarpathian *oblast* (region) of Western Ukraine. From 1919 to 1939 Transcarpathia (then called Ruthenia) was part of Czechoslovakia. During the second World War, the region was occupied by Hungary. In 1945 the region was transferred to the Soviet Union under a treaty with Czechoslovakia and thus forms part of present-day Ukraine. The potential therefore existed for Czechoslovak, Slovak, or Ruthene revanchist claims against Ukraine. There are also small Ruthene and Slovak minorities in Ukraine and a smaller Ukrainian minority in Eastern Slovakia, creating potential problems over minority rights.[82]

After the 'velvet revolution', a Ruthene Renewal movement was formed in Czechoslovakia, demanding a special minority status – denied during the communist period – for Ruthenes. With regard to Transcarpathia, one Czechoslovak Ruthene leader also argued that the Ruthenes 'would like the border withdrawn . . . it was taken away from us by force'.[83]

This position was, however, supported by only a small minority of ultra-nationalist politicians and in January 1991 Foreign Minister Dienstbier ruled out any border changes.[84] The government's position was confirmed in October 1991 when a Foreign Ministry spokesman stated that Czechoslovakia would not initiate talks on Transcarpathia and would only support any territorial change with the agreement of the USSR and Ukraine.[85]

The situation was complicated, however, by the collapse of the Soviet Union at the end of 1991. In the December 1991 Ukrainian independence referendum 78 per cent of the population of Transcarpathia voted in favour of the region becoming 'a special self-governing administrative territory' (a free trade zone), within an independent Ukraine. Later that month the Society of Carpathian Ruthenians (SCR), based in Transcarpathia, requested that the 1945 treaty ceding the region to the Soviet Union be annulled and called for an independent 'Carpathian Republic'. In Czechoslovakia, the chairman of the Society of Friends of Subcarpathian Rus condemned the 'theft' of the region. The SCR repeated its demands for the annulment of the 1945 treaty and an independent Transcarpathia in January 1992.[86]

Despite this, relations with Ukraine remained good, as the Czechoslovak government consistently rejected any territorial revisions. When diplomatic relations were established at the end of January 1992 the Ukrainian Foreign Minister expressed satisfaction that Czechoslovakia had not raised the border issue,[87] a position reiterated by Prime Minister Calfa in March.[88] The absence of disputes between the two states allowed negotiations for a bilateral cooperation treaty to proceed. The treaty, signed at the end of May 1992, included a mutual commitment not to make any territorial claims.[89] Although Transcarpathia remained a point of tension, it did not appear likely to emerge as a serious source of conflict, at least in the short-to-medium term.

DEFENCE POLICY

De-politicizing the Military

One of the most immediate tasks facing the new Czechoslovak government in 1989–90 was the de-politicization of the military. During the November–December 1989 'velvet revolution' the army had issued a statement that it was 'ready to defend the achievements of socialism' and fear of an army supported suppression of the democracy movement was widespread.[90] Despite demands for the appointment of a civilian Defence Minister, however, the coalition government formed under Prime Minister Calfa in December 1989 retained the existing communist Defence Minister Lieutenant-General Miroslav Vacek (who had replaced the previous minister Milan Vaclavik during the short-lived reform communist government of November 1989). This decision was apparently driven by fears of provoking the still communist-dominated armed forces and the Soviet leadership, combined with assurances from Vacek that the military would not oppose reform.[91]

Steps to de-politicize the military, however, were taken rapidly. On 6 December 1989 changes to the constitution removed the commitment to the communist party's leading role from the military oath, invalidated rules enforcing ideological instruction in the armed forces and abolished mandatory instruction in Marxism–Leninism at military colleges. Communist Party cells were banned from the armed forces from 31 December. Prime Minister Calfa, acting as interim President, replaced a number of high-ranking general staff members. [92] In January 1990, however, rumours surfaced that the communist-dominated officer corps might support the secret police and the recently disbanded people's militia in a coup attempt.[93] Interior Minister Richard Sacher ordered special units of the Ministry of Internal Affairs onto the streets to reinforce the police – suggesting that the government did indeed fear a coup, although Sacher and President Havel denied this.[94] A coup attempt never occurred and whether a coup was ever planned and elements of the army would have participated remain unclear. The widespread rumours, however, indicated the extent to which doubts about the loyalty of the armed forces remained.

De-politicization of the armed forces was accelerated after this. In January 1990 Defence Minister Vacek introduced a 'screening' process for all professional soldiers. In the first stage of this process, 5,000 top-ranking officers and senior Ministry of Defence officials were screened, with over 20 per cent failing to be cleared.[95] By September 1990, 74 generals, 4,830 officers and 4,476 non-commissioned officers had left the armed forces.[96] Thus, quite rapidly those most closely associated with the communist system were removed. A new law on military service passed by the Federal Assembly in March 1990 also banned membership of and activity in political parties during military service, omitted all reference to the Soviet Union and socialism, limited the circumstances in which the army might be used to maintain internal security and put decisions on its internal use in the hands of the President as Commander-in-Chief.[97]

A more radical step was taken in October 1990 when President Havel sacked General Vacek and appointed a non-communist civilian – Lubos Dobrovsky – as Defence Minister. Vacek's dismissal coincided with the announcement of the findings of a presidential commission on the events of November 1989, which confirmed that the military, including Vacek, had prepared to intervene against the democracy movement.[98] Vacek's removal, therefore, seemed to indicate that doubts remained about the military's loyalty. In contrast, Dobrovsky, a close associate of Havel and Dienstbier, had been a leading member of Charter 77, a key activist in the 'velvet revolution' and Foreign Ministry spokesman and then First Deputy Minister of Foreign Affairs in the new government. His appointment signalled that the new democratic elite was taking more direct control of defence policy.

The background to Vacek's dismissal had been intensifying demands for purges of former-communists in the armed forces. Dobrovsky, however, opposed purging the armed forces, instead asking the Federal Assembly to verify the screening of the military.[99] The Defence and Security Committee of the Federal Assembly reported on the screening process in April 1991, arguing that there were no major problems. One committee member concluded that the 'Czechoslovak Army is creative, obedient, and guarantees the minister's decisions'. Dobrovsky ordered an end to further dismissals.[100] The first months of Dobrovsky's tenure as Defence Minister, therefore, seemed to indicate that the process of de-politicization had been successful. According to one analyst, 'by the summer of 1991, the military clearly had become a genuine state institution under the full control of elected bodies'.[101] Another observer concluded that 'the army is certainly not seen as a threat to the democratic reforms in the country anymore'.[102] Whilst a significant achievement, the rapid and apparently successfully de-politicization of the military also reflected the shallowness of its loyalty to the communist party and the Soviet Union.

Defence Strategy

The new government also faced the task of developing a new defence strategy. After the 'velvet revolution', although the military continued to implement changes which had been initiated by the communist regime early in 1989 (including significant reductions in the armed forces and their defensive restructuring), they continued to see the main threat as coming from the West and to think in terms of Warsaw Pact coalition warfare. Defence Minister Vacek argued that Czechoslovakia 'need make no change in relations with the Warsaw Pact'.[103] The new political leadership, however, wanted a more fundamental reform of defence policy. In May 1990 the Czechoslovak Defence Council – the highest defence decision-making body – instructed Vacek to develop a new doctrine not directed against a specific enemy.[104] By the autumn of 1990 the Defence Ministry had developed a draft doctrine, which was submitted to the federal assembly. Some Civic Forum deputies, however, distrusted the Ministry of Defence and prepared their own draft doctrine.[105] By March 1991 the basic principles of the document, based on elements of both drafts, had broad support and the Federal Assembly formally adopted Czechoslovakia's new military doctrine. The doctrine outlined a policy of territorial defence, did not define a specific enemy, called for an equal distribution of the armed forces throughout the country and envisaged exclusively defensive operations.[106]

The new military doctrine, however, was a general statement of principle. A more detailed three-stage plan for the development of the armed forces had been published by the Defence Ministry in June 1990 – the 'Army 2005' plan. From 1991 to 1993, manpower would be reduced by 40,000 to 160,000, equipment reduced by 40–60 per cent, forces redeployed to the East of the country, and professional soldiers increased from 30 to 50 per cent of the total. From 1994 to 2000, more modern equipment would be procured, further cuts in personnel made and the Czechoslovak armed forces integrated into wider European security structures. From 2000 to 2005, professional soldiers would rise to 75 per cent of the total; compulsory military service would be reduced to three-to-five months, with a system similar to the Swiss militia system; the armed forces reduced to between 80,000 and 90,000; and full integration into European defence structures achieved.[107]

Reducing the size of the armed forces was not a major problem. In June 1990 First Deputy Chief of the General Staff Lieutenant General Josef Vincenc stated that the Army would be cut by 60,000 to 140,000 within three years. The combination of screening, alternative service for conscientious objectors, resignations, retirements and planned reductions saw total active armed forces fall from 198,200 in 1990 to 145,800 in 1992. Since Czechoslovakia had one of the largest and best equipped armed forces in Eastern Europe, reductions in line with the CFE treaty would allow it to remove large amounts of old equipment while retaining newer equipment. Equipment modernization was therefore a less significant problem for Czechoslovakia than for Poland and Hungary. According to Vincenc, 'our army's equipment is such that we can afford to forego purchases during the next few years'.[108] By

Table 5.1   Czechoslovakia's Armed Forces in Transition

	1987	1988	1989	1990	1991	1992	CFE
Active	201,000	197,000	199,700	198,200	154,000	145,800	140,000
Reserves	280,000	280,000	295,000	295,000	295,000	295,000	—
Army	145,000	145,000	148,600	125,700	87,300	72,000	—
Airforce	56,000	52,000	51,100	44,800	44,800	44,800	—
Main Battle Tanks	3,500	3,400	4,585	3,995	3,200	3,208	1,435
Armoured Combat Vehicles	4,900	4,900	4,900	5,528	4,740	4,386	2,050
Artillery	1,795	1,975	2,100	3,685	3,446	3,414	1,150
Combat Aircraft	465	450	477	312	297	304	345
Attack Helicopters	40	45	50	60	56	56	75

Source: The International Institute for Strategic Studies, The Military Balance (London: Brassey's for the IISS, annually, 1987 to 1992).

1992 equipment levels had fallen significantly from those of the late 1980s (see Table 5.1).

Relatively rapid progress was also made in redeploying the Czechoslovak armed forces, although this was made difficult by the lack of bases in Slovakia. In September 1990 Defence Minister Vacek announced the redeployment of Czechoslovakia's armed forces in order to distribute them equally across the whole of the country's territory.[109] The redeployment would involve transferring one tank division, one mechanized division, one air-defence division and a number of specialized units to Slovakia. Scheduled to be completed in 1993, it would leave 38 per cent of the armed forces in Slovakia.[110] The new force structure also involved replacing Czechoslovakia's two existing Military Districts with three regional commands. By the summer of 1992 substantial progress had been made in redeploying the ground forces, but none of the Czechoslovak airforce was based in Slovakia, which had no military airfields.[111]

These developments, however, took place against a background of a rapidly declining defence budget (see Table 5.2). Czechoslovak defence spending fell by more than half in real terms between 1989 and 1991. Although some of this reduction was absorbed by the large reductions in manpower and equipment, the redeployment of forces was also costly. As a result, funding for training and operational readiness

Table 5.2   *Czechoslovak Defence Expenditure*

	1986	1987	1988	1989	1990	1991
mn. Koruny[1]	26,435	27,362	28,374	28,213	25,089	21,323
mn. US $[2]	3,962	4,097	4,241	4,159	3,363	1,768
% GDP	3.4	3.4	3.4	3.7	3.1	—

Note: 1. Current price figures.
        2. 1988 prices and exchange rates.

Source: S. Deger, E. Loose-Weintraub and S. Sen, 'Tables of world military expenditure', Appendix 7A, in Stockholm International Peace Research Institute, *SIPRI Yearbook 1992: World Armaments and Disarmament* (Oxford: Oxford University Press, 1992), pp. 254–64.

was reduced, while all new procurement was postponed. By November 1991 Chief-of-Staff Lieutenant General Karel Pezl was arguing that a 50 per cent increase in defence spending was needed to implement reform plans and maintain readiness. Despite similar calls from Defence Minister Dobrovsky,[112] the Federal Assembly refused to authorize increased spending. Reflecting the increasing budgetary squeeze, in May 1992 Dobrovsky announced that the armed forces would be further reduced from 135,000 to between 100,000 and 90,000 within five years.[113]

CZECHOSLOVAKIA'S DEMISE

Implicit in the security policy developed by the federal government and President Havel after 1989 was the assumption of a single, federal state with coherent security interests and objectives. Increasingly, however, this assumption was undermined by the Czech–Slovak tensions which led to the break-up of Czechoslovakia at the end of 1992.[114] After the June 1990 elections disputes rapidly emerged over the balance of power between the federal and republican governments. The Slovak government demanded increasing devolution of power. The federal and Czech governments supported a strong federal state. These differences produced increasingly bitter and protracted negotiations for a new constitution. By the autumn of 1991, nationalist Slovak deputies had issued a declaration of sovereignty and a declaration of independence was defeated by a single vote in the Slovak parliament.

These developments spilled over into security policy. In the spring and summer of 1990 the Slovak Republic established a parliamentary Commission on Foreign Policy, a Minister for International Relations and a Ministry of International Relations.[115] Although formally not interfering with the jurisdiction of the federal authorities, the role of these bodies remained ambiguous, appearing to be the first step towards an independent Slovak foreign policy. The Slovak government also began to assert distinct Slovak national interests. In the summer of 1990 Slovakia's then Prime Minister Vladimir Meciar called for a more rapid re-deployment of the Czechoslovak armed forces to Slovakia to counter possible Hungarian and Ukrainian threats.[116] During the debate over the cooperation treaty with Germany in 1991–2, the Slovak government argued that recognition of the wartime continuity of the Czechoslovak state was intended to humiliate Slovakia by denying its wartime existence as an independent state.[117] Czech–Slovak tensions also emerged in the armed forces.[118] In January 1991 an Association of Slovak Soldiers was formed, demanding recognition of Slovak rights within the military and the formation of separate Czech and Slovak armed forces. In the summer of 1991 a proposal for the formation of a Slovak Home Guard was narrowly defeated within the Slovak parliament.[119]

The June 1992 elections proved to be the decisive turning point in Czech–Slovak relations. The right-of-centre Civic Democratic Party (ODS), led by the new Czech Prime Minister Vaclav Klaus, emerged as the dominant force in the Czech Republic. The left-of-centre, nationalist Movement for a Democratic Slovakia (HZDS) emerged as the dominant force in Slovakia, under the leadership of the new Slovak Prime Minister Vladimir Meciar. The two differed radically on the future structure of the Czechoslovak state, with the ODS advocating a strong federal state and the HZDS supporting a vaguely defined confederal Czech–Slovak union. The formation of an effective federal government proved impossible and negotiations between Klaus and Meciar in July and August produced agreement that the Czechoslovak federation be dissolved by the end of 1992. Although the majority of the population in both the Czech Republic and Slovakia supported the maintenance of a single state, Czechs and Slovaks were, by and large, divided on whether the state should be a strong federation or a loose confederation. A referendum, therefore, was likely only to produce continued constitutional paralysis. In November, with the irreconcilability of the positions of the Czech and Slovak governments clear, the Federal Assembly voted in favour of dissolving the Czechoslovak state. Czechoslovakia formally ceased to exist on 1 January 1993, with the Czech and Slovak Republics becoming independent states.

Table 5.3   Czechoslovakia, the Czech Republic and Slovakia (1992–3)

	Population	Area (sq. km.)	Troops	Main Battle Tanks	Armoured Personnel Carriers	Artillery Pieces	Combat Aircraft	Attack Helicopters
Czechoslovakia	15,576,000	49,382	145,000	3,208	4,286	3,414	402	56
Czech Republic	10,302,000	30,449	110,010	1,703	2,462	1,612	231	37
Slovakia	5,274,000	18,933	55,005	851	1,231	806	116	18

Sources: J. Pehe, 'Czechoslovakia: Toward Dissolution', *RFE/RL Research Report*, 2 (1 January 1993) p. 85, Copyright © 1993 by RFE/RL, Inc.; 'Czechoslovakia: the two halves', *The Guardian* (28 December 1992); The International Institute for Strategic Studies, *The Military Balance 1992–1993* (London: Brassey's for the IISS, 1992); and *The Arms Control Reporter 1992 and 1993* (Cambridge, Mass.: Institute for Defense and Disarmament Studies, 1992 and 1993).

Throughout the second half of 1992, the Czech and Slovak governments negotiated over the division of federal assets and terms for future Czech–Slovak relations. In October and November agreement was reached on a wide range of issues, including a customs union, a border treaty, the rights of Czechs and Slovaks on the territory of the other republic, a good-neighbourly relations treaty, the division of federal assets (including the Czechoslovak armed forces), and a treaty on defence cooperation. The armed forces would be split on the basis of a 2:1, Czech–Slovak ratio, requiring the transfer of substantial amounts of weaponry and material from the Czech Republic to Slovakia (See Table 5.3).[120] The transfer of forces to Slovakia, accelerated in the autumn of 1992 when it became clear that the country would split, was virtually complete by the end of 1992.

In stark contrast to the violence unleashed by the disintegration of Yugoslavia, a key feature of Czechoslovakia's demise was its peaceful character. [121] Although federal leaders were opposed to the break-up of Czechoslovakia, there appears to have been no consideration of the use of force to maintain the federation. Minority rights and border disputes – the immediate causes of the conflict in Yugoslavia – did not emerge as serious sources of tension, nor do the two peoples have a history of violent ethnic conflict. The Czech Republic and Slovakia do not to view each other as security threats and conflict between them appears unlikely, at least in the short-to-medium term. Since the break-up of Czechoslovakia, however, relations although formally cooperative have been somewhat strained.[122] The establishment of separate currencies (despite an earlier agreement to maintain a single currency for some period of time), disagreements over the division of federal property and disputes over how open the border between the two states should be have all caused tensions. Underlying these issues is the broader question of how far the two states are pursuing divergent political and geo-strategic paths. Since independence, the Czech Republic has moved rapidly to establish a Western-style democracy and market economy and to integrate itself with the EU and NATO. Slovakia, in contrast, has been mired in political instability and has made less progress in instituting economic reforms and developing ties with the West. In this context, the Czech Republic has been reluctant to establish a close relationship with Slovakia.

THE CZECH REPUBLIC

Security Policy

The Czech Republic has made integration with the West its central foreign and security policy objective. Prime Minister Klaus has sought to establish the Czech Republic on a 'fast-track' for integration with Western institutions, particularly the EU, arguing that his country is the most advanced of the East European states in establishing democracy and a market economy. In September 1992, before formally gaining independence, the Czech Foreign Ministry outlined the Czech Republic's foreign policy priorities: strengthening ties with Western economic, political and security institutions and eventually joining them; establishing close bilateral relations with its neighbours; and preventing further de-stabilization of other post-communist states in the region.[123] In December 1992, Czech Foreign Minister Josef Zielienec stated that he wished to see negotiations for Czech membership of the EU begin in 1996, with membership achieved by 2000.[124] Progress in integration with the West was confirmed in 1993, with admission to the Council of Europe and the signing of an association agreement (based on Czechoslovakia's agreement) with the EU.[125] Throughout 1994, Klaus asserted his government's desire to apply for EU membership by 1996 and to join by 2000.[126]

The Czech Republic has also sought full membership of NATO. In the summer of 1993, Prime Minister Klaus appeared to raise some doubts over this, noting that NATO's relevance had been called into question by the end of the Cold War and that his government was examining the development of different European security organizations.[127] In a major speech to the Czech parliament in October 1993, however, President Havel outlined the reasons for the Czech Republics desire to join NATO: its situation at the centre of Europe, its commitment to Western values, and the need 'to be firmly integrated into a working system of collective defence'. Further, Havel argued, NATO must 'differentiate' the East–Central European states as the logical 'first candidates for NATO membership'.[128] The government accepted Havel's arguments. In October 1993 Foreign Minister Zieleniec, visiting the US, pressed for a clear US commitment to Czech membership of NATO.[129] In November he argued that NATO was the only functioning military alliance able to safeguard its members' security and that there was no alternative to NATO membership.[130] Although some Left Bloc deputies opposed joining NATO,[131] the main political forces within the Czech Republic all supported the idea.

The debate surrounding NATO's Partnership for Peace (PFP) programme in 1993–94 confirmed the Czech Republic's support for membership of NATO. When PFP was proposed in October 1993 President Havel stated that the Czech Republic would continue to press for NATO membership, warning that PFP could not be regarded as an alternative to membership.[132] Similarly, Prime Minister Klaus argued that PFP lacked 'clear signals, adequate for us' on NATO membership.[133] Klaus also suggested that the East–Central European states might join NATO 'à la France' – becoming members of the alliance, but not (yet) joining its integrated military structures – thereby overcoming the problem of compatibility with NATO forces.[134] Despite concerns over PFP, the Czech Republic became one of its first signatories in March 1994, with Klaus describing NATO as 'the most reliable way of safeguarding our security' and then NATO Secretary-General Manfred Woerner noting that the Czech Republic was one of the Alliance's most active partners.[135]

The Czech Republic has also been active in developing military cooperation with the West. In April 1993 a memorandum of understanding was signed with the UK on strengthening defence cooperation, including exchanges of personnel from training establishments.[136] In June 1993 NATO's then Supreme Allied Commander Europe (SACEUR) General John Shalikashvili visited Prague, meeting Prime Minister Klaus and President Havel, with the two sides agreeing to expand military cooperation.[137] By 1993–94, officers were being trained in the West (particularly in the US and Germany) and air defence ties (including military exchanges), designed to facilitate eventual integration with NATO air defences, were underway.[138] In May 1994 joint Czech–French military exercises were held for the first time in both the Czech Republic and France.[139] In August 1994 a defence cooperation agreement was signed with Canada, covering military training and possible cooperation in arms production.[140]

Unlike the previous Czechoslovak government, the Czech government sought to limit cooperation in the Visegrad group, believing that integration with the West might be delayed by close ties with what it saw as its less economically advanced and less politically stable neighbours.[141] Thus, in January 1994, it rejected a joint approach to NATO, stating that it supported free trade and economic integration within the Visegrad group, but wanted to maintain autonomy in its dealings with the West.[142] Klaus again rejected calls for closer Visegrad cooperation in March 1994, arguing that the Czech Republic was 'far ahead of all other countries in the region' in its reforms.[143] Klaus's view appeared to be gaining support in the West by the autumn of 1994, with the European Commission arguing that the Czech Republic and Slovenia were the most advanced of the East European states in terms of economic reforms and the best-placed to join the EU.[144] How far such considerations would shape EU policy or would affect the issue of NATO membership, however, remained unclear.

Relations with Germany

Germany is the largest foreign investor in the Czech Republic, its largest trading partner and a strong advocate of its integration with the EU and NATO. At the same time, however, Germany's growing economic influence has created fears of economic (and perhaps also political domination), while Sudeten German compensation claims remain a source of tension between the two states. The Sudeten German compensation issue re-emerged in May 1993, when the parties of the Czech coalition government proposed the establishment of a working group to take part in an informal non-governmental dialogue with the Sudeten Germans. The proposals, however, rapidly attracted great criticism. With the majority of Czechs clearly opposed to any discussion of compensation, Prime Minister Klaus called off the proposed dialogue.[145] Since then, the issue has remained a source of tension, with the Czech government continuing to oppose demands from Sudeten German bodies for compensation.

These tensions, however, have not spilled over into the security field. Germany has continued to support the Czech Republic's integration with the EU and NATO and bilateral security and defence cooperation has developed well. In May 1993 a defence cooperation treaty was signed, providing for the regular exchange of information; cooperation in humanitarian aid operations, environmental protection and arms control; and the development of contacts between Czech and German troops in the border region.[146] In August 1994 Czech, German and Polish soldiers undertook a symbolic joint friendship march along the border between their countries.[147] Thus, while some tensions between the Czech Republic and Germany seem likely to continue, President Havel has noted that these are 'not . . . explosive material'.[148]

Defence Policy

The first Czech Defence Minister, Antonin Baudys, was appointed on 31 December 1992, one day before Czechoslovakia's break-up. Thus, almost no time had been available for planning a new Czech defence policy. Despite the relative success of the de-politicization of the Czechoslovak armed forces undertaken since 1989, many officers from the 'old order' remained in place. In May 1993 Defence Minister Baudys announced the resignation of the Chief of Staff General Karel Pezl and introduced a new screening process, checking the 'moral, physical, and professional qualifications' of all 43,000 professional soldiers. All officers who had participated in the purges of the armed forces after 1968 or planning for a clampdown in 1989 would be dismissed. By August 1,620 officers had been screened, with only 618 surviving the process. The purge of the military (combined with many younger officers leaving by choice), however, has left it with a shortage of skilled officers, raising doubts about its combat-effectiveness.[149]

In June 1993 Baudys announced plans for the restructuring of the armed forces to create a 'semi-professional army'. The armed forces would be cut from their then strength of 88,500 to 65,000 by the end of 1995. The Soviet-model division structure would be replaced by a Western-style brigade structure. By 1995, the 28,000-strong ground forces would be equipped with 957 main battle tanks, 954 combat vehicles, 413 armoured personnel carriers and 767 artillery pieces. The force would be based on three elements: a mobilizable territorial defence force (15 brigades), an operational mobile ground force (9 brigades), and a rapid deployment force (1 brigade of 3,000 men). The air force would have 20,500 personnel, 150 aircraft and 36 attack helicopters.[150] These reforms seemed likely to create a more defensively oriented force, since the territorial forces would have little offensive potential and the size and offensive mobility of the mobile ground force and the rapid deployment force seemed limited.

Constraints on the defence budget have, however, created significant problems for the Czech armed forces. Under the 1993 budget of 20 billion koruny ($688 million), three per cent of gross national product

(GNP), the military did not have sufficient funds to maintain existing equipment or undertake required training. Prime Minister Klaus, however, wished to reduce defence spending to two-and-a-half per cent of GNP. The procurement of new equipment and the development of a fully professional force (Baudys' long-term goals) therefore seemed likely to be postponed indefinitely. The ability of the Czech armed forces to respond in the event of a military threat also seemed called into question.[151]

SLOVAKIA

Security Policy

Since gaining independence, Slovakia has been plagued by political instability and doubts about its democratic credentials. These problems have spilled over into foreign and security policy. After the June 1992 elections, Meciar's autocratic character and nationalist agenda, doubts over his government's commitment to economic reform, and worsening relations with Slovakia's Hungarian minority all raised questions about how far Slovakia would pursue a Western-oriented foreign policy or would meet the criteria for integration with Western institutions. Meciar warned that if the West shut the door on Slovakia, it might be forced to orient itself toward the East.[152] By November, with the prospect of independence looming, Slovak Foreign Ministry officials were noting that relations with the West, particularly NATO, would be a subject of 'political discussions', since there were some politicians who wanted 'a neutral Slovakia'.[153]

Foreign and security policy emerged as a contentious issue early in 1993. In a New Year speech heralding Slovak independence, Meciar gave priority to relations with Russia and Ukraine. Shortly after this, Meciar argued that Slovakia had to decide whether to remain neutral, move towards NATO or act within a new Central European security system. Meciar also criticised the reforms undertaken by Poland, the Czech Republic and Hungary, arguing for a 'third way' between capitalism and socialism. Foreign Minister Milan Knazko, however, argued that these were Meciar's 'private views' and that integration with the West, including the Western security system, was the only option. Knazko's criticism of Meciar's 'authoritarian attitudes' and their differences over foreign policy resulted in his replacement as Foreign Minister in March 1993 by Meciar's then ally Josef Moravcik, raising fears that Slovakia might pursue a more Eastern oriented foreign and security policy.[154]

After Moravcik's appointment, however, Slovakia began to pursue a more actively Western-oriented policy. By May 1993 Meciar had dropped ideas of a 'third way', arguing that the only option for Slovakia was 'to accept the requirements of the West'. Meciar, Moravcik and President Michal Kovac repeatedly called for closer integration with the West, including membership of the EU and NATO.[155] The shift in policy met with some success. In June 1993, after agreeing to alter its minority rights legislation, Slovakia was accepted as a member of the Council of Europe along with the Czech Republic (despite Hungarian opposition). In October Slovakia, again along with the Czech Republic, signed an association agreement with the EU. Although the West remained concerned about Slovakia's democratic and minority rights credentials, it appeared to be integrating it along with the other East–Central European states rather than allowing it to lag behind them.

The Slovak government also indicated more clearly its desire for NATO membership and sought to develop practical military cooperation with the West. By August 1993 Prime Minister Meciar was arguing that NATO was 'the only functioning security institution in Europe'.[156] Visiting the US in September, the chairman of the Foreign Affairs Committee of the Slovak parliament argued that 'the utmost priority of Slovak foreign policy is to enter European political, economic and security structures'.[157] In 1993 NATO SACEUR General Shalikashvili visited Slovakia and military cooperation was initiated with the US and the UK.[158] The Western orientation of Slovak security policy was confirmed in February 1994 when Slovakia became one of the first countries to join NATO's PFP programme.[159]

Although Slovakia continued to pursue a broadly Western-oriented security policy, it also sought good relations with Russia and Romania – suggesting that the options of a special relationship with Russia and a renewed 'Little Entente' were not entirely closed. For Russia, a close relationship with Slovakia might be seen as a way of limiting NATO's influence in the region. Thus, in November 1992, Russia's ambassador to Czechoslovakia stressed the 'great significance' of Slovakia as a partner for Russia and offered to 'support Slovakia in the military field.'[160] In the summer of 1993 the Slovak government supported a controversial clause in a draft Slovak-Russian treaty binding the two states not to make their territory available to other states in the event of a conflict with a third party. Criticism by Slovak opposition parties that this restricted Slovakia's sovereignty and undermined prospects for NATO membership led to the dropping of the clause and the revised treaty was signed in August 1993. A military cooperation agreement, however, was also signed at the same time, providing for close security ties and Russian military supplies to Slovakia. Prime Minister Meciar concluded that the treaties heralded 'a new type of Slovak–Russian cooperation'.[161] Good relations were confirmed in November 1993 when Russia agreed to pay back debt to Slovakia with deliveries of arms (including five MiG–29 aircraft), spare parts and ammunition. Russia, however, remained opposed to Slovak membership of NATO.[162]

Developments in Slovak–Romanian relations also raised fears of a possible renewed 'Little Entente'. In June 1993 Prime Minister Meciar met Romanian President Ion Illiescu, agreeing that 'good Romanian–Slovak relations were vital to dealing with the problem of Hungarian ethnic minorities'.[163] In September Illiescu visited Slovakia, signing a bilateral cooperation treaty, including a commitment to coordinate policies on ethnic minorities. Although a formal military alliance appeared unlikely, Illiescu said that the two countries should exchange experiences 'concerning their common neighbours' and that 'Slovakia would always find in Romania a loyal friend on whom it might rely in every situation'.[164]

Relations with Ukraine were also important for Slovakia. As one Slovak Foreign Ministry analyst noted, Ukraine is 'a superpower on our Eastern borders'.[165] Slovakia sought to persuade Ukraine (which also has a significant Hungarian minority) to agree to a statement on cooperation on minority issues. Ukraine, however, not wishing to jeopardise its good relations with Hungary, rejected the proposal.[166] Transcarpathia also remains a possible source of tension with Ukraine. However, as one observer noted, 'no one ever asked in Slovakia for the Subcarpathian–Ruthenia to be again attached to Slovakia . . . this should be some sort of reassuring element for the Ukrainians that this question is not going to jeopardise relations with Slovakia'.[167] The unproblematic state of relations was confirmed by the signing of a bilateral cooperation treaty and a military cooperation agreement in 1993.[168] Nevertheless, should pressure for an independent Ruthenian/ Transcarpathian state grow, Slovakia's relations with Ukraine could become complicated by the issue.[169]

In March 1994 Meciar's government was defeated in a parliamentary vote of no-confidence. Unlike its predecessor, the new government of Jozef Moravcik was unambiguously committed to establishing a Western-style democracy and market economy and pursuing membership of the EU and NATO. In the summer of 1994, therefore, the prospects for political stability and more concerted integration with the West appeared to improve. As a result, in June the International Monetary Fund (IMF) approved an economic stabilization loan of $263 million for Slovakia.[170] New elections in September–October 1994, however, returned Meciar to his position as Slovakia's dominant politician, with the HZDS winning 60 of the 150 seats in the parliament and in a strong position to form a coalition government. Meciar's most likely allies appeared to be the extreme nationalist Slovak National Party (SNS) and former-communists advocating political and economic alignment with Russia. Western observers feared that Meciar might try to establish an isolationist 'national socialism in one country'.[171] Should he follow this line, Slovakia's Western oriented foreign and security policy would clearly be called into question.

Relations with Hungary

Relations with Hungary have been the central security concern of the independent Slovakia. The creation of Czechoslovakia in 1918 ended 1000 years of Hungarian rule over Slovakia. Under the 1920 Treaty of Trianon, the new Czechoslovak state gained territory from Hungary, leaving it with a million-strong Hungarian minority. Throughout the inter-war period Hungary claimed the lost territory, temporarily regaining it during the second World War. When Slovakia became an independent state in 1993, therefore, it inherited a large Hungarian minority (over 10 per cent of its total population and 90 per cent in regions bordering Hungary) and a history of tensions with Hungary. Many Slovaks fear that the minority may secede or that Hungary will try to reclaim its lost territory – a fear exploited by nationalist politicians such as Meciar.

The June 1992 elections polarised the political situation in Slovakia, with Hungarian minority parties emerging as one of the main parliamentary opposition groups to Meciar's government and pressing for guarantees of minority rights. Meciar accused Hungary of conducting large-scale military exercises in the border region and warned that it could expect 'negative consequences' if it interfered in Slovakia's affairs. The Hungarian government denied the accusation and talks were held, resulting in the setting up of a hotline between the Hungarian and Slovak Prime Ministers' offices.[172]

Tensions, however, continued. In January 1993 the Council of Europe reported deficiencies in Slovakia's minority rights situation, including the forcible removal of Hungarian-language place signs; a ban on the use of Hungarian Christian names in birth registers; and a planned territorial reorganization of administrative districts designed to undermine the political representation of the Hungarian minority. In June, after agreeing to alter its minority rights legislation, Slovakia was admitted to the Council of Europe. The Slovak government and parliament, however, prevaricated, failing to implement the Council's recommendations.[173] The lack of progress led Hungarians in Southern Slovakia to hold an assembly in January 1994, calling for the implementation of the Council of Europe recommendations and greater Hungarian representation in state bodies. This, however, created Slovak fears that it might be a first step towards secession.[174] The dispute also prevented the signing of a bilateral cooperation treaty guaranteeing the current Hungarian–Slovak border, as Hungary was only willing to sign the treaty if it included specific guarantees of rights for the Hungarian minority (which the Slovak government was unwilling to accept).[175]

Slovakia's relations with Hungary were further complicated by the Gabcikovo–Nagymaros dam, a joint border region hydro-electric power project initiated by the two states in 1977. Although abrogated by Hungary in 1989, Slovakia continued with the project, unilaterally diverting the Danube in October 1992, thereby reducing the waterflow into Hungary and provoking a crisis. The EC intervened, mediating an agreement to halt further production, take the Slovak power plant out of operation, restore much of the water to its original course and submit the dispute to the International Court of Justice. Although the agreement temporarily defused the issue, disputes continued over Slovakia's failure to redivert the water or stop the operation of the plant.[176]

Despite these problems, military relations between the two states remained reasonably good. The Czechoslovak and then Slovak Defence Ministries and armed forces maintained regular and close contacts with their Hungarian counterparts, exchanging information on force strengths and doctrines. Meciar's assertions that Hungary was increasing military activities in the border region were denied by the Slovak Defence Minister Imrich Andrejcak. When Hungary began to modernize its airforce, Andrejcak argued that the modernization was legitimate and so long as Hungary observed Conventional Armed Forces in Europe (CFE) Treaty limits Slovakia had no reason to object. In October 1993 a military cooperation agreement was signed, including confidence-building measures such as exchanges of information on large-scale troop movements, exchanges of military observers, and coordinated air defence in border areas.[177]

The formation of the new Slovak government in March 1994 and the victory of the Hungarian Socialist Party (MSP) in Hungary's May 1994 elections led to improved relations. The new Slovak government was more sympathetic to the Hungarian minority's demands and proved able to cooperate with them in the Slovak parliament. In May the Slovak parliament approved a law allowing the use of Hungarian-language names.[178] The new Hungarian government was also more willing to include a commitment to the current Hungarian–Slovak border in a bilateral treaty and less strident in support of Hungarian minority rights. By the time of Slovakia's September–October 1994 elections, however, the Council of Europe's recommendations had not been fully implemented and the cooperation treaty had not been signed. Vladimir Meciar and his likely coalition partners opposed the minority rights legislation passed by the Moravcik government and campaigned in the election on a nationalist platform. Meciar's election victory, therefore, raised doubts about the prospects for continued rapprochement.

Defence Policy

In December 1992, just prior to Czechoslovakia's break-up, the Slovak parliament approved the establishment of a Defence Ministry and armed forces.[179] Although the Czechoslovak government appeared to have been relatively successful in de-politicizing the armed forces, questions about the politicization of the Slovak armed forces have emerged. Early in 1993 General Imrich Andrejcak was appointed as Defence Minister, raising questions about civilian control of the military. During his 1992–94 term as Prime Minister, Meciar was also accused of placing people loyal to him in the armed forces and seeking their political support.[180] Thus, it was notable that the Slovak Soldiers Association (a body representing the armed forces interests) endorsed the October 1993 coalition agreement between Meciar's HZDS and the SNS.[181] The Moravcik government made efforts to de-politicize the military, appointing Pavol Kanis as Slovakia's first civilian Defence Minister. In August 1994 Kanis announced reforms, including reductions in the number of military personnel working for the Defence Ministry and the conversion of the Army Headquarters into a smaller General Staff.[182] Meciar's October 1994 election victory, however, raised questions about how far he might seek to assert his political influence within the military.

In December 1992, when the Defence Ministry and armed forces were formed, it was announced that the armed forces would number 35,000.[183] Since most of the Czechoslovak armed forces were deployed in the Czech Republic, however, Slovakia faced particular problems in establishing its own armed forces and developing a defence policy. While Slovakia inherited personnel and equipment, it did not have ground and air bases, accommodation for personnel or ammunition depots. In 1993, the Slovak defence budget was 8.6 billion korunas ($283.3 million), representing 5.4 per cent of total government expenditure. The Defence Ministry, however, stated that 92 per cent of the budget covered maintenance costs, leaving only eight per cent for procurement, construction and research and development.[184] The delivery of five MiG-29s from Russia in January 1994 (as part of Russia's repayment of its debt to Slovakia) helped to strengthen the armed forces, taking the total strength of the airforce to 115 combat aircraft, the maximum permitted under the CFE treaty.[185] Given economic constraints and the absence of a decisive military threat, however, it seems likely to be some years before Slovakia will be able to construct the infrastructure it requires or fully modernize its armed forces. In the meantime, as with the other East–Central European states, the ability of the Slovak armed forces to respond in the event of a crisis is open to doubt.

CONCLUSION

Very rapidly after the 'velvet revolution' of November 1989, Czechoslovakia's new democratic leadership enunciated a visionary new security policy, aiming to develop the CSCE into a strong pan-European collective security system, which within a few years would replace NATO and the Warsaw Pact and could guarantee the security of all European states. From late 1990 onwards, however, the Czechoslovak leadership was forced to rethink this policy. With the CSCE failing to meet their initial expectations and increasing instability in the Soviet Union, they turned to NATO, seeking close relations with, and eventually membership of, the Alliance.

Since the break-up of Czechoslovakia at the end of 1992, the two new states have followed different paths. The Czech Republic has established itself as perhaps the most stable state in Eastern Europe, with good prospects for membership of the EU and NATO. By the autumn of 1994, however, whether Czech Prime Minister Vaclav Klaus's hopes of a 'fast-track' to membership of the EU and NATO (ahead of the other East–Central European states) would be fulfilled was unclear. Slovakia, in contrast, has followed an uncertain path. Although the overall direction of integration with the West has been maintained, doubts over its democratic and minority rights credentials, the continuing possibility that it might seek a special relationship with Russia or a renewed 'Little Entente' with Romania, and tensions with Hungary all raised questions about how far it would continue to follow the Western-oriented security policy of the other East–Central European states.

6 Hungary

After the collapse of the Austro-Hungarian empire at the end of the First World War, the central foreign and security policy question facing the new Hungarian state was that of relations with its immediate neighbours. Under the 1920 Treaty of Trianon, Hungary lost over two thirds of its pre-First World War territory to its neighbours (primarily to Romania, Czechoslovakia and Yugoslavia), leaving three million Hungarians outside Hungary as ethnic minorities in neighbouring states. During the inter-war years the desire to revise the Trianon borders dominated Hungary's foreign policy, leading it into an alliance with the Axis powers and conflict with its neighbours. Between 1938 and 1945 Hungary regained some of its lost territories, particularly those areas with large Hungarian populations. Defeat in the Second World War, however, saw Hungary returned to its Trianon borders.

With the establishment of a communist regime in the late-1940s Hungary became part of the Soviet bloc. Hungary's foreign and security policy was subordinated to that of the Soviet Union and the earlier problems of relations with neighbouring states were suppressed. The 1956 uprising against Soviet-imposed communist rule led the reformist Hungarian leadership to announce that their country was withdrawing from the Warsaw Pact and would become neutral. The Soviet suppression of the uprising, however, prevented the withdrawal from the Warsaw Pact and Hungarian policy was once more subordinated to Soviet policy.

Since the mid-1980s Hungary's domestic and international environment has, however, been radically transformed. In the late-1980s Hungary's ruling communist party – the Hungarian Socialist Workers Party (MSMP) – emerged as the leading reformist force in Eastern Europe. The democratic elections of March and April 1990, however, brought to power a non-communist, centre-right coalition government led by the Hungarian Democratic Forum (MDF). In May 1994, new elections returned the Hungarian Socialist Party (MSP) – the reformed successor of the MSMP – to government. This chapter examines the evolution of Hungarian national security policy since the late 1980s, exploring the impact of democratization and the way in which Hungary's governments have coped with the re-emergence of tensions with neighbouring states over borders and minorities.

REFORM UNDER THE MSMP

In the late 1980s Hungary's ruling MSMP was the first East European government to test how far increasing independence from Moscow night extend into foreign policy. In May 1988 MSMP leader Janos Kadar argued that there was no 'internal Hungarian reason' for the Soviet military presence in Hungary, only 'international reasons', expressing the hope that by the year 2000 Soviet forces would no longer be required. Officials suggested that Hungary could become 'experimental terrain' for a European conventional arms reductions agreement, implying that Soviet forces might be withdrawn.[1]

In 1989, with radical reformers dominating the MSMP and Soviet acceptance of East European autonomy becoming clearer, Hungary began to assert an independent security policy. In June, the reburial of the leaders of the 1956 Hungarian uprising in front of a crowd of 300,000 in Budapest symbolically rehabilitated the anti-Soviet revolt, implicitly questioning the rationale for the Soviet troops stationed in Hungary ever since.[2] By August the government was declaring that its 'central strategic goal' was for Hungary to join 'the community of the developed democratic nations'.[3] MSMP leaders began to argue that Romania represented a greater threat to Hungary's security than the West and proposed confidence-building zones along Hungary's borders with Austria and Yugoslavia.[4] Debate also began to emerge about neutrality – a concept popularized by its association with the 1956 uprising. Reformers connected with the MSMP argued for gradual 'Finlandization'.[5] The democratic opposition openly supported a negotiated withdrawal from the Warsaw Pact and neutrality.[6] By September senior government officials were suggesting that Hungary might become neutral.[7] Whether the Soviet leadership would tolerate a neutral Hungary, however, was unclear.[8] The MSMP's official position remained that demands for a withdrawal from the Warsaw Pact were 'irresponsible' and neutrality should be a long term aim.[9]

The accelerating pace of democratization within Hungary increased pressure on the MSMP to break the alliance with the Soviet Union. By October 1989, when the new Hungarian Republic was proclaimed, demonstrators were calling for a withdrawal of Soviet forces. In December a motion in the National Assembly called for all Soviet troops to be withdrawn by the end of 1990. The government, however, rejected the deadline as unrealistic, arguing that a withdrawal should be linked to the on-going Conventional Armed Forces in Europe (CFE) negotiations. The Foreign Affairs and Defence committees of the National Assembly eventually brokered a compromise, whereby the government would negotiate a complete withdrawal of Soviet forces 'if possible'.[10]

The January 1990 announcement that the Soviet Union had agreed to withdraw its forces from Czechoslovakia altered the situation. With the MSMP facing defeat in the elections in March, the government changed its position. On 13 January Prime Minister Miklos Nemeth, after meeting with his Soviet counterpart Nikolai Ryzhkov, announced that the two sides had agreed that Soviet forces be withdrawn as soon as possible.[11] Negotiations opened in February, with the Soviets agreeing to a total withdrawal, but disputing Hungarian demands that it be completed by 30 June 1991 (the same deadline as the Soviet withdrawal from Czechoslovakia). After further negotiations (and a Hungarian agreement to buy fuel and equipment which the Soviets argued they would be unable to withdraw by the deadline) an agreement was reached. On 10 March the agreement for a complete Soviet withdrawal by 31 June 1991 was signed. The first troops left two days later.[12] Debate over neutrality intensified. All the democratic opposition parties adopted it as part of their electoral programmes, isolating the MSMP, which still formally supported Warsaw Pact membership.[13] Foreign Minister Gyula Horn was forced to concede that neutrality might be achieved in the 'not too distant future'.[14]

TRANSFORMATION UNDER THE MDF

The victory of the democratic opposition in the March–April 1990 elections accelerated the breaking of the alliance with the Soviet Union. Announcing his government's programme, the new Prime Minister Jozsef Antall argued that Warsaw Pact membership was 'contrary to the will expressed by the nation in 1956 and reaffirmed in the latest election' and proposed negotiations on the alliance's future. Foreign Minister Geza Jeszenszky called for withdrawal from the Pact, but argued for caution over the method and a Finnish model for relations with the Soviet Union.[15] At the June 1990 meeting of Pact leaders Antall made clear that Hungary wished either to see the Pact dissolved or to leave it. The summit's declaration was altered at Hungarian request from a call for 're-organization, democratization, and improvement of cooperation' to a more radical 'review of the character, functions, and activities of the Warsaw Pact'. However, according to Antall, because Hungary depended on the Soviet Union for raw materials and energy, it wished to achieve its objectives by negotiation. Hungarian officials later noted that they also came 'under terrible pressure from the West not to withdraw from the Warsaw Pact before CFE' was signed.[16] Following the summit, the new Defence Minister Lajos Fur announced that Hungary would not participate in Pact exercises and would remove its armed forces from the Pact's joint command.[17]

Despite the pre-election debate over neutrality, the MDF stated from the outset that the focus of its foreign and security policy would be integration with Western Europe:

> The government commits itself to European unity . . . It is the aim of the government to gain membership of the European Community during the course of the forthcoming decade.[18]

According to Foreign Minister Jeszenszky:

> Above all, we want to re-orient Hungary's foreign policy toward the West, to move as close as possible to Western Europe economically, culturally, and politically. . . . I do not think neutrality will be the general line Hungary will follow. . . . if the Cold War is over . . . it no longer makes sense to declare oneself neutral.[19]

The Hungarian government supported a pragmatic, multi-institutional approach, seeking security through ties with the EC, NATO and the CSCE. The policy was summarized by the head of the Hungarian Ministry of Defence's policy planning department:

> in 1989 and 1990 . . . various ideas were floated. . . . Some people advocated neutrality, but because this concept has lost its validity and its coherence as a result of the historical changes, it was discarded and we started to elaborate a security policy which is a multi-tiered system. The basic aim is to try to create virtual security guarantees – which are not hard security guarantees, but mechanisms which could compensate for the lack of hard security guarantees.[20]

In July 1990 Prime Minister Antall met EC and NATO officials in Brussels, stating Hungary's aim of joining the EC by 1995. Antall argued that 'the point is not that Hungary wishes to become a member of NATO, rather that it establishes relations with the Atlantic Treaty in the diplomatic field'.[21] In August 1990, Antall added a new dimension to Hungarian security policy, calling for a Central–East European Union, initially involving Hungary, Czechoslovakia and Poland, but perhaps later joined by other East European and neutral states. The body would be 'a loose, consultative organization similar to the West

European Union', facilitating 'cooperation'. Later on, it might merge with the WEU.[22] While Antall's proposal remained vague and received no direct response from Poland or Czechoslovakia, it should be seen as one of the antecedents of the security cooperation that emerged between the three countries in 1991.

From the autumn of 1990, tensions with the Soviet Union (over financial issues arising from the Soviet troop withdrawal, suspension of Soviet oil supplies to Hungary, and Soviet opposition to Hungary's desire to withdraw from the Warsaw Pact) led the MDF government to look increasingly to the West for security guarantees.[23] By November 1990, when NATO Secretary-General Manfred Woerner visited Budapest, Prime Minister Antall was urging NATO to make a statement guaranteeing the East European states' security.[24] In January 1991 the Hungarian parliament agreed to join the North Atlantic Assembly and called for 'close and institutionalized relations' with the EC and NATO.[25] By the spring of 1991, officials were indicating that Hungary was considering eventual membership of NATO and the WEU.[26] Prime Minister Antall indicated how far Hungarian security thinking had changed: 'one thing for sure, we don't want to be neutral'.[27]

The January 1991 Soviet crack-down in the Baltic states accelerated these trends. Although Hungary stopped short of recognizing the Baltic states, the government supported NATO and EC criticisms of the Soviet action and the parliament condemned the use of force and called for a Soviet withdrawal. As was seen in chapter 4, Hungary joined Poland and Czechoslovakia in calling for the abolition of the Warsaw Pact's military structures by 1 July 1991 and its complete dissolution by the end of 1991 or March 1992 at the latest. Foreign Minister Jeszenszky warned that 'if this should fail, we shall step on the path of independent action'.[28] Hungary, like Poland and Czechoslovakia, opposed the 'security clauses' proposed by the Soviet Union for bilateral treaties with the East European states. According to Foreign Ministry officials, Hungary would not accept any commitments that would prevent it from 'holding discussions, consultations with, and joining' NATO or the WEU.[29]

The withdrawal of the last Soviet troops from Hungary on 19 June 1991 and the dissolution of the Warsaw Pact at the beginning of July marked the formal end of the alliance with the Soviet Union. When the events in the Soviet Union came to a head with the August 1991 coup, the Hungarian government and all six parties in the parliament condemned the coup. Prime Minister Antall stressed that Hungary was a sovereign state, no longer a member of the Warsaw Pact, with no

Soviet troops on its soil. After the collapse of the coup, Foreign Minister Jeszenszky indicated that the government had been concerned: 'in the case of a successful coup . . . Hungary would have become some kind of front-line state'.[30]

Hungary made significant progress in broad political integration with the West, becoming the first East European state to join the Council of Europe in November 1990 and signing its association agreement with the EC in December 1991 (along with Poland and Czechoslovakia). The break-up of the Soviet Union and the conflict in Yugoslavia, however, confirmed the need for closer security relations with the West. After meeting US President George Bush in October 1991, Prime Minister Antall argued that there were 'good opportunities to attain that NATO's security umbrella be spread over Central-Eastern Europe'.[31] Later that month Antall visited NATO's headquarters in Brussels, calling for 'special treatment' of the East–Central European states by NATO, differentiating them from their neighbours. It was 'extremely important' that NATO 'make an unequivocal stand against outside aggression'.[32] Hungary supported NATO's December 1991 decision to establish the NACC. The NACC, however, did not fulfil Hungarian hopes, since it neither differentiated the East–Central European states from their neighbours nor gave any formal commitment to respond to aggression in the region. In May 1992 members of the Hungarian parliament's Foreign Affairs and Defence Committees told NATO officials that their country needed security guarantees, pointing to the threat posed by the war in Yugoslavia.[33]

The war in the former-Yugoslavia provided the first test of Hungary's new security policy. The severity of the test was indicated by the incursion of Yugoslav aircraft into Hungarian airspace in the autumn of 1991, including the 'accidental' bombing of a Hungarian village in October – indicating the inability of Hungary's air defences to respond to attack by modern combat aircraft. These developments led the Hungarian government to seek more concrete assistance from the West. In September 1991 Prime Minister Antall wrote to EC member-states, offering cooperation in monitoring of Hungary's border with Yugoslavia.[34] During his October 1991 visit to NATO and the EC, Antall reiterated his call for observers to be sent to the Hungarian–Yugoslav border.[35] Discussions on the question began in mid-November,[36] leading to the deployment of observers. In 1992 Hungary also allowed NATO AWACS reconnaissance aircraft to use Hungarian airspace to conduct surveillance flights over Bosnia (the first NATO operations in Europe outside the NATO area), the transit of UN peacekeeping forces across its territory and use of its airspace by US planes dropping aid to Bosnia.[37] Hungary also moved forward with practical military cooperation with the West, developing bilateral military contacts and exchange programmes with NATO states, including the US, Germany, the UK, France and Italy. The US also agreed to sell Hungary a modern aircraft identification system and train Hungarian military air traffic controllers in order to modernize Hungary's air defences.[38]

Hungary's response to the Yugoslav conflict clearly indicated that it viewed Western support, including the deployment of Western forces on Hungarian territory, as central to its security. Gyorgy Csoti, vice-president of the National Assembly's Foreign Affairs Committee argued that Hungary could provide the base for a 'quick-reaction peace-keeping force' under CSCE auspices, but based on NATO forces.[39] By early 1993 Gyula Horn, former Foreign Minister, now chairman of the MSP, was arguing that the National Assembly should debate Hungary's future membership of NATO.[40] Wide political support for the overall direction of Hungarian security policy was confirmed in March 1993 when the National Assembly passed, with only one vote against, a resolution on the basic principles of security policy.[41] The principles had been drafted by the parliament's Foreign Affairs Committee, with the participation of the opposition parties, and represented a broad consensus. The principles confirmed Hungary's central goals of integration with Western institutions, particularly the EU and NATO, whilst also stressing the importance of good relations with Hungary's neighbours.

The Yugoslav conflict, however, created some problems in coordinating policy with the West. While the West was happy to use Hungarian airspace, when Hungary informally asked for security guarantees and the supply of anti-aircraft missiles in May 1993 it rejected the request.[42] Hungary, therefore, remained vulnerable to cross-border escalation of the conflict (as the 1991 incursions of its airspace had indicated) and possible retaliation against the Hungarian minority in Serbia. In February 1994, when NATO first authorized possible airstrikes against the Bosnian Serbs, Hungary responded by announcing that it would not take part in any military action, would not allow NATO to use its airspace for airstrikes and would request the departure of NATO AWACS planes during airstrike operations.[43] While subsequent NATO airstrikes did not result in a significant split with the West, the issue highlighted the extent to which Hungary might (in the absence of security guarantees from the West) have to look to regional diplomacy for its security.

While integration with the West was the central element of the MDF government's security policy, it also sought to develop good relations with the region's two largest powers, Germany and Russia. The Hungarian government's decision to allow East Germans free access across its border with Austria in September 1989 – a decision on which it consulted its German counterpart[44] – earned Hungary much gratitude from the German government and people. Hungary was also strongly supportive of German unification and a united Germany's membership of the EC and NATO. A bilateral cooperation treaty, signed in February 1992, called for regular political dialogue on international issues and expanded cooperation in international organizations; committed the two states to cooperate in supporting CSCE principles on minority rights; and committed Germany to support Hungary's membership of the EC.[45] The two states also developed good security relations, with German Defence Minister Gerhard Stoltenberg visiting Hungary in July 1990, his Hungarian counterpart Lajos Fur visiting Germany in May 1991, and close cooperation between their armed forces. In autumn 1992 Germany agreed to supply Hungary with parts and maintenance equipment from the former-East German army as a gesture of gratitude for Hungary's role in German unification.[46]

Hungary also moved rapidly to develop good relations with Russia. In November 1992 Russian President Boris Yeltsin visited Budapest, signing a cooperation treaty, which both sides heralded as a 'historical turning point'.[47] An important feature of the new relationship was military cooperation. Russia agreed to pay $800 million of former-Soviet debt to Hungary in spare parts and equipment for the Hungarian military. The two countries' defence ministries signed a military cooperation agreement, providing a framework for cooperation, including exchanges of views and information, Hungarian air force use of Russian firing ranges and training of Hungarian officers at Russian military schools.[48] In the summer of 1993 final agreement was reached on the supply to Hungary of 28 MiG-29 interceptor aircraft, including spare parts, ammunition and training for Hungarian pilots, as payment for the former-Soviet debt.[49] The first planes were delivered in October 1993. With parallels between the Hungarian minorities outside Hungary and the 25 million Russians outside Russia, the two countries also found common ground on minority rights. At the November 1992 meeting, the two governments signed a 'Declaration on the Principles of Cooperation in Guaranteeing the Rights of Ethnic, Religious, and Linguistic Minorities'. The declaration committed them to cooperate in promoting minority rights in international forums, the international legal codification of minority rights and various forms of autonomy for minorities.[50] Hungarian critics, however, argued that the relationship was a 'major tactical mistake', since it was 'a total misinterpretation' to see Russia as a reliable partner.[51] The potential for differences was confirmed in the autumn of 1993 when Hungary rejected President Yeltsin's proposal of joint NATO–Russian security guarantees as an alternative to NATO membership for East–Central Europe.[52] Hungary's position was confirmed in February 1994 when it joined NATO's Partnership for Peace Programme, with Foreign Minister Jeszenszky stating that this was a first step to NATO membership.[53]

CONSOLIDATION UNDER THE MSP?

The campaign for the May 1994 Hungarian elections opened renewed debate on Hungarian foreign and security policy, with the opposition parties criticizing the government for its conduct of policy. The debate, however, focussed on policy priorities and nuances, rather than larger strategic questions – reflecting the consensus on basic foreign and security policy objectives which had emerged after 1990. All the main political forces supported the objectives of integration with the West, developing good relations with Hungary's neighbours and supporting the rights of the Hungarian minorities abroad. Debate focussed on the degree of priority to be given to good relations with Hungary's immediate neighbours as opposed to the rights of the Hungarian minorities. The debate, however, was characterized as much as by political 'point-scoring' as by substantive discussion and did not appear to have a major impact on the outcome of the election.[54]

The victory of the former-communist MSP in the May 1994 election, however, did raise questions about how far the foreign and security policy established since 1990 would be continued. Some critics argued that the MSP would slow the pace of Hungary's integration with the West, particularly NATO. The MSP, however, formed a coalition government with the liberal Alliance of Free Democrats (SDK) and reaffirmed the strategic objective of integration with the West, including membership of the EU and NATO. The new government did, however, place greater emphasis on developing good relations with Slovakia and Romania.[55] By the autumn of 1994, therefore, while the overall objective of integration with the West seemed unlikely to change, the pace of that integration and the balance between that objective and policy towards Hungary's immediate neighbours appeared less fixed.

'EASTERN' POLICY

The most controversial issue in Hungary's post-1989 foreign policy
has been relations with its immediate neighbours – 'Eastern' policy.
As was noted in the introduction to this chapter, the 1920 Treaty of
Trianon left large Hungarian minorities outside Hungary and created
the possibility of Hungarian territorial claims against its neighbours.
Hungary's neighbours long experience of Hungarian domination and
Hungary's inter-war attempts to regain its lost territories created a legacy
of distrust which continues to shape relations. With the collapse of
communism, Hungary's desire to protect the rights of the Hungarian
minorities and its neighbours' fears of Hungarian revisionism re-emerged
as major issues. The risk that disputes with Romania, Serbia, Ukraine
and Slovakia over borders and minority rights may escalate to armed
conflict is probably the central threat to Hungary's security in the
post-Cold War era, (see Map 6.1 and Table 6.1).

Map 6.1   Hungary: Borders and Minorities

Source: G. Schopflin, *Hungary and its Neighbours*, Chaillot Papers No. 7
(Paris: The Institute for Security Studies of Western European Union, May
1993) pp. 16–17.

Table 6.1 The Hungarian Minorities

	Official figure	Estimate
Romania	1,600,000	2,000,000
Slovakia	567,000	600,000
Serbia	341,000	400,000
Ukraine	155,000	200,000
Croatia	26,000	40,000
Austria	10,000	16,000
Slovenia	8,500	10,000

Source: A. A. Reisch, 'Hungary's Foreign Policy toward the East', *RFE/RL Research Report*, 2 (9 April 1993) p. 42. Copyright © 1993 RFE/RL, Inc.

When Prime Minister Antall outlined his government's programme in May 1990 he stressed the importance of developing good relations with Hungary's neighbours, but also that his government would support the rights of the Hungarian minorities.[56] The Antall government pressed its neighbours to allow and support the use of the Hungarian language at all levels of education; to support Hungarian culture, including giving cultural autonomy to minorities; to accept the principle of collective (i.e., group) minority rights; to establish forums for discussion of minority issues between government and minority representatives; to enshrine these rights in bilateral treaties; and, in cases where the Hungarian population forms a majority within a particular region, to accept political autonomy. Within the CSCE, the Council of Europe and the United Nations, Hungary pressed for a charter defining collective minority rights. While many states were unwilling to adopt such a charter, the EU has accepted that its relations with East European states should be conditional on respect for minority rights and in July 1992 the CSCE established a High Commissioner on National Minorities, tasked with providing early warning and action in relation to minority conflicts.

For the governments of Romania, Slovakia and Serbia, Hungary's demands were unacceptable. Further, the MDF's support for Hungarian minority rights also led its leaders to make statements which raised fears that they harboured revisionist intentions. In August 1990 Antall stated that he was 'in spirit' the Prime Minister of all Hungarians. In February 1992 Defence Minister Lajos Fur argued that protection of Hungarian minority rights was inseparable from the security of the nation and that the government 'should do everything in their power' to protect those rights.[57] In August 1992, Istvan Csurka, one of the

MDF's six deputy chairmen and the leader of the party's right wing, published a pamphlet provocatively referring to Hungary's need for 'living space'. Although Csurka was subsequently expelled from the MDF and all the main Hungarian political parties committed themselves to Hungary's current boundaries, Hungary's neighbours still feared possible revisionism.

Although the MDF government stated that it did not seek revisions of Hungary's borders, it was only willing to include commitments to the borders in bilateral treaties with its neighbours if those treaties also included commitments to collective rights for the Hungarian minorities. Antall argued that it was 'impossible to have good relations with a country that mistreats its Hungarian minority'.[58] As a result, relations with Romania, Serbia and Slovakia remained tense. According to one senior Hungarian Foreign Ministry official, this created:

> a very difficult contradiction in Hungary's security interests. . . . we have to reconcile our interests in securing the country and securing the Hungarian minorities . . . this is a contradiction which you cannot resolve, you have to manage it.[59]

The Hungarian government managed this contradiction by combining support for Hungarian minority rights with active pursuit of bilateral military confidence and security-building measures (CSBMs). In order to foster good relations and makes its defence policy transparent, detailed information on Hungary's armed forces is shared with the military attaches of Hungary's neighbours.[60] Hungary has also pressed for military cooperation treaties and border confidence-building measures with its neighbours. In effect, the Hungarian government appears to have taken a strategic decision to use CSBMs as a way of preventing latent conflicts from escalating. In November 1990 Defence Minister Fur argued that military cooperation with Hungary's neighbours could act as a safety net against unexpected developments.[61] According to the above quoted Foreign Ministry official, 'to avoid conflicts must be the focus of our policy'.[62]

'Eastern' policy became controversial in the 1994 elections. The MSP and SDK accused the MDF government of making minority rights the sole focus of its 'Eastern' policy and seriously undermining relations with Slovakia and Romania. Critics of the MDF suggested that its approach was provocative and achieved little for the minorities, since it exacerbated fears that the minorities wanted to secede, providing fuel for extreme nationalist politicians within neighbouring states. Such critics argued that Hungary should focus on universal human rights and accept an unequivocal commitment to its existing borders.[63] Prior to the 1994 election, MSP leader Gyula Horn (to become Prime Minister after the election) visited Romania and Slovakia, offering both states a 'historic reconciliation' with Hungary. After the formation of the MSP government, however, it became clear that progress would be difficult. Despite changes in rhetoric, the MSP government still sought commitments to minority rights from its neighbours – commitments which Romania and Slovakia remained reluctant to give. Csaba Tabajdi, the MSP's leading expert on the minorities, argued that the issue remained a 'minefield' which would take decades to clear.[64]

Romania

Since the late 1980s Hungary's relations with Romania have been troubled, in particular by disputes over the two million strong Hungarian minority in Transylvania. Romanian President Nicolae Ceausescu's policy of forced re-settlement of rural villagers in agro-industrial centres resulted in the wholesale destruction of Hungarian villages in Transylvania.[65] The leaders of the two countries met in Transylvania in August 1988, the first bilateral talks at this level since 1977. The communique from the meeting, however, failed to mention the minority issue, with the Hungarian side receiving no tangible Romanian commitments on minority rights. The Hungarian government was widely criticized within Hungary for failing to make any progress on the minority issue.[66]

Relations between the two states worsened in 1989. In February Hungary demanded that the UN Human Rights Commission investigate violations of the human rights of the Hungarian minority in Transylvania.[67] With Hungary moving toward a multiparty democracy, the Romanian government became increasingly hostile, suggesting a link between Hungary's political reforms and Hungarian territorial revisionism. Reports suggested that Romania was pressing other Warsaw Pact countries to intervene in Hungary to forestall further reforms.[68] In July the Hungarian and Romanian leaderships held bilateral talks during a Warsaw Pact summit in Bucharest. The Hungarian delegation demanded an end to the resettlement programme and 'cultural autonomy' for the Hungarian minority. Ceausescu argued that minority rights were not a problem in Romania, rejecting Hungarian calls for the UN Human Rights Commission to examine the situation. Hungary's then Foreign Minister, Gyula Horn, concluded that relations had 'reached the bottom point'.[69] Throughout the summer and autumn of 1989 Ceausescu attempted to marshal East European opposition to the political reforms in Hungary and Poland, seeking Warsaw Pact intervention to prevent the installation of non-communist governments.[70]

Tensions spilled over into the military sphere. In June 1989 the Hungarian government announced that troops would be redeployed from the border with Austria to the border with Romania, arguing that 'today the great majority of Hungarians know that an attack would not come from the West but from the South-east'.[71] However, it appears that the Hungarian leadership was exaggerating the 'Romanian threat' in order to gain domestic political support. Few analysts took Ceausescu's boasting of Romania's capability to produce nuclear weapons seriously, while Romania's poorly trained conscript army and strategy of territorial defence gave it little offensive potential. The Hungarian government pressed ahead with defence cuts, while the Defence Ministry stated that it saw no Romanian threat and 'the traditional friendship-of-arms between the two armies' remained.[72]

The collapse of the Ceausescu regime at the end of December 1989 altered the situation. The Romanian government's efforts to exile an ethnic Hungarian priest sparked the revolution and united Hungarians and Romanians in opposition to the Ceausescu regime. Hungarian aid poured into the country. At the end of December Gyula Horn became the first foreign minister to visit Romania since the revolution, reaching agreement with the new Romanian government on constitutional guarantees of individual and collective rights for the Hungarian minority.[73] The improvement in relations, however, proved short-lived. Early in 1990 opposition emerged in Transylvania to the separation of Romanian and Hungarian schools, with ethnic Hungarians accused of separatism. Romania's new National Salvation Front (FSN) government backed down on the issue, supporting the accusations of separatism. In January and February, conflicts occurred between ethnic Hungarians and Romanians, with sizable anti-Hungarian demonstrations.[74] By February the Hungarian government had renewed earlier calls for the UN Human Rights Commission to investigate the situation.[75]

In March 1990 the situation escalated. Disputes in Transylvania over Hungarian-language education and bilingual signs led to violence between the two communities, with the Romanian army intervening to restore order. Reports suggested eight people were killed and over 300 injured in the town of Tirgu-Mures. It appeared that the incidents had been incited and organized by the extreme Romanian nationalist organization Vatra Romaneasca.[76] The Romanian government, however, argued that the Hungarian minority and irredentist statements from the Hungarian government were responsible for the violence.[77] The Hungarian government accused the Romanian government of failing to take action to prevent the violence, notified the UN Commission on Human Rights and the UN Secretary-General, and called on the Council of Europe to protect the Hungarian minority.[78] It also accused the Romanian government of increasing the readiness of its armed forces in order to give the impression that Hungary was preparing to invade.[79]

The elections in Hungary and Romania, in March–April and May 1990 respectively, failed to improve relations. Although the new Hungarian parliament issued a statement committing Hungary to its current borders, the statement failed to reassure the Romanian government, as it implied that the borders were unjust and might still be changed by peaceful means.[80] As has already been seen, Hungary's new MDF government was also committed to securing collective rights for the Hungarian minorities. Romania's FSN government, however, had dropped its earlier commitments to supporting minority rights, adopted an increasingly nationalistic stance and maintained that many Hungarians questioned the border between the two countries. The Hungarian Democratic Union in Romania, a body formed to press for rights for the Hungarian minority, emerged as Romania's largest opposition party, further polarizing relations between the two communities. Prime Minister Antall warned that good relations with Romania would be impossible so long as Romania's Hungarian minority was oppressed.[81]

Negotiations for a new bilateral treaty became the focus of relations. Hungary insisted that any treaty give clear commitments on collective minority rights. Romania insisted that Hungary commit itself absolutely to the existing border between the two countries. Hungary, however, would only accept the border commitment if Romania guaranteed collective Hungarian minority rights, which the Romanian government refused to do. The result, from the start of the negotiations in 1990, was stalemate. By the end of 1992, although eighty per cent of the treaty had apparently been agreed, the core issues of the border and minority rights remained unresolved.[82]

In stark contrast to general political relations, security and military relations improved significantly after Ceausescu's fall. During the Romanian revolution, the Hungarian and Romanian armed forces set up a hotline allowing their defence ministers to remain in direct contact and a direct radio link between their general staffs. The Romanian armed forces informed their Hungarian counterparts that they would not be used outside Romania's borders and protected the Hungarian embassy in Bucharest. The Hungarian armed forces supplied food and medical supplies to Romania by road, rail and air, and made transport available for the evacuation of wounded. Hungary also reinforced its Eastern border to prevent Securitate members escaping through Hungary and monitored Securitate radio broadcasts, locating their transmitters and passing intercepted information on to the Romanian authorities. Hungary even went so far as to offer weapons and ammunition to the Romanian armed forces, although the offer was declined.[83] Given the sensitivity of relations between the two states and the nature of the crisis within Romania at this point, the extent of military cooperation was quite remarkable.

Military security relations continued to improve, remaining unaffected by worsening political relations. In February 1990 Defence Minister Ferenc Karpati visited Romania discussing the establishment of technical cooperation and receiving a Romanian order for telecommunications equipment. During the clashes in Tirgu-Mures in March 1990, Karpati telephoned his Romanian counterpart, Colonel General Victor Stanculescu, to deny rumours that Hungary had massed troops on its border with Romania and to ask Stanculescu to protect the Hungarian minority. Stanculescu expressed regret over the violence and said that a large force had been brought into Tirgu-Mures to restore order.[84] Good military security relations continued after Lajos Fur became Hungarian Defence Minister under the new MDF government. In October 1990 Fur visited Romania to meet Stanculescu, discussing mutual exchanges of information, documents and expertise and visits by officers and soldiers. In November a bilateral military cooperation agreement was signed, calling for familiarization with each other's military doctrines; visits to training centres, military schools and academies; the setting up of joint committees at various levels; and the expansion of technical cooperation. Fur described his relationship with Stanculescu as better than with any other defence minister. Fears of military conflict between Hungary and Romania were 'unrealistic', as tension could not 'extend to the military sphere'.[85]

Security cooperation was taken a step further in 1991, with the conclusion of a unique bilateral 'open skies' treaty. The treaty, concluded after only a few months of negotiations and signed in May, allows four unarmed surveillance flights over each state's territory annually. The first flights were successfully conducted in June 1991.[86] The agreement was particularly notable since it was concluded over a year ahead of the wider European 'open skies' agreement – a testament to the desire of Hungary and Romania to press ahead with bilateral cooperative security measures. In May 1991 Fur invited Romania's new Defence Minister Lieutenant General Nicolae Spiriou to visit Hungary, leading to a series of visits to both countries at various levels. Spiriou concluded that relations were 'excellent'. The two militaries agreed to maintain good relations in order to 'stave off possible political friction'.[87] Cooperation continued in 1992, with visits under the bilateral military cooperation programme and surveillance flights under the 'open skies' treaty. In October the Romanian Defence Ministry denied accusations by Romanian nationalists that Hungarian army units had been brought up to the border.[88] Spiriou argued that Hungary posed no military threat to Romania and that the two militaries' good relations could help hinder nationalist forces.[89]

In the autumn of 1993 Hungary initiated an attempt to improve broader political relations with Romania. In September Foreign Minister Jeszenszky paid an official visit to Romania, the first such visit since Gyula Horn's in December 1989. Meeting with Foreign Minister Teodor Melescanu and Prime Minister Nicolae Vacaroiu, Jeszenszky argued that tensions in relations had been exaggerated, stressed that Hungary had no border claims against Romania and called for greater dialogue. In both countries, the visit was viewed as the first step in a Hungarian–Romanian detente. Indicating a significant shift in policy, later that month Hungary did not oppose Romania's accession to the Council of Europe, seeking instead to use negotiations on the issue to moderate Romania's minority policy. The underlying issues of minority rights and their linkage to the border issue, however, remained unresolved.[90]

As was seen earlier, during the 1994 Hungarian election the MSP advocated improved relations with Romania and Gyula Horn offered a 'historic reconciliation'. After the elections, however, it became clear that progress would be difficult. The MSP government still sought specific commitments on minority rights. Despite having agreed to some of these commitments as part of its membership of the Council of Europe, it remained unclear how far Romania would implement them.[91] Further, the Romanian government depended on the support of extreme nationalists within the parliament and ethnic tensions within Transylvania were increasing.[92] Progress on minority rights and a bilateral treaty, therefore, appeared likely to be difficult. The new Hungarian government, however, also appeared likely to continue to seek good military relations with Romania. The new Defence Minister Gyorgy Keleti met his Romanian counterpart in July 1994, discussing possible joint manoeuvres.[93] The present pattern of Hungarian–Romanian relations – political tension and military cooperation – seems likely to continue until one side changes its position on the central issues of minority rights and the border. Much may depend, therefore, on how far and how quickly Romania implements the commitments on minority rights made as part of its membership of the Council of Europe. Alternatively, should nationalism within Romania increase and ethnic tensions in Transylvania intensify, relations could worsen. Hungarian Foreign Ministry officials, however, believe that relations with Romania are 'a long term problem . . . a problem in the refrigerator: every time you open the door, you see the problem. But it's not a problem which will explode, it's manageable'.[94]

The Former Yugoslavia

From 1990 onwards, the escalating conflict in Yugoslavia became a major security concern for Hungary. While the Hungarian government and people were sympathetic to the independence movements in Slovenia, Croatia and Bosnia, support for those movements might risk incurring retaliation against the Hungarian minority in Vojvodina or, in the worst case, military conflict with the Serb dominated Yugoslav People's Army (JNA). Shortly after the MDF government came to power in May 1990, Foreign Minister Jeszenszky indicated its policy. Croatia and Slovenia were following a democratic path and Hungary should develop relations with them, while a confederation was the best solution to the Yugoslav crisis. However, the position of the Hungarian minority in Vojvodina meant that it was 'very important to talk to the Serbs and to show them how enlightened our attitude toward them is'.[95]

Early in 1991, however, relations with Serbia were undermined by the revelation that Hungary had sold 10,000 Kalashnikov assault rifles to Croatia in October 1990. Although it appears that the arms sale resulted from confusion within the Hungarian government rather than a strategic decision to provide military support for Croatia,[96] the incident nevertheless provoked a crisis. The Serbian press accused Hungary of 'gross interference with Yugoslavia's interests and national integrity'.[97] Attempts to negotiate a bilateral military cooperation agreement broke down and tensions increased. The worsening situation of the Hungarian minority in Vojvodina exacerbated these tensions. Until the late 1980s, the Vojvodina Hungarians were the best treated of all the Hungarian minorities, with guaranteed educational and cultural rights and Vojvodina an autonomous province within Serbia. In the late 1980s, however, Serbia's new President Slobodan Milosevic removed Vojvodina's autonomy and began a campaign against ethnic minorities in Serbia.[98] In response, early in 1990, the Democratic Community of Vojvodina Hungarians was formed, demanding cultural autonomy, minority self-rule, a multiparty democracy and a market economy – placing it in direct political conflict with the government in Belgrade.[99] From mid-1990 onwards, the Hungarian government, whilst declaring that it did not wish to interfere in Yugoslavia's internal affairs, called for a peaceful solution to the growing political dispute between Serbia, Croatia and Slovenia, suggesting that a confederal state might be the best option. When the war broke out in Yugoslavia following Slovenia and Croatia's June 1991 declarations of independence, the Hungarian government continued to follow this policy, supporting EC calls for a cease-fire, negotiations and a ban on arms shipments. Despite popular sympathies for Slovenia and Croatia, Hungary's policy remained cautious, rejecting unilateral recognition of the two states or direct involvement in the war.[100] However, a controversial statement by Prime Minister Antall that the 1920 Trianon and 1947 Paris treaties applied to Yugoslavia not Serbia (implying that if Yugoslavia broke up Vojvodina might not be part of Serbia) provoked Serb fears that Hungary might harbour revisionist intentions. Despite subsequent statements that Hungary had no territorial claims, the Yugoslav government accused Hungary of encroaching on its sovereignty and territory and interfering in its internal affairs.[101]

As the war in Yugoslavia escalated from July 1991 onwards, JNA aircraft violated Hungarian airspace a number of times, drawing Hungarian protests.[102] In August 1991, Prime Minister Antall's foreign policy adviser warned that if violations continued Hungary would be 'obliged to do something'. A Defence Ministry spokesman, however, acknowledged that Hungary's inadequate air defences meant that it could not respond effectively.[103] By October, JNA aircraft had violated Hungarian airspace eighteen times in order to attack targets in Croatia, leading Antall to write to EC member-states offering cooperation in EC monitoring of Hungary's border with Yugoslavia.[104] Hungary's response to these developments emphasized the extent to which its policy was predicated on cooperation with Western institutions, rather than unilateral action. According to one Hungarian Defence Ministry official:

> We had to demonstrate very much self-restraint . . . It was very difficult to preserve our neutrality and to not get involved in armed conflict, because some people in Serbia obviously tried to pick Hungary as their enemy . . . we have no troops stationed in the border region. We don't want to create the impression that militarily we are present or acting in the border region.[105]

At the end of October 1991, the most serious incident occurred, with

Yugoslav aircraft bombing a Hungarian village and destroying some houses. Whether the attack was deliberately directed against Hungary or unintended spill-over from the war in Yugoslavia remains unclear.[106] The Hungarian government reported the incident to the CSCE's Conflict Prevention Centre, the UN Secretary-General and the UN Security Council, and called on the JNA to take steps to keep military operations away from the border.[107] The Hungarian military also increased the readiness of forces near the border and the frequency of border patrols and reinforced some units, although no general mobilization was ordered.[108] At Hungary's request, the Hungarian and Yugoslav militaries rapidly agreed bilateral confidence-building measures designed to prevent further incidents. In mid-November the Hungarian Defence Ministry announced that the two countries had agreed on a neutral airspace zone of ten miles on either side of their shared border.[109] A hotline was also established between the two countries' air-defence commands to enable them to 'clarify risky situations in time'. After this, the violations of Hungarian airspace stopped and fears of escalation receded.[110]

Tensions, however, increased in Vojvodina. When the war broke out in Yugoslavia in June 1991, the Democratic Community of Vojvodina Hungarians issued a statement condemning growing political pressure and intimidation against the Hungarian minority, demanding the right to self-government and the restoration of Vojvodina's autonomy, and supporting a confederal solution to the Yugoslav crisis.[111] By October 1991 Prime Minister Antall was accusing the Serbian leadership of treating the Vojvodina Hungarians 'like hostages'.[112] The situation worsened when the war spread to Bosnia in 1992. 'Ethnic cleansing' spread to Vojvodina, with Serbian nationalists, joined by Serbian refugees from Croatia and Bosnia, violently forcing Croatians and Hungarians to leave their houses and villages. Throughout 1992 and 1993, increasing numbers of nationalist Serbs moved into the area, anti-Hungarian demonstrations occurred and fears of large-scale inter-ethnic violence grew.[113] In November 1993 ultranationalist Serbian leader 'Arkan', campaigning in Vojvodina for the December Serbian elections, warned that citizens who looked to Budapest 'should pack their bags'.[114]

In 1994, however, Hungary initiated a cautious, but potentially significant rapprochement with Serbia. In January Foreign Minister Jeszenszky visited Serbia, meeting with his counterpart Vladislav Jovanovic and President Milosevic. Jeszenszky expressed hope that relations could improve and that President Milosevic might be willing to accept cultural and educational autonomy for the Vojvodina Hungarians. Both sides looked forward to the lifting of sanctions on the former-Yugoslavia.[115] The new MSP government continued the cautious rapprochement. In July the new Hungarian Foreign Minister Laszlo Kovacs met Foreign Minister Jovanovic in Belgrade. Jovanovic described relations as favourable and said Serbia was willing to normalize relations and supported Hungary's active participation in solving regional problems. Kovacs called for an upgrading of ties, but noted that Hungary would continue to pay 'particular attention' to the situation of the Vojvodina Hungarians.[116]

The shift in Hungarian policy appeared to be driven by a growing recognition of the limits of Western policy. By 1993–94 it was clear that the West had failed to protect minority rights in the region and that its ability to put pressure on Serbia was limited. At the same time, Serbia's desire to have UN economic sanctions lifted was leading it to seek some form of accommodation with the West and its neighbours. In these circumstances, an accommodation with Serbia perhaps appeared the best way to improve the situation of the Vojvodina Hungarians and prevent escalation of the conflict. One senior Western diplomat concluded that Hungary 'had realised that Western policy has failed, that Serbia will be a key power in the region and that Western policy will do nothing for their security or vital interests. It's a new realpolitik'.[117] Progress, however, would be difficult, since Serbia was unlikely to accept many of the demands of the Vojvodina Hungarians. Further, if the Bosnian peace process failed or renewed war broke-out between Serbia and Croatia, the possibility of escalation remained.[118]

In contrast to its relations with Serbia, Hungary's sympathy for Slovenia and Croatia's independence moves and the three countries' shared difficulties with Serbia led to good relations. The Hungarian minorities in Slovenia and Croatia fared well in terms of minority rights. In 1990 the Croatian government formed a Nationality Committee and the Slovenian government appointed a Minister for Nationalities, both of which worked well with the Hungarian minorities.[119] After Hungary followed the EC in recognizing Slovenia and Croatia in January 1992, cooperation treaties – including commitments to collective minority rights – were signed with both states.[120]

Ukraine

With the collapse of the Soviet Union at the end of 1991, Ukraine became the only former-Soviet state bordering Hungary. The main potential source of conflict between the two states is the Transcarpathian *oblast* (region) of Ukraine, which contains a Hungarian minority of between 150,000 and 200,000. Until the end of the first World War, the region, then known as Subcarpathia, was part of Hungary. In 1919 it was transferred to Czechoslovakia and its name altered to Subcarpathian Rus. Throughout the inter-war period, Hungary sought, as part of its revisionist foreign policy, to regain the territory. The region gradually came under Ukrainian influence and in 1939 gained autonomy as the Carpatho-Ukrainian republic. Hungary, however, regained the territory later in 1939, controlling it throughout the second World War. After the war, the region was seceded to the Soviet Union, becoming the Transcarpathian *Oblast* of the Ukrainian republic.[121]

After Ukraine's July 1990 declaration of sovereignty, the two states moved rapidly to develop good relations. In August Ukrainian Foreign Minister Anatolii Zlenko visited Budapest, meeting Prime Minister Antall and Foreign Minister Jeszenszky. Agreement was reached on the need to expand cooperation and uphold the rights of the Hungarian minority. In September Hungary's President Arpad Goncz became the first foreign head of state to visit Ukraine since the declaration of sovereignty, meeting Ukrainian Supreme Soviet Chairman Leonid Kravchuk. The two sides signed a communique on expanding cooperation and agreed to draw up a nationality charter incorporating the concept of collective minority rights. Goncz concluded that the talks had been a 'one hundred and five per cent success' and the situation in Transcarpathia was an 'island of peace' compared to that of the Hungarian minorities elsewhere.[122]

Negotiations following Goncz's visit were successful and in May 1991 Kravchuk visited Budapest, signing statements of intent on bilateral cooperation and minority rights. Both sides agreed to respect citizens' rights to decide their nationality and to help ensure the preservation of national identities. State bodies, including minority representatives, were to be set up in minority areas to take minority interests into account. Minorities were to be guaranteed the right to study in their mother tongue at all levels of education. Minority rights were also to be regarded as universal humans rights. Most significantly, Ukraine accepted that minority rights must be guaranteed both for individuals and for groups. Ukraine thus became the first of Hungary's neighbours to accept the concept of collective minority rights.[123] When Ukraine formally gained independence in December 1991, Hungary was the first country to establish diplomatic relations with the new state. Within days, the two states had also signed a cooperation treaty confirming their current border and committing Ukraine to respect the rights of the Hungarian minority.[124]

The December 1991 Ukrainian independence referendum, however, complicated the situation in Transcarpathia. Prior to the August 1991 Soviet coup, the Hungarian minority had been united with the Ukrainian national and democratic movements in their opposition to communist rule. After the coup, the Hungarian minority began to press for autonomy, pitting them against the Ukrainian national and democratic movements (which saw autonomy as a threat to Ukraine's territorial and political integrity). In the December 1991 referendum, 78 per cent of the voters in Transcarpathia supported granting the region 'a special self-governing administrative' status within an independent Ukraine – a free-trade zone with some form of autonomy. In one Hungarian county, 81 per cent of the electorate also supported the granting of a special status of Hungarian national district. The position of Leonid Kravchuk, elected President in the December 1991 referendum, was unclear, although he appeared to be sympathetic to the Hungarian demands.[125]

Despite the uncertainties about the position of Transcarpathia, the two states quickly developed good relations. In April 1992 Foreign Minister Jeszenszky met his Ukrainian counterpart Anatolii Zlenko again, with Ukraine agreeing to respect the rights of its Hungarian minority and Hungary agreeing to support Ukraine's efforts to join various European bodies.[126] In February 1993 President Kravchuk made his second official visit to Hungary, meeting with President Goncz and Prime Minister Antall and signing agreements on the opening of new border crossings and immigration control. A joint statement confirmed the two countries' intention to promote regional security through regular, high-level meetings. Hungary agreed to support Ukrainian membership of regional groupings, including the Central European Initiative.[127] The two countries' Presidents and Foreign Ministers met again in April 1993, once more stressing their excellent relations.[128] Despite protests by some deputies wishing to hold open the possibility of peaceful border changes, the bilateral cooperation treaty was ratified by a large majority in the Hungarian parliament in May 1993.[129]

Military relations also progressed well. Defence Minister Fur met his Ukrainian counterpart Konstantin Morozov in December 1991, agreeing to establish cooperation.[130] In February 1992 it was announced that officials were holding talks about the possibility of exchanging Ukrainian military equipment for Hungarian agricultural machinery.[131] In March a military cooperation agreement between the two states was signed, committing them to cooperate on disarmament and training.[132] In February

1994 Ukrainian Defence Minister Vitalij Radeckij visited Hungary, discussing future Ukrainian spare parts deliveries to Hungary.[133] In August the two countries defence ministers met again, discussing the possibility that Ukraine might transfer some of the equipment it had to destroy under the CFE treaty to Hungary in order to allow Hungary to modernize its armed forces.[134]

Despite differences over Transcarpathia's future, inter-ethnic relations remained very good compared with those in Transylvania, Vojvodina and Southern Slovakia. In April 1992 the newly-appointed Ukrainian presidential commissioner for Transcarpathia informed Foreign Minister Jeszenszky that the Ukrainian government wanted to guarantee the rights of the Hungarian minority, although the question of autonomy rested with the Ukrainian parliament.[135] In July the Ukrainian–Hungarian Commission on Minorities (agreed to during the May 1991 summit) held its first session, agreeing to open more border crossing points in order to make travel between the two countries easier.[136] Ukraine's language law, adopted in the same month, guaranteed the rights of the Hungarian minority, permitting the use of Hungarian names and symbols. In June 1993 the Hungarian–Ukrainian joint committee met again, reaching agreement on a range of issues, including the placing of Hungarian schools under their own administration.[137] The Ukrainian parliament, however, opposed establishing a free economic zone or granting full regional autonomy (which some Hungarians were advocating), fearing that such steps might promote separatism.[138]

By the autumn of 1994, therefore, Hungarian–Ukrainian relations were very good and Transcarpathia did not seem likely to become a major source of tension. Hungary viewed its relationship with Ukraine and Ukraine's approach to minority rights as a model for its other neighbours. Nevertheless, the uncertain political and economic situation within Ukraine meant that continued stability could not be guaranteed. If serious political and ethnic conflict emerges in Ukraine, the position of the Hungarian minority could worsen, undermining Hungarian–Ukrainian relations.

Slovakia

As was seen in the last chapter, Hungarian–Slovak relations emerged as a significant source of tension after the 1989 revolutions. From a Hungarian perspective, the core of the problem has been Slovakia's treatment of its Hungarian minority. After the 'velvet revolution' the Slovak Hungarians formed various groups to press for minority rights, demanding the restoration of Hungarian language schools, the right to decide the language of instruction in local schools, the establishment of Hungarian cultural and educational institutions, the right to use the Hungarian language at all levels of public administration, greater representation in the Czechoslovak and Slovak parliaments and the establishment of a federal Ministry of Nationalities. The Hungarian government, first under the MSMP, then under the MDF, pressed the Czechoslovak and Slovak governments to accept these demands. The Slovak government and parliament, however, rejected them.[139]

Although the Hungarian minority gained representation in both the federal and Slovak parliaments in the June 1990 Czechoslovak elections, their situation remained a source of tension. In particular, the October 1990 Slovak language law sparked controversy. The law declared Slovak the official language of the Slovak republic, stated that all place and sign names must be in Slovak and limited the right to use Hungarian in official dealings to those areas where Hungarians were 20 per cent or more of the population. The law was a step backwards, as bilingual signs and the use of Hungarian for official dealings were widespread. As a result, some Hungarian groups began to press for cultural and territorial autonomy.[140]

The June 1992 Czechoslovak elections further polarized the situation, with Hungarian parties emerging as one of the main opposition forces to the nationalist Slovak government of Prime Minister Vladimir Meciar. Meciar's opposition to the minority's demands and Hungary's pressure to accept those demands led to worsening relations between the two countries.[141] At the same time, the dispute over the Gabcikovo–Nagymaros hydro-electric project also came to a head. Widespread opposition to the environmental costs of the project had led Hungary to stop work on it in 1989.[142] Negotiations proved fruitless and in July 1991 the Slovak government decided to press ahead with its own part of the project, including a new diversion of the Danube. The Hungarian government argued that, since the Danube formed the border between the two countries, diverting it would be a violation of the border.[143] In May 1992 the Hungarian government unilaterally annulled the 1977 treaty on the project.[144] Hungary, however, was now in a weak position, as it had little leverage over a Slovak government committed to the project. In October Slovakia unilaterally diverted the Danube, reducing the waterflow into Hungary and creating a crisis.[145] The EC mediated an agreement whereby construction on the project would be stopped, the Slovak government would re-divert much of the original volume of the Danube, the hydro-electric turbines would not be put into operation and both sides agreed to accept an International Court of Justice (ICJ) ruling on the issue. With an ICJ ruling some years away, however, the dispute continued, with Slovakia operating the turbines and failing to redirect the Danube.[146]

Worsening relations and the onset of Slovak independence, led Hungary to attempt to mobilize international opposition to Slovakia's minority policies in the EC, the Council of Europe, the CSCE and the United Nations. Hungary's efforts had a significant impact in terms of putting pressure on Slovakia to alter its minority rights legislation and moderate its position on the Gabcikovo–Nagymaros project. The EC's October 1992 mediation efforts resulted in part from Hungarian demands and did put pressure on Slovakia to moderate its position. More significantly, as was seen in the last chapter, Slovakia's June 1993 accession to the Council of Europe was made conditional on its agreement to alter its minority rights legislation. The CSCE High Commissioner on National Minorities also examined the situation, putting further pressure on Slovakia to alter its legislation. Hungarian policy, however, also had negative effects, exacerbating the perception of Hungary as an 'enemy' in Slovakia and leading some in the West to view Hungary as contributing to its troubled relations with its neighbours.

Worsening political relations with Slovakia also led Hungary to pursue military confidence-building measures. Prime Minister Meciar's summer 1990 accusations that the redeployment of Hungary's armed forces threatened Slovakia led Hungarian Defence Minister Lajos Fur to meet with his Czechoslovak counterpart Miroslav Vacek. Fur and Vacek agreed to exchange information on the redeployment of troops and to hold regular meetings on troop exercises and movements.[147] Meciar's 1992 accusation that Hungary was conducting large-scale military manoeuvres near its border with Slovakia resulted in the establishment of a hotline between the two Prime Minister's offices.[148] After meeting their Slovak counterparts in November 1992, Hungarian Defence Ministry officials were 'very pleasantly surprised' at the attitude of the Slovak military and the prospects for cooperation.[149] The positive state of military relations was confirmed in 1993, with the signing of a military cooperation agreement, including commitments to exchange information on large-scale troop movements, exchanges of military observers, and coordinated air defence in border areas.

In 1994, the willingness of the Moravcik government in Slovakia to accept some of the Hungarian minority's key demands and the new MSP government's desire for a reconciliation with Hungary's neighbours appeared to offer the prospect of an improvement in relations.

In August Prime Minister Horn visited Slovakia, meeting with Moravcik and President Kovac. Both sides praised the constructive attitude of their talks. By the autumn of 1994, however, the two sides had still not resolved their differences over minority rights and the Gabcikovo–Nagymaros project. The re-election of Meciar as Slovak Prime Minister in October 1994 raised new uncertainties. The prospects for Hungarian-Slovak rapprochement appeared likely to depend on whether Meciar followed an anti-Hungarian nationalist line or whether he might moderate his position and implement the Council of Europe's requirements. Despite the MSP government's desire for a reconciliation with Slovakia, therefore, relations seemed likely to be difficult for some time to come.

DEFENCE POLICY

De-politicizing the Military

By the late 1980s, the radical reformers who were dominating the MSMP had accepted the need to de-politicize the military and were beginning to take practical steps towards this goal.[150] In June the National Assembly approved a new military oath obliging soldiers to serve the Republic of Hungary and the Constitution and expressing the independence of the armed forces from party politics and ideology. In November the new oath was signed by over 99 per cent of the officer corps.[151] The MSMP also broke up party cells in the military, dismantled the Main Political Administration, replaced political officers with apolitical education officers, banned the operation of political parties within the armed forces and placed the paramilitary Workers' Guard (an internal security force previously under the direct role of the MSMP) under the control of the Defence Ministry, removing its political role.[152] In December Prime Minister Miklos Nemeth announced that the Defence Ministry would be divided into two separate bodies: a Defence Ministry dealing with policy issues, accountable to the government, and a 'Command of the Hungarian People's Army' dealing with day-to-day military issues, accountable to the President as Commander-in-Chief. According to one observer, this was a 'momentous change' ensuring 'that the armed forces would be controlled not by any party organization but by the government and, ultimately, the President'.[153]

By the time the democratically elected MDF government came to power, therefore, substantial progress had been made in de-politicizing the military. Thus, there was little fear that the armed forces might intervene to prevent Hungary's transition to democracy. When Prime Minister Antall appointed the civilian MDF deputy Lajos Fur as Defence Minister in May 1990, the decision was seen not as a radical departure but as the logical and expected next step. Fur indicated that he would not institute purges of the armed forces. While some senior military commanders were opposed to the reforms, they were not a significant political force. By the end of 1990, only 44 of 87 generals in office in December 1989 had retained their posts.[154] By 1992 observers were arguing that 'the Hungarian army is politically absolutely loyal. There is no significant influence of the KGB or the communists . . . that's not a problem'.[155] As with Poland and Czechoslovakia, the rapid and successful de-politicization of the Hungarian military appears to reflect the reality that their apparent politicization was in fact relatively shallow.

Somewhat more controversial was the question of political control of the armed forces. Although under the constitution the President is Commander-in-Chief, there was broad acceptance that the government and the Defence Minister should direct defence policy. Opposition parties, however, were reluctant to give complete operational control to the government (fearing that such power might be open to abuse in a crisis). At the same time, however, the government needed to be able to respond rapidly in the event of a crisis. After much debate, a compromise defence law (passed by a large parliamentary majority in December 1993) gave the government the right to respond to foreign invasions without prior approval from the parliament, as long as the parliament and President were informed immediately.[156]

Defence Strategy

In the late 1980s, the MSMP also initiated significant cuts in and restructuring of Hungary's armed forces. In December 1988 it was announced that the defence budget would fall by 17 per cent in real terms in 1989 and the armed forces would be cut by nine per cent.[157] In June 1989 Hungary announced that it would exercise full control over its armed forces, deploying them in accordance with its own threat perceptions. Forces along the borders with Austria and Yugoslavia would be reduced and re-deployed to the border with Romania.[158] In December 1989 Prime Minister Nemeth announced 'drastic and expedient' reductions in the armed forces (cutting the armed forces by 20–25 per cent by 1991) and a new 'territorial defence' doctrine involving significant cuts in offensive forces.[159]

Table 6.2 Hungary's Armed Forces in Transition

	1989	1990	1991	1992	1993	1994	CFE
Active	91,000	94,000	86,500	80,800	78,000	74,500	100,000
Reserves	168,000	134,400	210,000	192,000	195,000	195,000	—
Army	68,000	72,000	66,400	63,500	60,500	56,500	—
Airforce	23,000	22,000	20,100	17,300	17,500	18,000	—
Main Battle Tanks	1,435	1,516	1,482	1,357	1,331	1,191	835
Armoured Fighting Vehicles	2,310	2,353	2,092	1,982	1,675	1,645	1,700
Artillery	866	1,084	1,087	1,040	787	991	810
Combat Aircraft	101	87	111	91	91	171	180
Attack Helicopters	40	64	39	39	39	39	108

Source: The International Institute for Strategic Studies, *The Military Balance* (London: Brassey's for the IISS, annually, 1989 to 1994).

Prime Minister Antall stated that the MDF government would 'continue the policy of change', developing a 'defensive and non-offensive type military force'.[160] Defence Minister Fur argued that, while a fully professional force might emerge eventually, the conscript based army would remain in place for the 1990s.[161] By the end of 1992, the Ministry of Defence and the National Assembly's Defence Committee had reached agreement on a new military doctrine – a formal statement of defence policy to be approved by the parliament. Under the doctrine, Hungary's armed forces have a purely defensive mission, envisaging no operations outside national territory (except under United Nations auspices), Hungary regards no country as its enemy, takes into account the legitimate security interests of its neighbours and does not wish to take military steps that would threaten them. It regards armed force as a last resort to be used only in the case of aggression against it and does everything in its power to avoid becoming involved in military conflicts and to ensure that its territory is not used as base for aggression.[162]

The MDF government continued the redeployment of forces begun under the MSMP, aiming to replace the deployment of forces predominantly along Hungary's Western border with an equal deployment across the whole country. By the end of 1992 the redeployment was largely completed.[163] The military also developed new operational plans and a new force structure, involving three components.[164] First, the new

70–75,000 strong regular army is being re-organized into motorized infantry and armoured brigades – smaller, more mobile and more defensively oriented formations than before. Second, 2–3 per cent of the re-organized regular army (i.e., approximately 2000 soldiers) will be centrally based airmobile rapid reaction forces, including reconnaissance and anti-tank battalions. Third, 12–14 territorial defence brigades, modelled on the Austrian and Swiss militia systems, will be created, composed of reservists to be called up in the event of a general mobilization. Hungary would be able to count on a total of 300,000 such reservists.[165]

The aim of the new strategy is to provide a defensively oriented deterrent force, capable of engaging in defence-in-depth should Hungary face sustained attack. The airmobile rapid reaction forces would provide the first line of defence, rapidly engaging any attacking force, providing time for regular forces to move to meet any attack and for territorial forces to mobilize. The rapid reaction forces are of such a small size, and armed largely with defensive weapons, that they could not constitute a significant offensive threat to any of Hungary's neighbours. The breaking up of the regular armed forces into smaller brigade-sized units limits their already small offensive potential. The territorial brigades will also have little offensive potential since they will be relatively lightly armed. According to head of the policy planning department of the Hungarian Defence Ministry:

> We re-organised the army in a way that it cannot be seen as presenting any serious threat to the security of any our neighbours. We have only three brigades which are fully active . . . these three brigades are based in different parts of the country and they cannot be concentrated anywhere . . . we cannot stage a large-scale offensive on land against anyone. It is structural incapacity to attack.[166]

The extent to which the Hungarian armed forces are currently able to provide an effective defence, however, remains open to doubt. The majority of the planned rapid reaction forces and territorial brigades are not yet operational. The equipment of the main ground forces is out of date (largely dating back from the 1970s or earlier). In particular, the air defence system is ineffective – as the violations of Hungarian airspace by JNA aircraft in 1991 made clear.[167] To supplement the armed forces, the government decided in November 1991, in response to the crisis in Yugoslavia, to set up 28 rapid reaction border guard companies armed with modern arms such as anti-tank weapons, under the jurisdiction of the Ministry of Internal Affairs. The task of these

Table 6.3   Hungarian Defence Expenditure

	1986	1987	1988	1989	1990	1991
mn. forints[1]	38,800	41,500	49,200	47,760	44,440	55,440
mn. US $[2]	2,321	2,285	2,343	1,944	1,411	1,354
% GDP	3.6	3.4	3.5	2.8	2.1	—

Note: 1. Current price figures.
2. 1988 prices and exchanges rates.

Source: S. Deger, E. Loose-Weintraub and S. Sen, 'Tables of world military expenditure', Appendix 7A, in Stockholm International Peace Research Institute, *SIPRI Yearbook 1992: World Armaments and Disarmament* (Oxford: Oxford University Press, 1992), pp. 254–64.

forces is to deal with small armed groups which might cross the Hungarian border as a result of conflicts in neighbouring countries. By the end of 1992 nineteen companies had been created, with six deployed along Hungary's border with Yugoslavia. The new border guard companies have, however, proved controversial as some fear that they might be used in cases of civil disturbance.[168]

Defence spending, however, has been contentious because of demands to modernize much of the armed forces' equipment. With sizable cuts in spending since the late 1980s (see Table 6.3), the majority of the defence budget is now spent on maintaining operational readiness, leaving little for modernization.[169] Defence cuts forced the Ministry of Defence to cut back manoeuvres and training and postpone procurement of new equipment.[170] When the MDF proposed reducing the defence budget to 42.5 billion forints for 1991, Defence Minister Für argued that at least 75 billion forints was needed to maintain readiness and buy new equipment. The National Assembly eventually agreed to increase the allocation to 54.46 billion forints.[171]

The inadequacy of Hungary's air defences was of particular concern. State Secretary for Defence Erno Raffay noted in 1991 that the Czechoslovak, Romanian and Yugoslav airforces were larger and more modern than Hungary's, concluding that Hungary would not be able to defend itself.[172] After the violations of Hungarian airspace by JNA aircraft in 1991, the Hungarian parliament approved an extra budget allocation of 1.1 billion forints for the modernization of air defences. In December 1992 a US firm was contracted to supply Hungary with a modern IFF (Identification Friend or Foe) system for its airforce and four ground-based radar stations, to be effective within two years.[173]

Hungary's improved relations with Germany and Russia offered a partial solution to the problems faced by its armed forces. Germany's autumn 1992 decision to supply parts and maintenance equipment from the former East German army should allow Hungary to maintain and improve the operational readiness of its forces. The 1993 agreement with Russia for the supply of 28 MiG-29s should also allow Hungary to modernize its air defences.[174] Notably, Hungary made special efforts to reassure its neighbours that this modernization would not threaten them, pointing out that the MiG-29s would replace outdated aircraft (rather than increase the total size of the airforce), that Hungary was only gaining aircraft which its neighbours already possessed and that Hungary would still be well below its CFE treaty limits for aircraft. It also deliberately based the MiG-29s in central Hungary, rather than near its borders.[175]

Defence spending, however, remained controversial. In June 1992 the Defence Ministry requested a 'minimal budget' for 1993 of 75–80 billion forint. The opposition Free Democrats and Socialists argued that this was unjustified given the countries economic and social problems. After negotiations, the National Assembly approved a compromise budget of 64.5 billion forint. The National Assembly's Defence Committee argued that no further cuts were possible without endangering the army's combat effectiveness.[176] After the 1994 elections, whilst the MSP government appeared likely to continue the reforms of its predecessors, it seemed no more likely to increase defence spending and might reduce it further.

CONCLUSION

Since 1989, Hungary's national security policy has been fundamentally transformed. Reporting to the National Assembly in February 1993, Foreign Minister Jeszenszky summarized the central elements of the new policy:

> In the present situation the security of the Hungarian Republic has two key questions. The process of our integration into the European or Western European community and the establishment and strengthening of settled relations with our immediate and more distant neighbours.[177]

Although the election of the MSP in May 1994 raised fears of a reorientation away from the West, the new government continued to seek membership of the EU and NATO and no major political forces within Hungary questioned the strategic objective of integration with the West. Parallel to this, Hungary has sought cooperation with the other East–Central European states in the Visegrad group, a strengthened CSCE and the development of a defensively oriented, territorial defence policy.

Hungary's relations with its immediate neighbours have, however, proved more difficult and have become the subject of domestic political debate. In essence, Hungary has had to balance its competing interests in protecting the rights of the Hungarian minorities abroad and avoiding conflict with its neighbours. It has sought to do this by combining support for specific rights for the minorities with the active pursuit of military CSBMs with its neighbours. The inability of the MDF government to establish good relations with Romania, Slovakia and Serbia led the MSP to criticize it and propose a 'historic reconciliation'. The prospects for that reconciliation, however, appear limited, as the central issue of minority rights remains unresolved and any Hungarian government will find it difficult to abandon support for the minorities.

Hungary's troubled relations with its neighbours might also have implications for its relations with the West. With Western governments afraid of the consequences of bringing East European conflicts into key Western institutions, Hungary's difficult relations with its neighbours might risk slowing its integration with the West. This risk, however, may lead Hungary to moderate its position in relations with its neighbours in order to improve its prospects for integration with the West. At the same time, as was seen earlier, the West's reluctance to guarantee Hungary's security was leading it to seek a bilateral accommodation with Serbia. By the autumn of 1994, however, how far these dynamics might affect Hungary's prospects for membership of the EU and NATO remained unclear.

7 East–Central Europe and the New European Security Order

Since 1990 the central feature of East–Central European security has been the emergence of the East–Central European states as a distinct Visegrad group with an increasingly close, special relationship with the West. This chapter traces this development, analyzing the position of the East–Central European states in the European security order of the mid-1990s. The chapter begins by examining the development of the East–Central European states as a distinct group, analyzing the nature of the regional cooperation process between them. It then examines the evolution of their relations with the EU and NATO, highlighting the increasingly close character of these relations and the East–Central European states emergence as the primary Eastern candidates for membership of both bodies. It then examines the role of the CSCE in East–Central European security. The chapter concludes by arguing that, while the East–Central European states have reasonable prospects for joining the EU and NATO, their membership of these bodies is still not guaranteed and should the possibility of integration with the West become closed to them a return to historical patterns of instability and conflict may be likely.

THE VISEGRAD GROUP

The emergence of the East–Central European states as a distinct Visegrad group was a gradual process. This process reflected the convergence of their domestic and foreign policy transitions, their shared concerns about the situation in the Soviet Union and the West's decision to treat them as a distinct group deserving of close ties with it. In 1989 and early 1990, Poland, Czechoslovakia and Hungary were at different stages in their domestic and foreign policy transitions and pursued substantially different national security policies. Polish concerns focussed on German unification. Czechoslovak policy focussed on developing the CSCE. Hungary maintained cautious support for the Warsaw Pact.

As was seen in chapter 5, President Havel's call for a coordinated 'return to Europe' resulted in the unsuccessful April 1990 meeting of Presidents, Prime Ministers and senior officials from the three countries in Bratislava (marred by disputes over the Hungarian minority in Slovakia and the Polish and Hungarian rejection of a Czechoslovak proposed joint declaration).[1]

By late 1990, however, the East–Central European states' security policies were converging. With German recognition of the Oder–Neisse border, Polish policy shifted towards integration with the West. The slow development of the CSCE led Czechoslovakia to re-focus on the same objective. In Hungary, the new MDF government indicated that its priority was integration with the West. Growing concern about the situation within the Soviet Union led all three to seek closer ties with NATO. At the same time, the West, particularly the EC, began to treat them as a distinct group. In June 1990 the EC's Council of Ministers approved a British suggestion that East European states be granted associate status. In August the European Commission proposed that association agreements be concluded with those states where there was evidence of substantive political and economic reform, arguing that only Poland, Czechoslovakia and Hungary met these criteria. The Council approved these ideas in September, authorizing the Commission to open negotiations in December. The move to negotiate association agreements was a significant strategic decision, establishing the East–Central European states as a distinct group likely to be the first Eastern states to be integrated with Western institutions. This was confirmed when Poland, Czechoslovakia and Hungary became the first East European states to join the Council of Europe in 1990 and 1991.[2]

The recognition that they faced essentially the same problems in their relations with the Soviet Union and that they might increase their diplomatic strength by cooperating with each other was the main catalyst for cooperation between the East–Central European states. As the Soviet Union became increasingly reluctant to reform or dismantle the Warsaw Pact, they began to cooperate in opposing the Soviet position:

> work in the Warsaw Pact Political Consultative Committee between June and November 1990 brought the three states together in a negotiating environment that enabled them to clarify the commonalities in their security needs and juxtapose these needs to those of Moscow.[3]

In September 1990 the three countries' civilian deputy defence ministers met in Zakopane in Poland to discuss the de-politicization of their armed forces – the first post-Cold War meeting of East European defence officials to which the Soviet Union was not invited. The three countries' deputy foreign ministers met in Warsaw in October, creating a consultative committee to address shared regional problems, establishing working groups to implement regular meetings and prepare a trilateral declaration, and agreeing to replace their negotiators in the Warsaw Pact's Political Consultative Committee and focus on dismantling rather than reforming the Pact.[4] President Havel and Prime Ministers Mazowiecki and Antall met during the Paris CSCE summit in November 1990, agreeing to increase cooperation.[5] At a meeting of deputy foreign ministers in December 1990 it was announced that a summit would be held at Visegrad near Budapest early in 1991.[6]

The emerging cooperation process was given a significant boost by the January 1991 Soviet crack-down in the Baltic republics. As was seen in the last three chapters, the East–Central European foreign ministers met in Budapest in mid-January, amidst rumours that their countries might withdraw from the Warsaw Pact. Despite their differences over whether or not to withdraw from the Pact, they were able to agree to a statement supporting the independence aspirations of the Baltic republics, condemning the Soviet action and, most significantly, demanding that the Pact's military structures be abolished by 1 July 1991 and the organization dissolved within a year. The statement, and the implied threat of withdrawal from the Pact, led President Gorbachev to accept the dissolution of the Pact – clearly indicating how cooperation might strengthen the East–Central European states' diplomatic hand.

Presidents Havel and Walesa and Prime Minister Antall met at Visegrad in February 1991. The declaration from the summit stated that the three countries' 'essentially identical' goal was 'total integration into the European political, economic, security, and legislative order'. As a result, they would 'harmonize their efforts to foster cooperation and close relations with European institutions' and 'consult on questions concerning their security'.[7] Thus, the East–Central European cooperation process became the Visegrad group. After the summit, consultative meetings were held at ministerial, deputy ministerial and working group level to coordinate policies towards the Soviet Union, NATO, the EC, the crisis in Yugoslavia and military reforms.[8] The growing confidence of the group was reflected in their united and successful opposition to the Soviet Union's demands for the inclusion of special 'security clauses' in new bilateral treaties.

After the Visegrad summit, the East–Central Europeans focussed their cooperation on pressing for closer security ties with the West. As was seen in the last three chapters, in a series of major policy speeches in

1991 East–Central European leaders indicated that they feared their countries were falling into a security vacuum and wanted membership of the EC and NATO. When the West made clear that it was not yet willing to consider this, they pressed for some form of special relationship, extending – preferably formally, but, failing that, informally – Western security guarantees to their countries.

The Western response was ambiguous. The West had an interest in ensuring that East–Central Europe did not once again become a Soviet sphere of influence and that stability in the region was not seriously undermined. Yet it feared provoking renewed confrontation with the Soviet Union or being dragged into conflicts in the East. Western governments attempted to square the circle by refusing early membership of the EC and NATO or formal security guarantees, but making an increasingly clear political commitment to the East–Central Europe states' security. Meeting in Copenhagen in June 1991 NATO foreign ministers declared:

> Our own security is inseparably linked to that of all other states in Europe. The consolidation and preservation throughout the continent of democratic societies and their freedom from any form of coercion or intimidation are therefore of direct and material concern to us.[9]

Despite being vague, the statement was clearly a signal to the Soviet Union of NATO's interest in the East–Central European states' security. NATO Secretary-General Manfred Woerner warned that any Soviet interference in Eastern Europe would have 'grave consequences'.[10] The growing Western commitment to East–Central Europe was confirmed in August 1991 when the United States lifted its Cold War ban on weapons sales to Poland, Czechoslovakia and Hungary.[11] The latter step also implied close collaboration in export control policy indicating that the West saw the East–Central Europeans as reliable partners.

Cooperation within the Visegrad group and the groups' emerging special relationship with the West were boosted by the August 1991 Soviet coup. The Polish, Czechoslovak and Hungarian deputy foreign ministers met in Warsaw during the coup, drawing up a joint assessment of the situation. They also established a standing committee to coordinate policies (particularly on security issues), agreed to coordinate policies on bilateral treaties with the Soviet Union and association negotiations with the EC, and agreed the key points of letters to be sent to Western governments by Presidents Havel and Walesa and Prime Minister Antall pressing for the association negotiations to be accelerated.[12] NATO leaders reiterated their conviction that the Alliance's security was 'inseparably linked to that of all other states in Europe, *particularly to that of the emerging democracies*', stated that they expected the Soviet Union 'to respect the integrity and security of all states in Europe' and committed themselves to 'further strengthening' ties with the new democracies.[13] EC foreign ministers agreed to accelerate the negotiation of the association agreements.[14]

The August 1991 Soviet coup and the outbreak of the war in Yugoslavia confirmed in the eyes of the East–Central European governments both the utility of their own cooperation and the need for accelerated integration with the West. The three countries' leaders met again in Cracow in October 1991. The declaration from the summit described their cooperation as 'an essential contribution in shaping a new democratic international order in the region'. The leaders called for the 'institutionalization' of ties with NATO, the 'extension' of ties with the WEU and their integration with the EC's common foreign and security policy decision-making process. Committing themselves to a new level of cooperation, they agreed to 'accord their position' in association negotiations with the EC and undertake a 'common policy' toward the Soviet Union.[15]

The East–Central European leaders met again in Prague in May 1992. Intensifying cooperation, they agreed to submit a joint application for EC membership and to cooperate in their relations with the WEU and NATO and in the further development of the CSCE.[16] By this point, however, foreign and security policy cooperation was already quite well established and the agenda was shifting towards economic issues. The most significant outcome of the Prague meeting, therefore, was an agreement to negotiate a free-trade zone between the three countries.[17] Havel, Walesa and Antall declared the Prague summit the most successful to date.[18] The West's treatment of the Visegrad group as a distinct group deserving of a special relationship with it was highlighted when the East–Central European prime ministers met as a group with EC leaders for the first time in October 1992.[19] Broader cooperation within the Visegrad group seemed confirmed in December 1992, when, after difficult negotiations, the three countries signed an agreement establishing a Central European Free-Trade Area (CEFTA).[20] By 1992, therefore, the Visegrad group was becoming an established feature of the new European security landscape.

The nature and the character of the Visegrad group was, however, complex and ambiguous. Czech Prime Minister Vaclav Klaus, a key critic of the group, argued that it was 'an artificial process created by the West'. While it is clear that the EC's decision to conclude parallel association agreements with the East–Central European states played an important role in the emergence of the Visegrad group, Klaus's argument was exaggerated. The convergence of the East–Central European states' domestic transitions and security concerns, and the active support of Presidents Walesa and Havel and Prime Minister Antall, also played a key role in the emergence of the Visegrad group.

The Visegrad group was characterized, in the words of one observer, by a combination of 'cooperation, competition, and coexistence'.[21] The East–Central European states cooperated with each other in their relations with the Soviet Union and the West because cooperation increased their diplomatic influence. Since each country's primary goal was integration with the West, they also competed with each other in this area. The West's policy of treating the group as a whole, however, denied any country the opportunity of achieving integration alone, thereby re-inforcing the dynamic of cooperation. At the same time, given the possibility of conflicts between the East–Central European states over borders, minority rights, environmental issues and trade, they also had to coexist with each other or risk the possibility of their conflicts escalating. Here again, the West's indication that conflicts within East–Central Europe might delay integration reinforced the dynamic of cooperation.

The Visegrad group, therefore, became a loose framework for cooperation and consultation within East–Central Europe. While cooperation took the form of regular meetings and policy coordination at many levels, there was no desire to create a permanent institution. The East–Central European leaders were clearly sensitive to the danger of creating a formal institution which might provoke the Soviet Union or its successors. Thus, the Visegrad summit declaration stressed that their cooperation was 'in no way ... directed against the interests of any other state.'[22] Perhaps even more importantly, the East–Central Europeans feared that creating a distinct regional institution might delay their integration with the West by creating an alternative to EC and NATO membership.[23]

Cooperation in the Visegrad group contributed to the East–Central European states' security in two main ways. First, it increased their diplomatic power and influence by enabling them to present united positions. As was seen above, the East–Central Europeans successfully pressured the Soviet Union into accepting the demise of the Warsaw Pact and opposed the Soviet proposal for special 'security clauses' in new bilateral treaties. The East–Central European states also gained diplomatic influence by coordinating their policies towards the West. This enabled them to extract additional concessions from the EC during the negotiation of their association treaties.[24] Most significantly in security terms, however, the East–Central European states' consistent demands for the expansion and institutionalization of their ties with NATO clearly put pressure on the Alliance to address their concerns.[25] Cooperation in the Visegrad group also indicated to the West that the East–Central European states were behaving 'responsibly', further improving their prospects for eventual membership of the Alliance. As President Havel argued:

> coordination has, above all, considerably helped all three countries in their entry into democratic European structures. The democratic world to a certain extent measures our trustworthiness by our ability to reach agreement. They consider us a troika.[26]

Second, the Visegrad group acted as a form of confidence-building measure within East–Central Europe, particularly in the military sphere. The process of cooperation was in itself a signal that the three countries wished to put historical disputes behind them and resolve their differences peacefully. The effectiveness of trilateral cooperation in this sphere was, however, limited. While Poland signed bilateral cooperation treaties with both Czechoslovakia and Hungary at the October 1991 Cracow summit, the Hungarian–Czechoslovak treaty remained unsigned because of the disputes over the Hungarian minority in Slovakia and the Gabcikovo–Nagymaros dam. Key issues were dealt with bilaterally rather than within the Visegrad group – indicating the limits of the cooperation process.

Military cooperation was, however, more successful. When the Polish, Czechoslovak and Hungarian civilian, deputy defence ministers first met in September 1990, they agreed to exchange information on the social and human aspects of military reform.[27] Following this, the East–Central European defence ministers met in Cracow in August 1991, agreeing on a system of regular consultation at all levels and examining possibilities for closer cooperation in arms production and procurement. During the Soviet coup, the East–Central European militaries maintained constant liaison and defence officials were involved in the meeting in Warsaw during the crisis. Further discussions were held at deputy defence minister level in Budapest in November 1991.[28] Defence ministers met again in Budapest in March 1992, discussing military cooperation, coordination of defence industries, joint air space control and a possible 'open barracks' regime.[29]

Most practical military cooperation, however, was bilateral. Bilateral military cooperation agreements between the three states were signed early in 1991. The agreements, signed by the countries' defence ministers, lasted for five years but were automatically renewed unless one side objected. The agreements committed defence ministers to consult on a range of issues: military doctrines, training and education; possible cooperation in weapons production; de-politicization of the military; and maintaining equipment. Forces from one country might also use training facilities in another. The Polish–Czechoslovak and Czechoslovak–Hungarian treaties also incorporated transparency provisions, including prior notification of troop movements into or within border regions.[30]

The break-up of Czechoslovakia at the end of 1992, however, created new tensions within the Visegrad group, raising serious doubts as to how far the cooperation established since 1990 would be maintained. As was seen in chapter 5, Czech Prime Minister Vaclav Klaus was an opponent of cooperation within the Visegrad group, believing that the Czech Republic was more advanced that its neighbours in establishing democracy and a market economy and that cooperation in the Visegrad group might delay his country's integration with the West, particularly the EU. Klaus's views raised the possibility that the Czech Republic might abandon or significantly downgrade cooperation with its neighbours. Czechoslovakia's demise also raised doubts as to how far Slovakia would continue to follow the same domestic and foreign policy path as the other East–Central European states. Should it follow an authoritarian, nationalist line, the prospects for cooperation within the Visegrad group and for its integration with the West might be seriously undermined. Slovak independence also exacerbated tensions with Hungary, further calling into question the prospects for cooperation within the Visegrad group.

The Polish, Hungarian and Slovak leaders indicated their desire for continued cooperation within the Visegrad group, including a coordinated approach to the West.[31] Klaus, while accepting CEFTA, rejected the May 1992 agreement to apply jointly for EC membership, arguing that the Czech Republic would be ready to join before its neighbours. Despite Klaus's rhetoric, however, a coordinated approach to the West was maintained to some extent in practice. In June 1993 the four states jointly appealed to the EC to 'set the date and define conditions for full membership in the community'.[32] In September the Polish, Czech, Hungarian and Slovak deputy defence ministers and chiefs of general staffs met in Cracow, agreeing to develop a program for supplying each other with arms and spare parts and to increase the volume of orders from each other for technological improvements to their military equipment.[33] Bilateral military cooperation also continued, with Poland, the Czech Republic and Hungary all concluding military cooperation agreements with Slovakia. Hungary's opposition, in the summer of 1993, to Slovakia's membership of the Council of Europe, however, indicated that tensions between the two states might undermine a coordinated approach towards the West.

The West also indicated that it wished to continue to treat the East–Central European states as a group and signalled its support for cooperation within the Visegrad group, putting pressure on the East–Central European states to maintain that cooperation. The EU concluded its association agreements with the Czech Republic and Slovakia in parallel. At its June 1993 Copenhagen summit the EU referred to the Visegrad states as a group, supporting their cooperation.[34] More generally, as was seen in chapter 5, the West appeared to be seeking to encourage reform in Slovakia by integrating it along with the other Visegrad states, rather than isolating it.

President Clinton's January 1994 Prague summit with the heads of state of the Visegrad countries, however, highlighted growing divisions within the group. With Poland, Hungary and Slovakia advocating a coordinated approach to NATO, Czech Defence Minister Antonin Baudys refused to attend a meeting with his Visegrad group counterparts to discuss such an approach. Czech Foreign Minister Josef Zieleniec stated that 'we don't believe in organising lobbies or pressure groups to knock on doors'.[35] Although the four countries' heads of state did meet as a group with President Clinton, this reflected the fact that the Czech government had little alternative but to accept the US proposed meeting. Indicating the growing divisions within the group, a public walkabout by Presidents Clinton and Havel led Poland to accuse the Czechs of hijacking the summit.[36] The public Czech rejection of a coordinated approach to NATO signalled a major break-down in cooperation within the Visegrad group, perhaps even its end (at least in terms of a coordinated approach to Western institutions). This seemed confirmed in April 1994 when Poland and Hungary formally applied for EU membership and the Czechs refused to join a common application.[37]

The break-down in cooperation within the Visegrad group coincided with new uncertainties about how far the West would continue to treat the four East–Central European states as a distinct group. Bulgaria and Romania's conclusion of association agreements with the EU removed the Visegrad states' special status as associates. This shift was confirmed in October 1994 when EU foreign ministers agreed that the ministers of the six East European associate states should join meetings of EU ministers, including annual meetings of heads of states and six monthly meetings of foreign ministers, in preparation for eventual membership.[38] Polish Foreign Minister Andrej Olechowski said that he expected the EU to treat the six East European states as a group, but that within that context separate membership negotiations would take place for each country and Poland would not worry if the Czech Republic joined the EU before it.[39] In terms of which states might join the EU and NATO first, however, the picture was less clear. A September 1994 European Commission report argued that the Czech Republic and Slovenia were significantly ahead of the other Visegrad states in meeting the economic criteria for EU membership and might be the only countries economically strong enough to join the Union by the year 2000. A joint Franco-German government paper, in contrast, continued to place the Visegrad states (with Slovenia) as a distinct group, ahead of Bulgaria, Romania and the Baltic states in terms of admission to the EU.[40] Other Western sources suggested Poland, the Czech Republic and Hungary were the primary candidates for EU and NATO membership, viewing Slovakia as too unstable.[41] No clear overall Western position on future EU and NATO membership had emerged, therefore, and the West appeared to be keeping its options open in terms of whether and how far to differentiate between the various East European states. The absence of a clear Western position diminished pressure on the four East–Central European states to maintain close cooperation.

By the autumn of 1994, therefore, the earlier foreign and security policy cooperation within the Visegrad group appeared to be in decline. While the Visegrad states had agreed to speed up implementation of CEFTA[42] and bilateral military cooperation remained strong, the central element of a coordinated 'return to Europe' appeared to have been seriously undermined by the events of January 1994. While a shift in Czech policy and stabilization in Slovakia could not be ruled out, a return to the earlier pattern of close collaboration seemed unlikely. Even President Havel, earlier a leading advocate of cooperation within the Visegrad group, had accepted Klaus's position, arguing that the East–Central European states should join Western institutions when they were ready and not wait for each other.[43] Whether the West would continue to treat the East–Central European states as a group, however, remained unclear. Even in the absence of close policy coordination between the East–Central Europeans themselves, the West might continue to treat them as a group in terms of either EU or NATO membership.

RELATIONS WITH THE EUROPEAN UNION

From 1990 onwards Poland, Czechoslovakia and Hungary made clear that their central foreign policy goal was membership of the EC. This was driven as much by political and security concerns as by economics. For the new East–Central European leaders the EC was the institutional framework which had facilitated the development of democracy, prosperity and security in Western Europe after the second World War. Integration with the EC would underpin democracy in East–Central Europe, provide the region with a sense of security and symbolize its 'return to Europe'.

In 1990–91, the EC was preoccupied with the Maastricht negotiations on closer integration between its existing members and was unwilling to seriously consider the possibility that the East–Central European states might become full members. The EC's 1990 decision to negotiate association agreements with Poland, Czechoslovakia and Hungary indicated that they would have to be satisfied with a relationship short of membership for some years to come. With the EC discussing the development of a common foreign and security policy, the East–Central European states began to press for integration in this area ahead of full membership. At the Cracow summit in October 1991 the East–Central European leaders called for their countries' forthcoming association agreements to 'lead to an integration . . . into the system of European Political Cooperation' (EPC – the EC's foreign and security policy-making process) and an 'extension of relations' with the WEU.[44]

The EC, however, rejected the East–Central Europeans' proposal. The association agreements, signed in December 1991, focussed on economic integration and lower level political ties and did not bring the East–Central European states into the EPC process. They did, however, provide some limited possibilities for discussion of security issues. The agreements are supervised by Association Councils, at the level of Ministers and Commissioners, able to take decisions by mutual agreement and to discuss wider international questions. Each Council's work is prepared by an Association Committee of senior offiicials. Parliamentary Association Committees, involving members of the East–Central European national parliaments and the European Parliament, are able to make recommendations to the Association Councils. As one observer noted, 'the right of the Association Councils to discuss wider questions beyond the working of the agreements opens the way to general political dialogue'.[45] According to another analyst, through this process 'the new democracies in Europe are thus gradually familiarised with the foreign policy cooperation of EC members within the framework of European Political Cooperation, insofar as this relates to issues of common interest'.[46] Such limited, medium level discussions, however, hardly satisfied the security demands of the East–Central European states. The association agreements did, however, include the politically significant recognition that 'the ultimate aim is accession to the EC' – the EC's first recognition that the East–Central European states were on a 'track' leading to membership.[47]

The East–Central European states remained dissatisfied, arguing that the association agreements gave them no timetable or criteria for EC membership and no direct involvement in EC foreign policy-making. The EC, while remaining reluctant to establish a timetable or criteria, accepted the case for closer political and security dialogue. The 'troika' of EC foreign ministers met with their East–Central European counterparts during the May 1992 Prague Visegrad group summit, discussing political and economic ties; the roles of the WEU, NATO and the CSCE; and the Yugoslav conflict.[48] Dutch Foreign Minister Hans van den Broek described the East–Central Europeans as 'partners with which we wish to develop more political dialogue, economic cooperation and discussions on the future security system in Europe'.[49] Hungarian Foreign Ministry Geza Jeszenszky noted that the meeting was the group's first substantial exchange of views with EC leaders.[50]

In October 1992 the East–Central European foreign ministers joined for the first time a regular meeting of EC foreign ministers. The East–Central Europeans asked the EC to assess by 1996 their progress in meeting the conditions for EC membership and, if this assessment was positive, to begin negotiations so that they could join by the year 2000.[51] The EC argued that it could not yet draw up a timetable. Later in October a special meeting of East–Central European leaders with British Prime Minister John Major (as the current holder of the EC Presidency) and EC Commission President Jacques Delors resulted in a joint declaration committing the EC to 'consolidation and intensification of dialogue', including regular meetings of foreign ministers and more frequent meetings at high administrative levels.[52] According to Prime Minister Major, this 'set the framework for regular discussions . . . on major foreign policy issues'.[53]

By 1993, however, there was growing recognition that the EC should reduce barriers to East European goods, expand foreign and security policy contacts and make a clearer political commitment to the East European states eventual membership. At their June 1993 Copenhagen summit EC leaders agreed to reduce some trade barriers and formally stated for the first time that they expected the East European states to join the EC once they had met membership criteria. The EC leaders, however, gave no timetable for membership and the criteria remained general, including stable democracy, rule of law, respect for human and minority rights, a functioning market economy, ability to meet the obligations of membership, and support for further EC integration.[54] Nevertheless, the Copenhagen summit was an important political commitment in terms of formally opening up the prospect of EC membership to the East–Central European states.

Following the success of Vladimir Zhirinvosky's neo-fascist Liberal Democratic Party in Russia's December 1993 elections and Russian attempts to reassert a sphere of influence in East–Central Europe, European Union (as the EC had become when the Maastricht Treaty came into force) leaders sought to further accelerate the integration of the East–Central European states. In March 1994 EU foreign ministers agreed to an annual summit of the President of the European Council and the Commission with associate states' heads of state and government; bi-annual meetings of foreign ministers; regular working-level meetings on security, terrorism and human rights; formal cooperation at international conferences; and 'joint foreign policy actions' between the EU and associates.[55] In October 1994 EU foreign ministers took further steps, agreeing to annual meetings of heads of governments and of other relevant ministers and that the associate states should participate in EU ministerial meetings on foreign and security policy.[56] The latter step was particularly significant since it meant that, despite not being formally part of the EU's common foreign and security policy, the associate states would participate in shaping that policy and would have a high level forum where their security concerns might be directly expressed to Western leaders. EU foreign ministers also agreed to draw up details of the measures the East European states would need to adopt in order to become members – a further significant step, since it implied laying out detailed membership criteria for the first time.[57]

A further dimension was added to the EU's relations with the East–Central European states by French Prime Minister Edouard Balladur's April 1993 proposal for a European stability pact. The proposal envisaged the EU promoting stability in Eastern Europe by supporting the negotiation of a stability pact guaranteeing ethnic minority rights and borders amongst those East European states seeking to join the Union.[58] Central to the plan was the idea that the EU make economic aid and future membership conditional on East European states resolving minority and border disputes. EU foreign ministers endorsed the idea in

December 1993 and the initial conference opened in Paris in May 1994, agreeing to establish regional negotiating tables for Eastern Europe (covering the six EU associates) and the Baltic region. The Paris conference was, however, marred by disputes over the nature and role of the proposed stability pact and tensions between Hungary and its neighbours and Russia and the Baltic states.[59]

The stability pact faced a number of serious problems. East European states feared that it might be used to delay or prevent their membership of the EU. They also feared that it was discriminatory since it did not address disputes involving existing EU members and might impose standards of minority rights on Eastern Europe which EU states themselves did not have to accept. It also faced the danger of duplicating the roles of the CSCE, the Council of Europe and existing bilateral negotiations within Eastern Europe. The range of issues it would cover and the types of negotiating forums were unclear. Further, given the very real differences between some East European states over minority rights, it was far from clear that the negotiations would be able to resolve these issues.[60] While a successful resolution of ethic minority conflicts might make a significant contribution to East–Central European security and improve the region's prospects for integration with the EU, by the autumn of 1994 the outlook for the European stability pact was uncertain.

Parallel to their relations with the EU, the East–Central European states also developed relations with the Western European Union (WEU), the 'defence arm' of the EU. Unlike NATO (where the NACC and Partnership for Peace were open to all East European and former-Soviet states), the WEU followed 'the pattern of ... differentiation' established by the EC, focussing its cooperation efforts on those states associated with the EC.[61] In June 1991 WEU foreign and defence ministers proposed *ad hoc* meetings at ministerial level and links between the embassies of the East European countries and the WEU Secretariat-General and between the government of each Eastern European country and the embassy of the country acting as WEU President. Meeting in Bonn in November 1991 WEU foreign and defence ministers agreed to enhance this security dialogue, formalizing their differentiation of Eastern Europe from the Soviet Union by inviting the foreign and defence ministers of Bulgaria, Czechoslovakia, Hungary, Poland and Romania to a special meeting with the WEU Council.[62] In June 1992 the first meeting of the WEU Forum of Consultation (WEU foreign and defence ministers plus their counterparts from Poland, Czechoslovakia, Hungary, Romania, Bulgaria and the three Baltic states) took place after a normal meeting of the WEU Council. The ministers agreed to meetings at least once a year, with the possibility of additional meetings; consultations between the WEU Permanent Council and East European ambassadors at least twice a year; and the possibility of meetings at a senior official level with an *ad hoc* WEU troika.[63]

By 1993–94 there was growing recognition within the WEU of the need to develop closer relations with prospective EU members. In November 1993 the WEU agreed that those states associated with the EU be given enhanced status in relations with the WEU.[64] The WEU's parliamentary assembly also offered the East European states 'special permanent observer' status, allowing them to participate in sessions, but without voting rights.[65] In May 1994 the WEU went further offering the EU associates 'associate partnership' in the WEU, including attendance of weekly working meetings of the WEU and participation in peacekeeping operations with WEU members.[66] By the time the new associate partners first formally joined a regular meeting of WEU foreign and defence ministers in November 1994, WEU Secretary-General Willem van Eekelan was noting that they were 'already contributing fully to the preparation of WEU meetings including our discussions on a common European defence'.[67] Thus, by 1994 the WEU, like the EU, was taking clear steps to bring the East European states into its discussions as active participants, preparing them for future membership. The relative military weakness of the WEU as an organization, however, meant that actual military cooperation remained very limited.[68] Further, since the Maastricht negotiations had established a link between EU and WEU membership, it was likely that the East–Central European states would only join the WEU when they joined the EU.[69]

By the autumn of 1994 the East–Central European states were developing increasingly close political, economic and security cooperation with the EU and had established themselves (along with Slovenia) as the primary Eastern candidates for membership. They were involved in a growing range of meetings with the EU and the WEU at various levels, enabling them to contribute directly to EU and WEU discussions and raise their security concerns. The EU had committed itself to accepting them as members once they had met general conditions. Practical security cooperation was also occurring in some areas. The EU was trying to promote the resolution of Hungary's disputes with Romania and Slovakia and monitoring Hungary's border with the former-Yugoslavia. The WEU was supplying boats and manpower to help Hungary enforce the UN blockade of the rump-Yugoslavia.[70]

The East–Central European states, however, remained disappointed

with the EU's response to their demands. Practical security cooperation, they argued, needed to be deepened. The EU's reluctance to open
its markets to East European goods undermined their economic reforms, thereby threatening their political and social stability. The EU
had still not established clear criteria or a timetable for their membership. Nor had it begun to seriously address the reforms of its own
political and economic structures which were certain to be necessary
if the East–Central European states were to join. While welcoming
growing political support for their membership, the East–Central European states remained wary that Western fears of the economic consequences of integrating them might seriously delay or postpone their
membership of the EU.

Eastward enlargement of the EU was set to be a central issue in the
1996 inter-governmental conference on the Union's future development.
Led by Germany, support was growing within the EU for the conference to make a clear political commitment to expanding the Union,
establish criteria and a timetable for expansion and seriously address
the political and economic reforms necessary for such a step. If the
conference successfully addressed these issues, the East–Central European states' prospects for EU membership might be significantly enhanced. If the conference failed to adequately address these issues,
however, their membership might be delayed. At the same time, EU
membership would remain dependent on political stability and continued progress in establishing democratic societies and market economies in East–Central Europe.

RELATIONS WITH NATO

From late 1990 onwards growing concern at developments within the
Soviet Union led the East–Central European states to seek closer relations
with NATO in order to guarantee their security. At its July 1990 London
summit NATO had offered to extend the 'hand of friendship' to Eastern
Europe and the Soviet Union through intensified diplomatic and military contacts.[71] These contacts, however, were relatively limited and did
not assuage East–Central European concerns. As was seen earlier in this
chapter, while NATO was unwilling to extend membership or formal
security guarantees to the region, growing pressure from the East–Central
European states for security guarantees led the Alliance – at the June
1991 Copenhagen meeting of NATO foreign ministers and during the
August 1991 coup – to express its direct interest in their security.

After the failure of the coup in the Soviet Union, NATO – led by the United States and Germany – showed increasing interest in institutionalizing its relations with the countries to its East.[72] Viewing this shift in policy as a significant opportunity, at the Cracow summit in October 1991 East–Central European leaders called for the 'extension of relations with the Atlantic treaty, including their institutionalization'.[73] The three countries' foreign ministers made a separate statement at Cracow calling for their countries existing 'diplomatic liaison' to be 'widened considerably in order to create conditions for direct involvement . . . in the activities of NATO'.[74] Later in October Czechoslovakia's President Havel and Hungary's Prime Minister Antall argued that NATO should provide more explicit guarantees to the countries of East–Central Europe and state clearly that it would support them militarily in the case of aggression against them.[75] NATO, however, rejected these demands. According to one NATO official, 'their security should be tied up with our own, but we are not prepared to entertain the notion of membership or a security guarantee of an explicit legal nature'.[76]

The November 1991 Rome NATO summit made clear the limits of what NATO was willing to offer. In the *Rome Declaration on Peace and Cooperation* NATO leaders called for their relations with Eastern Europe and the Soviet Union to be 'broadened, intensified and raised to a qualitatively new level', inviting these countries to meet annually with the North Atlantic Council in a North Atlantic Cooperation Council (NACC), to meet more regularly at ministerial and ambassadorial level and to meet with NATO's political, economic and military committees and other NATO military authorities. Within this framework, NATO would offer its experience and expertise in 'defence planning, democratic concepts of civilian-military relations, civil/military coordination of air traffic management, and the conversion of defence production to civilian purposes'.[77] The first meeting of the NACC took place at the end of December 1991, agreeing to meet annually at foreign minister level and bi-monthly at ambassadorial level, to hold additional meetings as necessary, and to hold meetings with NATO's political, economic and military committees and NATO military authorities.[78]

With the former-Soviet states joining the NACC in March 1992, agreement was reached on a 'Work Plan for Dialogue, Partnership and Cooperation', including a commitment to consultation on political and security issues, arms control and disarmament, defence planning, defence conversion, mid/long-term foreign and security policy planning, and civil–military coordination of air traffic management.[79] NACC defence ministers met in April 1992, agreeing a more detailed agenda for defence cooperation.[80] The NACC, however, was a disappointment for the East–Central Europeans, as it neither differentiated them from their neighbours nor gave them security guarantees.

The NACC did, however, expand the range of areas of possible cooperation, creating new opportunities for the East–Central European states to deepen their political and military relations with the West and to differentiate themselves from their neighbours. According to NATO Secretary-General Manfred Woerner, the NACC did 'not exclude the possibility of separate consultations with one or two or three (NACC members). We remain very flexible. It is not necessary in every instance for everybody to be present'.[81] Under the March 1992 work plan, 'cooperative activities' might involve 'only some' NACC members.[82] In April 1992, NACC defence ministers also agreed that 'small teams of civilian and military defence experts, drawn as appropriate from several Alliance countries, could be sent, on request, to countries desiring advice'.[83] Thus, while the NACC did not formally differentiate the countries of East–Central Europe, a degree of *de facto* differentiation occurred, with meetings between NATO delegations and the Visegrad states in 1992 to discuss the restructuring of their armed forces and NATO's role in providing expertise and practical support.[84]

The NACC also provided a forum for putting diplomatic pressure on its members to resolve disputes on some military issues. Early in 1992 the NACC provided the forum in which pressure was brought to bear on the post-Soviet states to accept the Soviet Union's commitments under the Conventional Armed Forces in Europe (CFE) Treaty and to agree armaments allocations amongst themselves.[85] NATO also brought pressure to bear on Russia to agree to withdraw its forces from the Baltic states at the end of 1992.[86] Notably, the countries of East–Central Europe had a strong interest in seeing the CFE treaty implemented by their new Eastern neighbours and, in Poland's case, in a Russian military withdrawal from the Baltic states.

Peacekeeping became a particular focus of discussions within the NACC. In 1992 NATO foreign ministers agreed in principle to support CSCE and UN peacekeeping operations (including making Alliance resources available).[87] In December 1992 NACC foreign ministers agreed to exchange experience and expertise and develop consultations and cooperation on peacekeeping.[88] The 1993 NACC workplan, agreed at the same meeting, detailed areas for possible cooperation, including peacekeeping planning, training and joint exercises.[89] During 1993, the NACC established an *ad hoc* group on peacekeeping, which developed

discussions on conceptual approaches to peacekeeping, operational principles, and possible NACC roles in peacekeeping.[90] In effect, the NACC
was preparing the way for possible joint peacekeeping operations, although actual military cooperation remained limited.

As was seen in the preceding chapters, the East–Central European
states also pursued bilateral security and defence ties with individual
NATO countries. At the political level this included the expansion of
diplomatic contacts and bilateral cooperation treaties, including commitments to consult and cooperate on security issues. These developments led to closer relations between Western and East–Central European
foreign and security policy-making elites and to some practical cooperation, such as joint proposals at the CSCE arms control negotiations.
At the military level cooperation included expanded military contacts;
the training of East–Central European officers in the West; advice from
the West on civil–military relations, defence planning and military strategy; and, on a small scale, purchases of Western military technology.

By 1992–93, therefore, a relatively close relationship was emerging
between the countries of East–Central Europe and NATO, *de facto*
differentiating the East–Central Europeans from their Eastern and Southern
neighbours and creating an informal special relationship with NATO.
The East–Central European states were among the most active participants in the NACC, had developed increasingly close political and military
cooperation with NATO and were developing close bilateral security
and defence ties with individual Western states. This practical cooperation helped the East–Central European states in reforming their own
militaries, by providing practical advice; models for civil–military relations, defence policy planning and military strategies; and direct contacts
with Western militaries.

More significantly, however, the East–Central European states emerging special relationship with NATO advanced the general perception
that they were increasingly part of the West and would be likely to
receive Western support in the event of a crisis. NATO's 1991 formula
that its security was 'inseparably linked' to that of all other European
states was clearly intended to convey this message. The growing Western
commitment to East–Central European security was confirmed by the
visits of NATO and US officials to the region during the August 1991
Soviet coup, reassuring the East–Central Europeans (as was seen in
Chapter 4) that they were 'not left alone in the face of a threat from
the East'.[91] Whether more formal commitments were made, however,
is not clear. The informal special relationship with the West was further confirmed in June 1992 when US officials held talks behind closed

doors with the East–Central European states to discuss the region's security.[92] Deepening military cooperation with the West might also facilitate practical support in a crisis. Thus, the idea that the countries of East–Central Europe were becoming part of the NATO air defence system without yet becoming members of NATO was being discussed in East–Central Europe by the end of 1992 – meaning that compatibility of communications, command and control, and identification systems might allow NATO airforces to participate in the air defence of East–Central Europe in a crisis.[93]

The East–Central European governments, however, continued to press for NATO to formally differentiate them from their neighbours and extend security guarantees. In March 1992 the Polish, Czechoslovak and Hungarian ambassadors to NATO argued that the development of their countries' relations with the Alliance had been too slow, calling for a 'privileged' relationship with NATO.[94] At their Prague summit in May 1992 Presidents Havel and Walesa and Prime Minister Antall stressed the need to develop qualitatively new relations with NATO, leading to membership of the Alliance.[95] The East–Central European states' pressure, combined with the increasingly unstable situation in Russia, prepared the way for more serious debate within the West about possible expansion of NATO.

By 1992–93 support was beginning to emerge within the West for extending NATO membership to the East–Central European states.[96] In March 1992 NATO Secretary-General Woerner described the East–Central European's relationship with NATO as a 'dynamic process' which would lead to the 'possibility' of membership.[97] In November 1992 US Defence Secretary Richard Cheney argued that 'eventually we will want to expand NATO'.[98] In March 1993 German Defence Minister Volker Ruhe argued that there was no reason for NATO membership to be denied to future EU members and that, given the economic hurdles to joining the EU, consideration should be given to expanding NATO before the EU.[99] By June 1993 Cheney's successor Les Aspin was arguing that, while the prospect of NATO membership was important for the East–Central European states, the Alliance needed to work out the 'actual modalities' and 'conditions and timing'.[100]

Western leaders, however, remained concerned about the risks of isolating Russia and, to a lesser extent, bringing East European conflicts into the Alliance. President Yeltsin's August 1993 visit to Poland brought these concerns to the fore. As was seen in Chapter 4, after apparently endorsing Polish membership of NATO, Yeltsin then retracted. In September Yeltsin wrote to Western leaders, opposing an

expansion of NATO on the grounds that it would isolate Russia. Instead, Yeltsin argued, relations between Russia and NATO should 'be
by several degrees warmer than those between the Alliance and Eastern Europe'. Russia and NATO might 'offer official security guarantees to the East European states' in a joint 'political statement or
cooperation agreement'.[101] The West was thus faced with the likelihood that early expansion of NATO would face direct Russian opposition and risk confrontation with Russia.

Against this background, the Clinton administration developed the
idea of a Partnership for Peace (PFP) programme, involving expanded
political and military cooperation with all of NATO's Eastern neighbours, including Russia. NATO's reluctance to extend membership to
East–Central Europe and its willingness to address Russian concerns
appeared to raise the possibility that the East–Central European states
might be refused NATO membership and consigned to a 'grey zone'
between the West and Russia, with their security interests subordinated
to NATO–Russian relations. Not surprisingly, the East–Central European states continued to press for NATO membership, rejecting Yeltsin's
position and remaining ambivalent about PFP.

NATO defence ministers, meeting in Travemunde in Germany in
October 1993, informally endorsed PFP, whilst indicating that NATO
membership would remain possible in the longer term.[102] Although the
East–Central European states continued to press for a clearer Western
commitment to their future NATO membership and Russia continued
to oppose this option, a consensus in favour of PFP had emerged within
NATO and the Alliance's January 1994 Brussels summit endorsed the
proposal. Under PFP, partners were invited to:

- participate in political and military bodies at NATO headquarters
  with respect to partnership activities.
- expand and intensify political and military cooperation with NATO.
- 'work in concrete ways towards transparency in defence budgeting,
  promoting democratic control of defence ministries, joint planning,
  joint military exercises, and creating an ability to operate with NATO
  forces in such fields as peacekeeping, search and rescue and humanitarian operations, and others as may be agreed'.
- participate in joint peacekeeping field exercises with NATO.
- send permanent liaison officers to NATO headquarters and a Partnership Coordination Cell at NATO's military headquarters.[103]

NATO also committed itself to consult with any active partner which
perceived 'a direct threat to its territorial integrity, political independ-

ence, or security'. Perhaps most significantly, NATO leaders stated 'that the Alliance remains open to the membership of other European countries' and that they expected and 'would welcome NATO expansion that would reach to democratic states to our East, as part of an evolutionary process, taking into account political and security developments in the whole of Europe'.[104]

Despite being ambivalent about PFP, the East–Central European were some of the first states to join the programme, signing the framework document in February and March 1994. Attention, however, shifted to the question of whether Russia would join PFP and under what conditions. Within Russia, conservative and nationalist forces opposed PFP. The Russian government responded by arguing that Russia should join, but that Russia's partnership agreement should give it a special relationship with NATO, including a possible right of veto over NATO decisions (including expansion of the Alliance). This again provoked fears in East–Central Europe that the region's interests would be subordinated to the West's relations with Russia and that Russia might gain a veto over the region's security. NATO, however, rejected any Russian veto over Alliance decisions. After much diplomatic pressure, Russia joined PFP, signing the framework document in June 1994. NATO agreed to pursue 'broad, enhanced dialogue and cooperation in areas where Russia has unique and important contributions to make', but rejected any formal commitment to a privileged relationship.[105]

PFP was a disappointment for the East–Central European states. It offered them neither NATO membership nor formal security guarantees. It laid out no clear criteria or timetable for NATO membership. Nor did it differentiate them from Russia and the other former-Soviet states. From a longer term perspective, however, the debate surrounding PFP may have addressed a number of the East–Central European states' concerns about their relationship with NATO and enhanced their prospects for closer integration with and eventual membership of the Alliance. For the first time, NATO leaders had formally stated that the Alliance was open to their Eastern neighbours and that they expected its expansion. While seeking a close relationship with Russia, Western leaders had also rejected any Russian veto over NATO decisions (including expansion of the Alliance) or over East–Central European security. The commitment to consult with any partner which felt threatened opened up new possibilities for cooperation in the event of crises and would make it difficult for NATO to ignore any serious threat to East–Central European security. The expanded political and military cooperation involved in PFP opened up new opportunities for the East–Central European states to integrate themselves with NATO, including the development of interoperability with NATO military forces. While PFP rejected formal differentiation, cooperation would take place 'at a pace and scope determined by the capacity and desire of individual participating states', giving the East–Central European states the opportunity to further develop a special relationship with NATO.[106] Further, while failing to provide formal criteria for NATO membership, the commitment involved in PFP to move towards transparent defence budgeting and planning, democratic control of defence ministries and armed forces, joint planning and exercises with NATO, and an ability to operate with NATO forces implied that these were *de facto* criteria for NATO membership.

By the autumn of 1994, further, there appeared to be growing support within NATO for expanding the Alliance to include the East–Central European states. NATO's new Secretary-General Willy Claes argued the Alliance's 'next task' was 'to begin to examine internally the way ahead, so that we can prepare the Alliance to accept new members in a way which enhances European security'.[107] US officials were acknowledging that PFP was insufficient and the US government had initiated discussions within NATO on accelerating expansion of the Alliance and wished to begin talks with prospective members on the steps they would be required to take to join the Alliance.[108] At the same time, however, an immediate expansion of the Alliance seemed unlikely. Thus, by 1994 the East–Central European states had developed an increasingly close political and military relationship with NATO, establishing them as the primary Eastern candidates for membership. While Western fears of isolating Russia or instability within East–Central Europe might still prevent expansion of NATO, it seemed increasingly likely that the East–Central European states would join the Alliance. With growing recognition of the economic obstacles to EU membership, it also appeared likely that they might join NATO before they joined the EU.

THE CSCE: THE LIMITS OF PAN-EUROPEAN SECURITY

In 1990 there were hopes that the CSCE might develop into a powerful pan-European security body, capable of guaranteeing the East–Central European states' security. The November 1990 Paris CSCE summit, however, highlighted the difficulties involved in developing an effective pan-European security regime. *The Charter of Paris for a New*

Europe, signed at the summit, committed all CSCE states to democracy, the rule of law, respect for human and minority rights, market economics, the rejection of the use of force in international relations, the principle that borders should not be changed by force, and the resolution of disputes by peaceful means. The Paris summit also initiated the institutionalization of the CSCE, with agreement that CSCE leaders meet every two years, CSCE foreign ministers meet as a Council at least once a year, a Committee of Senior Officials (CSO) be established to support the Council, and a Secretariat, a Conflict Prevention Centre (CPC) and an Office for Free Elections be created.[109]

The East–Central European states welcomed these developments as establishing the principles on which the new European order should be built. One Hungarian Foreign Ministry official later stressed the importance of the *Charter of Paris* norms as the 'common values ... the broadest definition of European civilization' on which states' behaviour should be based.[110] The former Chancellor of President Havel's office noted that 'the paramount question was that the conference should say that borders should not be changed'.[111] Reflecting the East–Central European states' active support for the CSCE, it was agreed that the Secretariat be located in Prague and the Office for Free Elections in Warsaw. The Paris summit, however, dashed East–Central European (particularly Czechoslovak) hopes that the CSCE would guarantee their security. The major Western powers were not willing to make the CSCE into a collective security organization extending security guarantees to its members. CSCE decisions remained bound by consensus decision-making, virtually precluding effective action in any serious crisis. This was starkly illustrated in October 1990 and January 1991 when the Soviet Union vetoed proposals for meetings to discuss its military crackdown in the Baltic republics.[112]

Recognizing the limitations of consensus decision-making the first meeting of the CSCE's Council of Foreign Ministers in Berlin in June 1991 agreed (after a Czechoslovak initiative) that any CSCE state affected or threatened by a dispute could, if supported by twelve other CSCE states, call a crisis meeting of the Council or the CSO which must take place within forty-eight hours.[113] The outbreak of the war in Yugoslavia in July, however, once more highlighted the weakness of the CSCE. Despite calling for a ceasefire, an arms embargo and a negotiated solution, the CSCE had no means to influence the conflict and rapidly became marginalized. Although the CSO met in almost permanent session from early 1991 onwards to discuss the conflicts in the former-Yugoslavia and the former-Soviet Union, its calls for cease-fires, dispatching of missions and active role in mediation and monitoring largely failed to bring a halt to on-going violence.[114]

Meeting in Helsinki in July 1992 CSCE leaders sought to strengthen the CSCE's capacity for conflict prevention and crisis management. The leaders mandated regular consultations in the CSO to provide early warning of conflicts; created a number of mechanisms for bringing situations to the CSO's attention; gave the CSO the right to recommend mechanisms to resolve disputes, dispatch rapporteur or fact-finding missions, initiate mediation and authorize peacekeeping operations; and created the post of High Commissioner on National Minorities to provide 'early warning' and 'early action' in relation to minority conflicts.[115] In December 1992 CSCE foreign ministers took further steps, agreeing to develop a more active role in conflict prevention and crisis management, to a 'consensus minus two' principle whereby the CSO could impose conciliation on two parties to a conflict, and to appoint a Secretary-General to coordinate human rights monitoring, conflict prevention and democratic development.[116] A year later, in Rome in December 1993, CSCE foreign ministers agreed to create a 'permanent body for political consultations and decision-making' – a Permanent Committee of the CSCE – operating beneath the CSO and a new CSCE Secretariat in Vienna.[117]

Despite these developments, from 1990 onwards the East–Central European states altered their attitude towards the CSCE. Once it became clear that the CSCE would not develop into a body providing formal security guarantees for its members, they rapidly shifted the focus of their security policies towards integration with Western security structures, particularly NATO. While early, idealistic hopes for the CSCE were dropped, however, the East–Central European states also developed a more pragmatic approach to the CSCE – supporting its development in other areas where it might still contribute to both their own and wider European security.

The East–Central European states played an active role in initiating and supporting the development of the CSCE's role in conflict prevention and crisis management.[118] As Chairman-in-Office (CIO) of the CSCE from 1990 to 1992, Czechoslovakia took a particularly active role, chairing the CSCE steering group on the Yugoslav conflict, which organized the various CSCE missions to the former-Yugoslavia.[119] The East–Central Europeans also played an active role in CSCE missions, providing personnel and support in a number of cases.[120] This work, however, focussed on conflicts elsewhere in Europe, rather than relating directly to the East–Central European states' security – reflecting their desire to play an active role in developing new European security structures and supporting stability in post-communist Europe.

One area in which the CSCE played a more direct role in East–Central European security was through the High Commissioner on National Minorities (HCNM).[121] In 1993–94 the HCNM played an active role in Hungary's disputes with Slovakia and Romania, visiting all three countries, seeking to promote resolutions of the disputes over Hungarian minority rights. In combination with the Council of Europe's linkage of Slovakia and Romania's membership to their respect for minority rights, the HCNM's visits increased pressure on Slovakia and Romania to improve the position of their Hungarian minorities, hence improving the prospects for avoiding conflict in the region. The HCNM (and the Council of Europe) also played an active role in promoting resolutions of the disputes between the Baltic states and Russia over Russian minority rights. Given that any conflict between the Baltic states and Russia would be a serious security concern for Poland, the HCNM's role in this area was a potentially important contribution to Polish security.

The East–Central European states were also strong supporters of arms control and confidence-building regimes within the CSCE framework. At their October 1991 Cracow summit East–Central European leaders stressed the 'fundamental importance for the future of Europe' of the November 1990 CFE Treaty.[122] The countries of East–Central Europe pressed strongly for the Western post-Soviet states, particularly Russia, Ukraine and Belarus, to accede to the CFE Treaty in 1992. The CFE Treaty formally entered into force in November 1992 and is to be fully implemented by December 1995. By placing strict numerical limits on the main offensive armaments of the East–Central European states and their neighbours, the CFE Treaty makes a major contribution to regional security, reducing the likelihood of new arms races and creating a context in which states have been able to radically reduce their armed forces and defence spending. By limiting those armaments most necessary for offensive action, the CFE Treaty also constrains potential for large-scale offensive military operations. According to one Hungarian Defence Ministry official, when the CFE Treaty is implemented Hungary's neighbours 'will not have a preponderant superiority in the most important arms . . . they will have superior strength but not so much to guarantee the success of an attack against Hungary . . . the balance of forces would favour us'.[123] The CFE Treaty also includes an extensive verification and information exchange regime, including annual exchanges of data on the size, structure and deployment of forces and inspections of a wide range of military bases at short-notice.[124] This gives the East–Central European states unprecedented information about their neighbours' armed forces, providing substantial early warning of any mobilization and constraining possibilities for surprise or short-warning attacks, thereby reducing uncertainty and promoting confidence. In short, the CFE Treaty, if fully implemented, will be a significant contribution to East–Central European security.

The 1990 and 1992 Vienna Confidence and Security-Building Measures (CSBM) agreements (involving advance notification of exercises and detailed exchanges of military data) and the 1992 Open Skies Treaty (involving surveillance overflights) were also actively supported by the East–Central European states.[125] Notably, Hungary became one of the first states to use two new measures incorporated in the 1990 CSBM agreement. The mechanism on unusual military activities allows any state to request that another state provide information on unusual military activities, to request a meeting with that state and to convene a CSCE meeting at the Conflict Prevention Centre (CPC) in Vienna. Hungary triggered the mechanism in August 1991 in relation to the Yugoslav conflict, resulting in a meeting of the two countries delegations at the CPC Secretariat, where military tensions along their border were discussed. When Yugoslav airforce planes bombed a Hungarian village in October 1991 the Hungarian government referred to the provision on cooperation with regard to hazardous military incidents (which commits CSCE states to cooperate in reporting and clarifying any such incidents and to prevent misunderstandings and mitigate their effects on other states). The mechanism on unusual military activities was triggered again in the spring of 1992, resulting in a written response from the Yugoslav authorities.[126] As was seen in Chapter 6, soon after Hungary used these mechanisms it successfully concluded bilateral CSBMs with Yugoslavia in relation to airspace along their joint border.

When the CSCE Forum on Security Cooperation (the successor to the CFE and CSBM negotiations) opened in Vienna in September 1992 the East–Central European states established themselves as leading participants. Hungary suggested that arms control measures, including force limits similar to those in the CFE treaty, might be applied to the post-Yugoslav states.[127] Poland showed particular interest in measures relating to the force structures and force readiness levels of its Eastern neighbours and the possibility of regional arms control measures with these states.[128] By late 1994 significant progress had been made on

harmonization of existing arms control agreements, a code of conduct
for security, new stabilizing measures, non-proliferation and conventional arms transfers, military contacts and cooperation, defence planning information exchange, and global exchange of military information.
In many of these areas, progress had been based on initiatives from
the East–Central European states.[129] One senior US negotiator concluded
that the East–Central Europeans 'really would like to use arms control
to enhance their security'.[130] By 1994, therefore, while early hopes
that the CSCE might provide them with security guarantees had been
abandoned, the East–Central Europeans were actively supporting the
development of the CSCE's role in conflict prevention and crisis management and as a framework for arms control negotiations.

CONCLUSION

After the East European revolutions of 1989, the countries of East–
Central Europe established themselves as a distinct regional group with
an informal special relationship with the West. The convergence of
their national security policies and the EU's decision to conclude association agreements with them led to the emergence of what became
the Visegrad group. The East–Central European states agreed to cooperate with each other in seeking membership of the EU and NATO
and emerged as the leading Eastern candidates for eventual membership of both bodies. While the West remained unwilling to extend EU
or NATO membership, consistent pressure from the East–Central European states led it to signal an informal commitment to their security
and to develop increasingly close political and military security relations. For the West, the EU association agreements, the NACC and
PFP were ways of extending this process of close cooperation without
isolating Russia or making definitive commitments to expanding the
EU and NATO. At the same time, the East–Central European states,
while abandoning early ideas that the CSCE might provide them with
security guarantees, continued to support the development of the CSCE's
role in conflict prevention, crisis management and arms control.

By late 1994 this picture was shifting somewhat. The Czech Republic's rejection of a concerted approach to the West (combined with
tensions between Hungary and Slovakia and uncertainties about the
future direction of Slovak politics) had called into question the very
concept of a Visegrad group. The EU's conclusion of association agreements with Romania and Bulgaria was leading it to treat the six East

European countries as a group, although the pace of each states' integration might be different. The consistent pressure of the East–Central European states for EU and NATO membership was also forcing the West to address whether or not it was willing to expand these two key bodies. While avoiding definitive decisions, the West had indicated that it expected Eastward expansion of both. Support for a relatively early expansion of NATO and the EU appeared to be growing in the West, with the four East–Central European states as the primary candidates.

Despite these developments, however, real uncertainties remained. The economic obstacles to EU membership remained significant, suggesting that full membership was some years off. While the internal obstacles to NATO membership appeared less problematic, the West remained concerned about the danger of isolating Russia. Whether the West could successfully integrate the East–Central European states with NATO, while maintaining a cooperative relationship with Russia remained a central question. The West also remained concerned about importing Eastern instabilities into Western institutions. Some within the West also questioned whether, in the post-Cold War world, East–Central Europe was really of strategic importance. There remained, therefore, a danger that the options of EU and NATO membership might become closed to the East–Central European states. If this occurred, they would be forced to fundamentally rethink their security policies. One option would be renewed regional cooperation within the Visegrad group, or perhaps amongst all six East European states. The historical record and the still simmering disputes between the various East European states, however, suggested that the prospects for such cooperation were not good (particularly in the absence of integration with the West as an incentive to cooperate). A second option would be to pursue a strengthened CSCE. The CSCE, even if strengthened by a UN-type Security Council (as proposed by Russia), however, appeared unlikely to be able to provide the East–Central European states with security in the event of a serious crisis or conflict.[131] Should the option of integration with the West become closed, therefore, there remained a real danger of a return to historic patterns of instability, sub-regional alliances and conflict.

8 Conclusion

Since the collapse of communism in 1989–90 the national security policies of the countries of East–Central Europe have been radically transformed. This book has examined this transformation, highlighting the strategic choices made by the East–Central European states and analyzing the factors shaping those choices. As was seen in Chapter 3, when the new, democratic East–Central European governments came to power in 1989 and 1990, what security policies they would adopt was an open question. By the mid-1990s it was clear that they had made a strategic choice to pursue integration with the West as the central objective of their foreign and security policies – what Vaclav Havel defined as the 'return to Europe'. At the same time, however, they were also pursuing broader security policies, encompassing regional cooperation within the Visegrad group, support for a strengthened CSCE, bilateral security cooperation with their Eastern and Southern neighbours and defensively oriented military policies. This conclusion summarizes the key elements of the post-Cold War transformation of East–Central European security, exploring the factors which have shaped this transformation. It ends by highlighting the fact that East–Central Europe has been characterized by a remarkable degree of stability when compared with the Balkans and the former-Soviet Union and discussing the prospects for continued stability.

'RETURN TO EUROPE'

The central element of East–Central European states' security since the end of the Cold War has been their desire to integrate themselves with the West, in particular to become members of the European Union (EU) and NATO. This desire has reflected the parallel processes of democratization within the region and radical change in its external environment. Initially, in 1989 and early 1990, the differing pace of democratization in each country, and the differing implications of the changing international environment for each, led the East–Central European states to pursue divergent national security policies. Poland's concerns over German unification and the continuing influence of the communist party over its security policy led to a cautious policy of

155

reforming the alliance with the Soviet Union. Czechoslovakia's more rapid transition to democracy and its new leaders previous involvement in pan-European peace and human rights movements led it to emerge as the leading advocate of a CSCE-based collective security system. In Hungary the communist party remained committed to the Warsaw Pact until its defeat in the March–April 1990 elections. The victory of the democratic forces in those elections, however, led to decisive moves to dismantle the Warsaw Pact and re-orient Hungary towards the West.

By late 1990 the convergence of their democratization processes, the settlement of issues relating to German unification and a shared concern at developments within the Soviet Union was leading the three East–Central European states to follow similar security policies focussed on integration with the West. This process was underpinned by the idea, in Havel's words, of the 'return to Europe'. Central to the political agenda of the new East–Central European governments was the idea that their countries were returning to the Western values of liberal democracy and the Western institutions which reflect these values. The West represented what the East–Central Europeans wanted to join: a stable, prosperous and secure community of democratic nations. In essence, the same set of political values and assumptions drove both the domestic and the foreign policies of Poland, Czechoslovakia and Hungary's new governments.

At the same time, the re-orientation of East–Central European security was also shaped by the rapidly changing external environment. The new East–Central European leaderships quickly concluded that the main threats to their countries' security lay in the unstable situation on their Eastern and Southern borders. The growing power of hardliners within the Soviet Union and the attempt to re-establish a Soviet sphere of influence in Eastern Europe led to increasing concern that developments in the Soviet Union might threaten East–Central European security. The outbreak of the war in the former-Yugoslavia and the break-up of the Soviet Union highlighted the danger that nationalist conflicts might spill over into the region.

The new East–Central European governments rapidly concluded that only the West, in particular NATO, was capable of guaranteeing their security in this new environment. Neutrality could not protect them from Soviet pressure or nationalist conflicts on their borders. It might also leave East–Central Europe as a 'grey zone' between the Soviet Union/Russia and the West, with its security and independence vulnerable to great power relations over which it had little influence.

While the CSCE might contribute to their security, it could not provide them with security guarantees or material support in a crisis and appeared unlikely to evolve into an organization capable of doing so. While regional and bilateral security cooperation might contribute to conflict prevention and confidence-building, they similarly appeared unlikely to be able to cope with serious security threats. The problems of reforming armed forces structured for Warsaw Pact operations and dependent on Soviet support and supplies suggested that the East–Central European states ability to defend themselves was, at best, limited.

In contrast, the process of German unification led the East–Central European governments to conclude that the EC and NATO were central to their security. When forced, early in 1990, to decide between a neutral – and hence independent – Germany and one integrated in the West, they came out decisively in favour of Germany's integration in the EC and NATO. At the same time, only the West seemed likely to provide them with security guarantees or material support in a crisis. Even short of membership of the EC and NATO, a close political relationship would provide informal, 'soft' security guarantees and increase the prospects for material support in a crisis. Close military cooperation would facilitate military support in a crisis.

WIDER SECURITY POLICIES

While integration with the West has been their central objective, the East–Central European states have also pursued other dimensions to their security policies. Rather than viewing these wider security policies as alternatives to the strategic goal of integration with the West, the East–Central European states saw them as complementary to that objective, reflecting a pragmatic view that such policies could still play a significant role in enhancing their security.

Although they rejected the option of an East European bloc, shared security concerns led the East–Central European states to cooperate with each other in the Visegrad group. Such cooperation contributed to their security in a number of ways. It increased their diplomatic leverage in relations with the Soviet Union and the West. It facilitated integration with the West by indicating their ability to behave 'responsibly'. It acted as a confidence-building measure to prevent conflicts re-emerging within East–Central Europe. It also allowed the East–Central European states to provide limited practical support to each other in reforming their armed forces. The Czech Republic's rejection of a coordinated approach to the West in 1994, however, appeared to signal a major breakdown in cooperation, reflecting the inherent limitations of the Visegrad group.

Similarly, while being unwilling to rely entirely on the CSCE, the East–Central European states recognized that it could contribute to their security in a number of ways. In particular, as was seen in the last chapter, they supported the development of the CSCE's role in conflict prevention and crisis management and as a forum for arms control and confidence-building measures.

A further significant element of the East–Central European states' new security policies has been security cooperation with their Eastern and Southern neighbours. Bilateral agreements on respect for existing borders, minority rights and military confidence-building measures indicated that the East–Central European states viewed cooperation with their Eastern and Southern neighbours as an important means of preventing the escalation of political conflicts. In this context, Hungary's Eastern policy was particularly notable, since its problems over minority rights with its neighbours led it to pursue close military cooperation and confidence-building measures in order to ensure that disputes did not spill over into the military sphere.

The new East–Central European governments also sought to re-orient their armed forces to reflect their new security policies. As was seen in Chapters 4, 5 and 6, they appear to have been remarkably successful in establishing civilian, democratic control of their countries' armed forces – reflecting the extent to which the military's commitment to communism was only skin deep. They also initiated radical defence reforms. Defence spending and overall force numbers have been reduced by about half compared with the late-1980s. Forces have been redeployed equally across national territories. New strategies and force structures (designed to impose costs on any attacker but limit offensive potential) have been introduced. Although not yet fully implemented, these measures already reflect a significant defensive restructuring of the East–Central European militaries. The major problems involved in restructuring, however, cast real doubts on their ability to act effectively in a crisis.

PROSPECTS FOR STABILITY?

Since 1989 East–Central Europe has been characterized by a remarkable degree of stability when compared with the Balkans and the former-

Soviet Union. Progress has been made in establishing functioning democracies and market economies. Despite political divisions and the hardships imposed by economic reform, large-scale social disorder has not broken out. Despite ethnic tensions, potential border conflicts, the on-going war in the former-Yugoslavia and the unstable situation in the former-Soviet Union, violent conflict has not broken out in the region. In terms of foreign and security policy, the East–Central European states have made significant progress towards the goal of integrating themselves with the West. Their ability to cooperate with each other in the Visegrad group reflected a wish to avoid returning to historic patterns of conflict and symbolized their relative stability. Their pursuit of bilateral security cooperation with their neighbours and the defensive restructuring of their armed forces indicated a serious attempt to avoid provocative foreign and security policies.

Nevertheless, by late 1994, the transformation of East–Central European security was not absolutely secure and continued stability could not be guaranteed. Three factors were likely to shape the future direction of the region's security and its prospects for stability: domestic politics within East–Central Europe, the impact of developments in the former-Soviet Union and the Balkans and the region's continued prospects for integration with the West, particularly membership of the EU and NATO.

As was noted earlier, the process of democratization played a central role in the transformation of East–Central European security, with integration with the West – the 'return to Europe' – a key part of the new governments' agendas. A serious reversal of the processes of democratization and economic reform in one or more of the East–Central European states could have a significant impact on its foreign and security policy. Should an authoritarian, nationalist regime emerge (perhaps similar to that in Romania), progress towards establishing democracy and introducing economic reforms might be delayed, nationalist interests reasserted in foreign and security policy and prospects for integration with the EU and NATO weakened. Such a development, however, would be a slowing down, rather than an abandonment, of the goal of integration with the West. Should a more overtly authoritarian and extreme nationalist regime emerge (as in Serbia) a more radical re-orientation of foreign and security policy might be likely, with the goal of integration with the West abandoned and nationalist objectives becoming central.

By late 1994, authoritarian and nationalist forces in Poland, the Czech Republic and Hungary were relatively weak. The elections in Poland

and Hungary in 1993 and 1994 had confirmed the weakness of such forces and indicated that the former-communist parties, now in government, were likely to continue to follow the strategic objective of integration with the West. While the possibility of social and economic instability leading to the emergence of authoritarian, nationalist regimes could not be ruled out, it did not appear likely. In contrast, as was seen in chapter 5, the re-election of Vladimir Meciar in October 1994 suggested that Slovakia might follow a more authoritarian, nationalist line and slow the pace of economic reform. How far this would slow (or even reverse) Slovakia's integration with the West and exacerbate tensions with Hungary was less clear.

Developments in the Balkans and the former-Soviet Union may also have a significant impact on the future direction of East–Central European security. If conflicts break out in these areas which more directly involve the East–Central European states' interests, they might find it increasingly difficult to avoid becoming embroiled in them. Should serious inter-ethnic violence break out in Vojvodina, for example, pressure might grow in Hungary for it to play a more active role in protecting the Hungarian minority there, perhaps leading to armed conflict with Serbia. Such a development might also trigger conflict with Romania and Slovakia. Should conflict break out in Ukraine or between Ukraine and Russia, pressure might grow in Poland to take action to protect the Polish minority in Ukraine or reclaim former Polish territories. Even short of deliberate decisions to become involved, escalation of cross-border incidents might drag the East–Central European states into such conflicts. The East–Central European states have, however, made very real efforts to avoid becoming involved in conflicts on their Eastern and Southern borders – as their pursuit of bilateral security cooperation with their neighbours indicates. Again, Hungary's efforts to avoid being dragged into the Yugoslav conflict are particularly notable.

East–Central Europe's continuing prospects for integration with the West, particularly membership of the EU and NATO, will also have a significant impact on the region's future security and stability. Whilst the East–Central European states have been disappointed with the pace of their integration with the West, the prospect of eventual membership of the EU and NATO has, in many ways, driven their foreign and security policies since 1990. Should the possibility of membership of the EU and NATO become closed – whether formally or through an indefinite postponement – they would be forced to radically re-orient their security policies. The prospects for renewed regional cooperation or a strengthened CSCE, however, may be relatively poor. Thus, as was argued in the last chapter, a Western rejection of the East–Central European states' bids for EU and NATO membership might trigger a return to historic patterns of antagonism and informal alliances, thereby undermining regional stability. Given East–Central Europe's geostrategic location between Germany and Russia, such a development could also threaten wider European peace and security. One of the primary European security challenges facing the West in the 1990s, therefore, is to reconcile the integration of the East–Central European states into the EU and NATO with the maintenance of cooperative security relations with Russia.

Notes and References

1 Introduction

1. I use the term 'East–Central Europe' to describe Poland, the Czech Republic, Slovakia and Hungary and the term 'Eastern Europe' to refer to these countries, plus Romania and Bulgaria.
2. 'Security' is a problematic concept, which may be understood in different ways. See B. Buzan, *People, States and Fear: An Agenda for International Security Studies in the Post-Cold War Era*, 2nd ed. (London: Harvester Wheatsheaf, 1991); and H. Haftendorn, 'The Security Puzzle: Theory-Building and Discipline-Building in International Security', *International Studies Quarterly*, 35 (1991) pp. 3–17. The definition of political–military security is my own.
3. For literature on the causes of war, see J. A. Vasquez, *The War Puzzle* (Cambridge: Cambridge University Press, 1993); G. Cashman, *What Causes War? An Introduction to Theories of International Conflict* (New York: Lexington Books, 1993); and S. Brown, *The Causes and Prevention of War*, 2nd ed. (New York: St. Martins Press, 1994).
4. On the concept of 'national security' see Arnold Wolfers, *Discord and Collaboration: Essays on International Politics* (Baltimore: The Johns Hopkins University Press, 1962), Chapter 10, 'National Security as an Ambiguous Symbol', pp. 147–65; and Buzan, *People, States and Fear*, Chapter 2, 'National Security and the Nature of the State', pp. 57–111. For criticism of the concept of 'national security', see Haftendorn, 'The Security Puzzle'; and K. Booth, 'Security and Emancipation', *Review of International Studies*, 17 (1991) pp. 313–26.
5. On 'strong' and 'weak' states, see Buzan, *People, States and Fear*, pp. 96–107.
6. On the differing factors which shape states' foreign policies, see J.N. Rosenau (ed.), *Comparing Foreign Policies: Theories, Findings and Methods* (London: Sage Publications, 1974); C.F. Hermann, C.W. Kegley, Jr., and J.N. Rosenau (eds), *New Directions in the Study of Foreign Policy* (London: Unwin Hyman, 1987); and R.C. Snyder, H. W. Bruck, and B. Sapin (eds), *Foreign Policy Decision-Making* (New York: The Free Press of Glencoe, 1962).

2 The New Europe

1. On German unification, see K. Kaiser, 'Germany's Unification', *Foreign Affairs*, 70 (1991) pp. 179–205.
2. S. Crow, 'The Changing Soviet View of German Unification', *Report on the USSR*, 2 (3 August 1990) pp. 1–4.
3. 'Final Settlement With Respect to Germany', *Arms Control Today*, 20 (October 1990) pp. 33–4.

4. B. Buzan, M. Kelstrup, P. Lemaitre, E. Tromer and O. Waever, *The European Security Order Recast: Scenarios for the Post-Cold War Era* (London: Pinter Publishers, 1990) p. 133.
5. K.W. Deutsch *et al.*, *Political Community and the North Atlantic Area: International Organization in the Light of Historical Experience* (New York: Greenwood Press Publishers, 1969).
6. Deutsch *et al.*, *Political Community in the North Atlantic Area*, p. 5.
7. J. Joffe, 'Europe's American Pacifier', *Foreign Policy*, 54 (1984) pp. 64–82.
8. R.O. Keohane and J. Nye, *Power and Interdependence*, 2nd ed. (Boston: Scott, Foresman and Company, 1989).
9. W. Wallace, *The Transformation of Western Europe* (London: Pinter Publishers/The Royal Institute of International Affairs, 1990).
10. B. Buzan, *People, States and Fear: An Agenda for International Security Studies in the Post-Cold War Era*, 2nd ed. (London: Harvester Wheatsheaf, 1991) pp. 97–107, 113–14 and 154–8.
11. J.S. Levy, 'The Causes of War: A Review of Theories and Evidence', Chapter 4 in P.E. Tetlock *et al.*, *Behaviour, Society and Nuclear War*, Volume 1 (Oxford: Oxford University Press, 1989) p. 270.
12. F. Fukuyama, 'Democratization and International Security', in *New Dimensions in International Security*, Part II, Adelphi Paper 266 (London: Brassey's for the International Institute for Strategic Studies, Winter 1991/92) p. 19.
13. H. Starr, 'Democracy and War: Choice, Learning and Security Communities', *Journal of Peace Research*, 29 (1992) pp. 207–13.
14. H. Bull and A. Watson, *The Expansion of International Society* (Oxford: Oxford University Press, 1984) p. 1.
15. J.J. Mearsheimer, 'Back to the Future: Instability in Europe After the Cold War', *International Security*, 15 (1990) pp. 5–56.
16. R. Jervis, 'The Future of World Politics: Will It Resemble the Past?', *International Security*, 16 (1991/92) pp. 46–55.
17. B. Buzan, 'New Patterns of Global Security in the Twenty-first Century', *International Affairs*, 67 (1991) p. 436.
18. J. Snyder, 'Averting Anarchy in the New Europe', *International Security*, 14 (1990) pp. 5–41; and V. Bunce, 'The Struggle for Liberal Democracy in Eastern Europe', *World Policy Journal*, 7 (1990) pp. 395–430.
19. C. Gasteyger, 'The Remaking of Eastern Europe's Security', *Survival*, XXXIII (1991) pp. 111–24.
20. F.S. Larrabee, 'Long Memories and Short Fuses: Change and Instability in the Balkans', *International Security*, 15 (1990/91) pp. 58–91.
21. M. Jopp, *The Strategic Implications of European Integration*, Adelphi Paper 290 (London: Brassey's for The International Institute of Strategic Studies, July 1994).
22. Title V, 'Provisions on a Common Foreign and Security Policy, Treaty on European Union', Signed at Maastricht on 7 February 1992, in *Selection of Basic Texts on European Security and Defence*, Political Series W1 EN-8-1992 (Luxembourg/Brussels: Political and Institutional Affairs Division, Directorate General for Research, European Parliament, August 1992) pp. 83–8.

23. Title V, 'Provisions on a Common Foreign and Security Policy, Treaty on European Union', *Selection of Basic Texts on European Security and Defence*, p. 85.
24. Jopp, *The Strategic Implication of European Integration*, pp. 27–8.
25. T.C. Salmon, 'Testing Times for European Political Cooperation: the Gulf and Yugoslavia, 1990–1992', *International Affairs*, 68 (1992) pp. 233–53.
26. Communiqué, WEU Council of Ministers, Bonn, 18 November 1991, (London: Peace Through NATO, Text 026, 1991) pp. 1–2.
27. London Declaration on a Transformed North Atlantic Alliance, *NATO Review*, 38 (August 1990) pp. 32–3.
28. The Alliance's New Strategic Concept, Agreed by the Heads of State and Government participating in the meeting of the North Atlantic Council in Rome on 7–8 November 1991, *NATO Review*, 39 (December 1991) pp. 25–32.
29. Declaration of the Heads of State and Government participating in the meeting of the North Atlantic Council held at NATO Headquarters, Brussels, on 10–11 January 1994, *NATO Review*, 42 (February 1994) pp. 30–3.
30. London Declaration on a Transformed North Atlantic Alliance, pp. 32–3.
31. Rome Declaration on Peace and Cooperation, Issued by the Heads of State and Government participating in the meeting of the North Atlantic Council in Rome on 7–8 November 1991, *NATO Review*, 39 (December 1991) pp. 20–1.
32. Declaration of the Heads of State and Government participating in the meeting of the North Atlantic Council held at NATO Headquarters, Brussels on 10–11 January 1994, pp. 30–3.
33. A.D. Rotfeld, 'New Security Structures in Europe: Concepts, Proposals and Decisions', Chapter 17 in *SIPRI Yearbook 1991: World Armaments and Disarmament* (Oxford: Oxford University Press, 1991) pp. 585–600.
34. *Charter of Paris for a New Europe*, 16 November 1990.
35. *CSCE Helsinki Document 1992: The Challenges of Change*, pp. 7–24.
36. V.Y. Ghebali, 'CSCE's velvet clout', *International Defense Review* (1993) pp. 285–6.

3 Strategic Options for East–Central Europe

1. For similar analyses, see C. Gasteyger, 'The Remaking of Eastern Europe's Security', *Survival*, XXXIII (1991) pp. 111–24; J.M.O. Sharp, 'Security Options for Central Europe in the 1990s', in B. Crawford (ed.), *The Future of European Security* (University of California, Berkeley: Center for German and European Studies, 1992) pp. 54–78; A.G.V. Hyde-Price, 'After the Pact: East European Security in the 1990's, *Arms Control*, 12 (September 1991) pp. 279–302; and J. Orme, 'Security in East Central Europe: Seven Futures', *The Washington Quarterly*, 14 (Summer 1991) pp. 91–105.
2. S. Crow, '"Who Lost Eastern Europe?"', *Report on the USSR*, 3 (12 April 1991) pp. 1–5.
3. I. Traynor, 'Moscow defers critical summit', *The Guardian* (24 October 1990).
4. S. Crow, 'International Department and Foreign Ministry Disagree on

Eastern Europe', *Report on the USSR*, 3 (21 June 1991) pp. 4–8.

5. 'The Links That Bind', Chapter 4 in K. Dawisha, *Eastern Europe, Gorbachev and Reform: The Great Challenge*, 2nd ed. (Cambridge: Cambridge University Press, 1990) pp. 81–124.

6. G. Urban, 'How to set Hungary free', *The Times* (14 March 1989); W.C. Clemens, Jr., 'Promote an Austrian Solution for Eastern Europe', *International Herald Tribune* (10 July 1989); I. Kristol, 'Why Not Neutralize Eastern Europe?', *International Herald Tribune* (13 September 1989); R.A. Bitzinger, 'Neutrality for Eastern Europe: Problems and Prospects', *Bulletin of Peace Proposals*, 22 (1991) pp. 281–9; and S. Kux, 'Neutrality and New Thinking', Chapter 5 in R.E. Kanet, D. Nutter Miner, and T.J. Resler, *Soviet Foreign Policy in Transition* (Cambridge: Cambridge University Press, 1992) pp. 100–17.

7. Kux, 'Neutrality and New Thinking', pp. 100–1; and E. Karsh, *Neutrality and Small States* (London: Routledge, 1988).

8. See J.H. Herz, 'Idealist Internationalism and the Security Dilemma', *World Politics*, 2 (1950) pp. 157–80; B. Buzan, *People, States and Fear: An Agenda for International Security Studies in the Post-Cold War Era*, 2nd ed. (London: Harvester Wheatsheaf, 1991) Chapter 8, 'The Power-Security Dilemma', pp. 294–327; and N.J. Wheeler and K. Booth, 'The Security Dilemma', Chapter 1 in J. Baylis and N.J. Rengger (eds), *Dilemmas in World Politics: International Issues in a Changing World* (Oxford: Clarendon Press, 1992) pp. 29–60.

9. Kux, 'Neutrality and New Thinking', pp. 100–1; Karsh, *Neutrality and Small States*; and A. T. Leonhard (ed.), *Neutrality: Changing Concepts and Practices* (Lanham, MD: University of America Press, 1988).

10. H. Hakovirta, *East–West Conflict and European Neutrality* (Oxford: Clarendon Press, 1988); J. Kruzel and M.H. Haltzel (eds), *Between the Blocs: Problems and Prospects for Europe's Neutral and Non-aligned States* (Cambridge: Cambridge University Press, 1989); R.E. Bissell and C. Gasteyger (eds), *The Missing Link: West European Neutrals and Regional Security* (London: Duke University Press, 1990); E. Karsh, 'Between War and Peace: European Neutrality', *The World Today*, 44 (August/ September 1988) pp. 150–4; and P.R. Viotti, 'Comparative Neutrality in Europe', *Defense Analysis*, 6 (1990) pp. 3–15.

11. The International Institute for Strategic Studies (IISS), *Strategic Survey 1990–1991* (London: Brassey's for the IISS, May 1991) p. 36.

12. A. Roberts, *Nations in Arms: The Theory and Practice of Territorial Defence* (Basingstoke: Macmillan for the International Institute for Strategic Studies, 1986); R.E.J. Pentilla, *Finland's Search for Security Through Defence, 1944–89* (London: Macmillan, 1991); J. Juusti and R. Matthews, 'Finland's Defense Posture', *Defense Analysis*, 6 (1990) pp. 85–9; and G.J. Stein, 'Total Defense: A Comparative Overview of the Security Policies of Switzerland and Austria', *Defense Analysis*, 6 (1990) pp. 17–33.

13. A. Bebler, 'The Neutral and Non-Aligned States in the New European Security Architecture', *European Security*, 1 (Summer 1992) pp. 133–43; J. Lukacs, 'Finland Vindicated', *Foreign Affairs*, 71 (Fall 1992) pp. 50–63; and W. Carlsnaes, 'Sweden Facing the New Europe', *European Security*, 2 (Spring 1993) pp. 71–89.

14. See Gasteyger, 'The Remaking of Eastern Europe's Security', pp. 119–20; Sharp, 'Security Options for Central Europe in the 1990s', pp. 58–9; and Orme, 'Security in East Central Europe', pp. 100–3.

15. A. Palmer, *The Lands Between: A History of East–Central Europe since the Congress of Vienna* (London: Weidenfeld and Nicolson, 1970); and, J. Rothschild, *East Central Europe between the Two World Wars* (London: University of Washington Press, 1974).

16. F. Blackaby *et al.*, *A New Security Structure for Europe* (London: The British American Security Information Council, 1990); and J. Joffe, 'Collective Security and the Future of Europe: Failed Dreams and Dead Ends', *Survival*, 34 (Spring 1992) pp. 36–50.

17. J. Mueller, 'A New Concert of Europe', *Foreign Policy*, 72 (Winter 1989–90) pp. 3–16; and P. Zelikow, 'The New Concert of Europe', *Survival*, 34 (Summer 1992) pp. 12–30. On the nineteenth century concert system, see R. Jervis, 'From Balance to Concert: A Study of International Security Cooperation', *World Politics*, XXXVIII (October 1985) pp. 58–79.

18. S. Croft, 'Cooperative Security in Europe', Chapter 7 in Centre for Defence Studies (ed.), *Brassey's Defence Yearbook 1993* (London: Brassey's, 1993) pp. 101–16; and A.B. Carter, W.J. Perry and J.D. Steinbrunner, *A New Concept of Cooperative Security*, Brookings Occasional Papers (Washington, DC: The Brookings Institution, 1992); and R. Jervis, 'Security Regimes', *International Organization*, 36 (Spring 1982) pp. 357–78.

19. I.L. Claude, Jr., *Power and International Relations* (New York: Random House, 1962); Joffe, 'Collective Security and the Future of Europe'; R.K. Betts, 'Systems for Peace or Causes of War? Collective Security, Arms Control, and the New Europe', *International Security*, 17 (Summer 1992) pp. 5–43; and C.L. Glaser, 'Why NATO is Still Best: Future Security Arrangements for Europe', *International Security*, 18 (Summer 1993) pp. 5–50.

20. H.J. Morgenthau, *Politics Among Nations: The Struggle for Power and Peace*, 5th ed. (New York: Knopf, 1978); K.N. Waltz, *Theory of International Politics* (Reading, Mass.: Addison-Wesley Publishing Company, 1979); and R.O. Keohane (ed.), *Neorealism and its Critics* (New York: Columbia University Press, 1986).

21. Waltz, *Theory of International Politics*, Chapter 6 'Anarchic Orders and Balances of Power', pp. 102–28; and S.M. Walt, *The Origins of Alliances* (London: Cornell University Press, 1987).

22. J.S. Nye, Jr., *Understanding International Conflicts: An Introduction to Theory and History* (New York: Harper Collins College Publishers, 1993) p. 54.

23. A. Goldstein, 'Robust and Affordable Security: Some Lessons from the Second-Ranking Powers During the Cold War', *The Journal of Strategic Studies*, 15 (December 1992) pp. 476–527.

24. S.P. Huntington, 'Conventional Deterrence and Conventional Retaliation in Europe', *International Security*, 8 (Winter 1983/84) pp. 32–56.

25. A. Boserup and R. Neild (eds), *The Foundations of Defensive Defence* (Houndmills: Macmillan, 1990); and B. Moller and H. Wiberg (eds), *Non-Offensive Defence for the Twenty-First Century* (Boulder: Westview Press, 1994).

26. Roberts, *Nations in Arms*.

27. G. Sharp, *Self-Reliant Defense Without Bankruptcy or War: Considera-*

tions for the Baltics, East–Central Europe and members of the Common-wealth of Independent States (Cambridge, Mass.: The Albert Einstein Institute, 1992); and A. Roberts, *Civil Resistance in the East European and Soviet Revolutions*, Monograph Series No. 4 (Cambridge, Mass.: The Albert Einstein Institute, 1991).

28. L. Ruhl, 'Offensive defence in the Warsaw Pact', *Survival*, XXXIII (September/October 1991) pp. 442–50; and A.R. Johnson, R.W. Dean and A. Alexiev, *East European Military Establishments: The Warsaw Pact Northern Tier* (New York: Crane Russak, 1982).

29. D.R. Herspring and I. Volgyes (eds), *Civil–Military Relations in Communist Systems* (Folkestone: Dawson, 1978); and R. Kolkowicz and A. Korbonski (eds), *Soldiers, Peasants and Bureaucrats: Civil–Military Relations in Communist and Modernizing Societies* (London: George Allen & Unwin, 1982).

30. A. Karkoszka, 'Transition to Defence-Oriented Configurations', *Disarmament*, XV (1992) pp. 106–11.

31. Gasteyger, 'The Remaking of Eastern Europe's Security', pp. 121–2.

32. J. Sharp, 'Europe's Nuclear Dominos', *Bulletin of the Atomic Scientists*, 49 (June 1993) pp. 29–33.

4 Poland

1. G. Sanford, 'The Polish Road to Democratisation: from Political Impasse to the "Controlled Abdication" of Communist Power', Chapter 1 in G. Sanford (ed.), *Democratization in Poland, 1988–90: Polish Voices* (Basingstoke: Macmillan, 1992) p. 18.

2. M. Simmons, 'Polish–Soviet links haunted by history', *The Guardian* (17 August 1989).

3. R. Cornwell, 'Moscow guarded on crisis for Poles', *The Independent* (18 August 1989); and M. Shafir, 'Soviet Reaction To Polish Developments: Widened Limits Of Tolerated Change', *RAD Background Report/179* (Radio Free Europe Research, Radio Free Europe/Radio Liberty, 20 September 1989) pp. 2–7.

4. Associated Press, 'Poles at odds over foreign ministry', *The Guardian* (31 August 1989); I. Traynor, 'Jaruzelski to run defence and interior', *The Guardian* (4 September 1989); A. Applebaum, 'Leaders stress Polish independence', *The Independent* (9 September 1989); Reuters, 'German Expert Is Nominee at Foreign Affairs', *International Herald Tribune* (9/10 September 1989); and I. Traynor, 'Warsaw declares intent to chart independent course', *The Guardian* (11 September 1989).

5. A. Swidlicka, 'A New Departure in Polish–Soviet Relations', *Polish Situation Report/16* (Radio Free Europe Research, Radio Free Europe/Radio Liberty, 14 November 1989) p. 14; and, J.B. de Weydenthal, 'Prime Minister Mazowiecki's Inaugural Speech to the Sejm', *Polish Situation Report/15* (Radio Free Europe Research, Radio Free Europe/Radio Liberty, 12 October 1989) p. 4.

6. A. Swidlicka, 'Government Spokesman Presents Foreign Policy Aims', *Polish Situation Report/16* (Radio Free Europe Research, Radio Free Europe/Radio Liberty, 14 November 1989) pp. 9–10.

7. Swidlicka, 'A New Departure in Polish–Soviet Relations', p. 15.

8. Reuters, 'Polish army protest', *The Guardian* (8 January 1989); 'Demonstration Against Soviet Troops', Weekly Record of Events, 13 January, *Report on Eastern Europe*, 1 (26 January 1990) p. 53; and 'Anti-Soviet Demonstration', Weekly Record of Events, 7 February, *Report on Eastern Europe*, 1 (23 February 1990) p. 56.

9. D. Fairhall, 'Calls for Soviet pullout', *The Guardian* (19 January 1990); and D. White, 'Hungary and Poland urge early exit of Soviet troops', *Financial Times* (19 January 1990).

10. *The Arms Control Reporter 1990* (Cambridge, Mass.: Institute for Defense and Disarmament Studies, 1990) pp. 407.E-1.5–6.

11. R. Boyes, 'Warsaw treaty reviewed', *The Times* (18 April 1990).

12. 'Poland seeks Soviet pullout', *Financial Times* (27 April 1990).

13. *The Arms Control Reporter 1990*, pp. 407.E-1.16.

14. L. Vinton, 'Soviet Union Begins Withdrawing Troops – But on Its Own Terms', *Report on Eastern Europe*, 2 (26 April 1991) p. 21.

15. A. Sabbat-Swidlicka, 'Senate Calls for Changes in Eastern Policy', *Report on Eastern Europe*, 1 (28 September 1990) pp. 24–5; and K. Skubiszewski, 'Change versus Stability in Europe: a Polish View', *The World Today*, 46 (August/September 1990) p. 149.

16. B. Harden, 'The Poles Are Seeking Guarantees on a Unified Germany', *International Herald Tribune* (11–12 November 1989).

17. K. Kaiser, 'Germany's Unification', *Foreign Affairs*, 70 (1991) p. 185.

18. I. Davidson, 'Polish premier seeks frontier guarantees', *Financial Times*, (31 January 1991); and Speech by Mr. Tadeusz Mazowiecki, Prime Minister of the Polish Republic, at the 41st Ordinary Session of the Parliamentary Assembly of the Council of Europe (Strasbourg, 30 January 1990) *WEU Press Review*, 31 January 1990.

19. P. Millar, 'Stalin's poisoned chalice unsettles Bonn', *The Sunday Times* (7 January 1990); and 'Expelled Germans Seek Polish Lands', *International Herald Tribune* (10 January 1990).

20. *The Arms Control Reporter 1990*, p. 407.B.322.

21. P. Stothard, 'Brutal diplomacy pulled off "two plus four" deal', *The Times* (17 February 1990).

22. 'Hans Modrow's Visit to Poland', Weekly Record of Events, 16 February, *Report on Eastern Europe*, 1 (2 March 1990) p. 60; and A. Husarka 'Modrow reassures Poles', *The Guardian* (17 February 1990).

23. R. Gedge, 'Kohl agrees to declaration on Polish borders', *The Daily Telegraph* (1 March 1990); S. Schemann, 'Kohl Takes Step Toward Meeting Polish Demands', *International Herald Tribune* (1 March 1990); and J. Kampfner, 'France urges guarantee on Polish border', *The Daily Telegraph* (2 March 1990).

24. S. Schemann, 'Kohl Ties Border to War Debt', *International Herald Tribune* (3–4 March 1990).

25. I. Murray, R. Boyes and M. Binyon, 'Kohl faces all-party outrage', *The Times* (5 March 1990); B. Johnson, 'Hurd urges border treaty', *The Daily Telegraph* (6 March 1990); and M. Fisher, 'Kohl, in a Turnabout, Affirms Polish Border', *International Herald Tribune* (7 March 1990).

26. 'Poland to Be Invited to Attend German Reunification Talks', *Inter-*

national Herald Tribune (15 March 1900); D. Gow, 'Way cleared for Poland to join talks', *The Guardian* (15 March 1990); E. Cody, 'Paris Backs Warsaw on German Border', *International Herald Tribune* (10/11 March 1990); and R. Gedge, 'Poland invited to talks as Bonn fights criticism', *The Daily Telegraph* (15 March 1990).

27. C. Bobinski, 'Poles and Germans to meet on border pact', *Financial Times* (3 May 1990); and A. Sabbat-Swidlicka, 'Polish–German Relations: Turning Borders into Bridges', *Report on Eastern Europe*, 1 (18 May 1990) p. 35.

28. 'Poland Hails Border Votes', *International Herald Tribune* (23–24 June 1990).

29. 'Poles Press Allies Anew On German Frontiers', *International Herald Tribune* (12 July 1990); F. Kempe, 'Polish Government Presses Border Issue Despite Assurances From Both Germanies', *The Wall Street Journal* (16 July 1990); and 'Poles worried over border treaty', *Financial Times* (12 July 1990).

30. J.B. de Weydenthal, 'Settling the Oder–Neisse Issue', *Report on Eastern Europe*, 1 (3 August 1990) pp. 46–8; W.S. Mossberg, 'Last Bar to United Germany Comes Down in Paris Talks', *The Wall Street Journal* (18 July 1990); 'Germany and Poland', *International Herald Tribune* (20 July 1990); and S. Lambert and S. Cranshaw, '"Two-plus-four" group clears way to German unity', *The Independent* (18 July 1990).

31. 'Final Settlement With Respect to Germany', *Arms Control Today*, 20 (October 1990) pp. 33–4.

32. A. Sabbat-Swidlicka, 'The Signing of the Polish–German Border Treaty', *Report on Eastern Europe*, 1 (7 December 1990) p. 18; and 'Poles urge treaty', *The Guardian* (19 October 1991).

33. R. Boyes, 'Polish border treaty leaves expelled Germans embittered', *The Times* (15 November 1990); and Sabbat-Swidlicka, 'The Signing of the Polish–German Border Treaty', p. 16.

34. Skubiszewski, 'Changes versus Stability in Europe', p. 151.

35. D. L. Clarke, 'The Military Institutions of the Warsaw Pact', *Report on Eastern Europe*, 1 (7 December 1990) p. 31.

36. Sabbat-Swidlicka, 'Senate Calls for Changes in Eastern Policy', pp. 21–2.

37. Sabbat-Swidlicka, 'Senate Calls for Changes in Eastern Policy', pp. 21–2.

38. M. Gorski, 'Poland presses for early pullout', *The Guardian* (10 September 1990).

39. 'Foreign Minister in the Soviet Union', Weekly Record of Events, 11 October, *Report on Eastern Europe*, 1 (19 October 1990) p. 51.

40. *The Arms Control Reporter 1990*, pp. 407.B.418–9.

41. Sabbat-Swidlicka, 'Senate Calls for Changes in Eastern Policy', p. 22.

42. 'Commission on Soviet Troop Withdrawal', Weekly Record of Events, 9 October, *Report on Eastern Europe*, 1 19 (October 1990) p. 50.

43. 'Polish–Soviet Negotiations on Troop Withdrawal', Weekly Record of Events, 15 November, *Report on Eastern Europe*, 1 (23 November 1990) p. 35.

44. 'Moscow Delays Warsaw Pact Session', *International Herald Tribune* (24 October 1990).

45. A. Sabbat-Swidlicka, 'Polish Reaction to the Lithuanian Crisis', *Report on Eastern Europe*, 2 (8 February 1991) pp. 32–5.

46. Reuters, 'Baltic crackdown was "threat to Poland"', *The Independent* (19 January 1991).
47. Associated Press, 'Poland Steps Up Soviet Border Security', *International Herald Tribune* (26 January 1991).
48. *The Arms Control Reporter 1990*, p. 407.E-1.24; and 'Progress in Soviet Troop Withdrawal', Weekly Record of Events, 12 December, *Report on Eastern Europe*, 1 (21 December 1990) p. 43.
49. 'Soviets Want Delay on Troop Withdrawal', Weekly Record of Events, 8 January, *Report on Eastern Europe*, 2 (18 January 1991) p. 58.
50. 'Soviet Military Train Stopped', Weekly Record of Events, 10 January, *Report on Eastern Europe*, 2 (18 January 1991) p. 58.
51. H. Plater-Zyberk, *The Soviet Military Withdrawal From Central Europe*, London Defence Studies No. 7 (London: Brassey's for The Centre for Defence Studies, 1991) pp. 5–7.
52. J. Kampfner, 'Poles fear the Red Army will never leave', *The Daily Telegraph* (30 January 1991).
53. Sabbat-Swidlicka, 'Polish Reaction to the Lithuanian Crisis', pp. 32–5.
54. Reuters, 'Walesa warns of "dark possibility" of Lithuanian crackdown spreading to Poland', *The Guardian* (19 January 1991).
55. V.V. Kusin, 'Gorbachev Agrees to Warsaw Pact Meeting on Military Structures', *Report on Eastern Europe*, 2 (22 February 1991) p. 44.
56. 'Soviet Treaty Demand Rejected', Weekly Record of Events, 19 June, *Report on Eastern Europe*, 2 (28 June 1991) p. 54.
57. 'More Polish–Soviet Talks on Troops', 'No Full Withdrawal of Soviet Troops this Year', and 'Foreign Minister on Soviet troops', Weekly Record of Events, 11, 12 and 14 February, *Report on Eastern Europe*, 2 (22 February 1991) pp. 49–50; and 'Poles Harden Stand on Soviet Troops', *International Herald Tribune* (15 February 1991).
58. *The Arms Control Reporter 1990*, pp. 407.E-A.30–2; 'Polish–Soviet Rift on Troops Ended', *International Herald Tribune* (12 March 1991); and P. Clough, 'Red Army starts to leave Poland in its own time', *The Independent* (10 April 1991).
59. M. Simmons, 'Poland urges West to help Eastern Europe survive Soviet collapse', *The Guardian* (30 May 1991).
60. L. Vinton, 'The Attempted Coup in the Soviet Union: East European Reactions – Poland', *Report on Eastern Europe*, 2 (30 August 1991) pp. 10–11.
61. '"State of Military Readiness" Maintained during Soviet Coup', Weekly Record of Events, 28 August, *Report on Eastern Europe*, 2 (6 September 1991) p. 41.
62. Interview with Dr. Janusz Prystrom, Head of Disarmament Department, Polish Institute of International Affairs, Warsaw, 9 November 1992.
63. Interview with Dr. Slawomir Dabrowa, Deputy Director, Department of European Institutions, Ministry of Foreign Affairs, Warsaw, 12 November 1992.
64. Weekly Record of Events, 19, 20 and 21 August, *Report on Eastern Europe*, 2 (30 August 1991) pp. 46–7; Reuters, 'Progress in Moscow–Warsaw Talks', *International Herald Tribune* (24 August 1991); 'Troop Withdrawal Proceeding Well', Weekly Record of Events, 23 August, *Report on Eastern Europe*, 2 (6 September 1991) p. 40.

65. 'Skubiszewksi Briefs Press on Foreign Policy', *Foreign Broadcast In-formation Service–Eastern Europe–91–196*, (9 October 1991) p. 21.
66. 'Troop Withdrawal Treaty Initialled', Weekly Record of Events, 26 October, *Report on Eastern Europe*, 2 (8 November 1991) p. 39; and *The Arms Control Reporter 1991* (Cambridge, Mass: Institute for 'Defense and Disarmament Studio, 1991), p. 407.E-1.51.
67. 'Polish–Soviet Treaty Initialled', Weekly Record of Events, 10 December, *Report on Eastern Europe*, 2 (20 December 1991) p. 43.
68. J.B. de Weydenthal, 'Polish–Russian Relations Disturbed by Troop Dispute', *REF/RL Research Report*, 1 (13 March 1992) p. 32.
69. J.B. de Weydenthal, 'Poland Free of Russian Combat Troops', *RFE/RL Research Report*, 1 (19 June 1992) pp. 46–8.
70. J.B. de Weydenthal, 'Poland: Finding a Place in Europe', *Report on Eastern Europe*, 1 (28 December 1990) p. 23.
71. *The Arms Control Reporter 1990*, p. 407.E-1.20.
72. C. Bobinski, 'Membership of the EC is the long-term objective', *Financial Times* (20 November 1990).
73. K. Skubiszewski, 'New Problems of Security in Central–Eastern Europe', Speech to the Royal Institute of International Affairs, London, 9 January 1990; and M. Simmons, 'Poles want more power for NATO', *The Guardian* (10 January 1991).
74. 'NATO Ties', Weekly Record of Events, 17 February, *Report on Eastern Europe*, 2 (1 March 1991) p. 44.
75. J. Palmer, 'Poland presses for full membership of EC', *The Guardian* (8 March 1991); and J. Wolf, 'Walesa warned not to rush into EC', *The Guardian* (4 April 1991).
76. W. Dawkins, 'French encouragement for Warsaw plan to join EC', *Financial Times* (9 April 1991); and H. Pick, 'Britain placates Poles with pact', *The Guardian* (25 April 1991).
77. 'More Contacts With NATO', Weekly Record of Events, 23 May, *Report on Eastern Europe*, 2 (31 May 1991) p. 34.
78. 'President Walesa visits NATO headquarters', 3 July 1991, Documentation, *NATO Review*, 39 (August 1991) pp. 33–4.
79. 'President Urges Faster EC Association', Weekly Record of Events, 25 August, *Report on Eastern Europe*, 2 (6 September 1991) p. 40.
80. J.B. de Weydenthal, 'Poland: Rapproachement with the West Continues', *Report on Eastern Europe*, 2 (20 December 1991) pp. 23–4.
81. 'NATO Described as Key to Poland's Security', Weekly Record of Events, 13 November, *Report on Eastern Europe*, 2 (22 November 1991) p. 36.
82. B. Johnson, 'History "turns inside out" as Russia asks to join NATO', *The Daily Telegraph* (21 December 1991).
83. J.B. de Weydenthal, 'Poland's Security Policy', *RFE/RL Research Report*, 2 (2 April 1993) p. 1.
84. Interview with Dr. Janusz Prystrom.
85. 'Prime Minister at NATO', Military and Security Notes, *RFE/RL Research Report*, 1 (23 October 1992) p. 45.
86. Interview with Dr. Tadeusz Chabiera, Senate Cᴜ   for International Studies, Warsaw, 12 November 1992.
87. J. Borger, 'Worried Poles warn that time is running out for reforms',

The Guardian (7 November 1992).
88. Interview with Ministry of Defence Official, Warsaw, 13 November 1992.
89. 'Poland Seeks Special Relations with WEU', Weekly Review, *RFE/RL Research Report*, 1 (17 April 1992) p. 63.
90. Interview with Ministry of Foreign Affairs Official, Warsaw, 12 November 1992.
91. 'Polish and Czechoslovak Presidents Urge CSCE Peace Force', Weekly Record of Events, 16 September, *Report on Eastern Europe*, 2 (27 September 1991) p. 42.
92. Interview with Dr. Slawomir Dabrowa.
93. Interview with senior official, Polish delegation, CSCE Forum on Security Cooperation, Vienna, 7 October 1992.
94. J.B. de Weydenthal, 'Poland Supports the Triangle as a Means to reach other Goals', *RFE/RL Research Report*, 1 (5 June 1992) p. 15.
95. *Tenets of Polish Security Policy and Security Policy and Defence Strategy of the Republic of Poland* (Warsaw: National Security Bureau, 1992) pp. 6 and 12.
96. Interview with Dr. Janusz Prystrom.
97. A. LeBor, 'Polish leaders cast doubt on entry into NATO', *The Times* (21 September 1993).
98. 'Experts in coalition talks favour early NATO membership', *Summary of World Broadcast – Eastern Europe*, EE/1817 (12 October 1993) A/4.
99. 'New Foreign Minister wants to focus foreign policy on European integration', *Summary of World Broadcasts – Eastern Europe*, EE/1832 (29 October 1993) A/8.
100. 'New Defence Minister say he is not sceptic over NATO', *Summary of World Broadcasts – Eastern Europe*, EE/1833 (30 October 1993) A/15.
101. C. Bobinski, 'Clinton plan fails to impress Poland', *Financial Times* (11 January 1994).
102. 'Poland, Denmark sign Military Agreement', *RFE/RL News Briefs*, 2 (1993) p. 17; and J.B. de Weydenthal, 'Poland Builds Security Links with the West', *RFE/RL Research Report*, 3 (18 April 1994) p. 29.
103. 'Polish Navy vessel takes part in NATO exercise in Baltic', *Summary of World Broadcast – Eastern Europe*, EE/1713 (12 June 1993) A1/5.
104. 'Poland wants to join Eurocorps', *Financial Times* (3 March 1994).
105. R. Gedge, 'Worried Poles seek fast entry into NATO', *The Daily Telegraph* (20 May 1994).
106. 'Poland given promise of NATO membership', *The Times* (8 July 1994).
107. 'Partners for what?', *The Economist* (24 September 1994) p. 39.
108. 'Polish–German Border Treaty', Weekly Record of Events, 14 November, *Report on Eastern Europe*, 1 (23 November 1990) p. 35.
109. J.B. de Weydenthal, 'The Polish–German Reconciliation', *Report on Eastern Europe*, 2 (5 July 1991) p. 20.
110. M. Fisher, 'Poles and Germans Sign Border Treaty', *International Herald Tribune* (18 June 1991).
111. De Weydenthal, 'The Polish–German Reconciliation', p. 19.
112. 'Germany Backs Its Polish Border', *International Herald Tribune* (18 October 1991); and 'Poland's parliament voted Friday to ratify', *International Herald Tribune* (19 October 1991).

113. 'Polish President Concludes German Visit', Weekly Review, *RFE/RL Research Report*, 1 (17 April 1992) p. 62.
114. 'Walesa Departs for Germany . . .', '. . . and holds talks with German leaders', Weekly Review, *RFE/RL Research Report* 1 (10 April 1992) pp. 58–9.
115. 'Polish and German defence secretaries for Poland joining NATO and WEU', *Summary of World Broadcasts – Eastern Europe*, EE/1855 (25 November 1993) A/9.
116. 'Poland, Germany to Strengthen Military Cooperation', *Periscope – Daily Defence News Capsules* (26 March 1992); and 'Joint Polish–German Military Action Possible', Military and Security Notes, *RFE/RL Research Report*, 1 (3 April 1992) p. 53.
117. Interview with Polish Defence Ministry official, September 1992.
118. Interview with official, Ministry of Defence, Warsaw, 13 November 1992.
119. 'German–Polish accord', *Jane's Defence Weekly* (6 February 1993) p. 12.
120. 'German offer', *The Times* (7 September 1993).
121. 'Foreign Ministers Meeting', Weekly Review of Events, 29 August, *Report on Eastern Europe*, 2 (6 September 1991) p. 41; and, '"Weimar Triangle" meets in Warsaw', *RFE/RL News Briefs*, 2 (15–19 November 1993) p. 10.
122. '"Weimar Triangle" agrees on Defense Contacts', *RFE/RL News Briefs*, 3 (28 February–4 March 1994) p. 19.
123. '"Weimar Triangle" Defense Ministers in Warsaw', *RFE/RL News Briefs*, 3 (18–22 July 1994) p. 12.
124. *Tenets of Polish Security Policy*, p. 10.
125. *Tenets of Polish Security Policy*, p. 14.
126. *Tenets of Polish Security Policy*, p. 5.
127. *Tenets of Polish Security Policy*, p. 11.
128. Interview with Krystian Piatkowski, National Security Bureau, Office of the President, Warsaw, 13 November 1992.
129. J.B. de Weydenthal, 'Poland and Russia Open a New Chapter in Their Relations', *RFE/RL Research Report*, 1 (19 June 1992) p. 46.
130. L. Vinton, 'The Katyn Documents: Politics and History', *RFE/RL Research Report*, 2 (22 January 1993) pp. 19–31.
131. 'The Central European Seesaw', in The International Institute for Strategic Studies, *Strategic Survey 1992–1993* (London: Brassey's for the IISS, May 1993) p. 106.
132. 'Moscow in U-turn over Poland's NATO entry', *The Daily Telegraph* (26 August 1993).
133. 'Russian ambassador says Poles "oversimplifying" Russia's declaration on NATO', *Summary of World Broadcasts – Eastern Europe*, EE/1797 (18 September 1993) A/6; and 'Foreign Minister in Washington comments on Kozyrev statement on NATO', *Summary of World Broadcasts – Eastern Europe*, EE/1801 (1 October 1993) A/11.
134. 'Polish TV reports Yeltsin change of mind on Central European states joining NATO', *Summary of World Broadcasts – Eastern Europe*, EE/1809 (2 October 1993) A/1.
135. 'Skubiszewski insists Poland's determination to join NATO is "irrevocable"', *Summary of World Broadcasts – Eastern Europe*, EE/1812 (6 October 1993) A/7.

136. 'Poland skeptical about NATO Partnership', *RFE/RL Research Report*, 3 (24–27 May 1994) p. 19.
137. 'Government sets up special teams to monitor effects of events in Russia', *Summary of World Broadcasts – Eastern Europe*, EE/1814 (8 October 1993) A/5.
138. I. Traynor, 'Serbian day out for wild bear', *The Guardian* (31 January 1994).
139. 'Poland, in reversal of policy, seeks better relations with Russia and CIS', *International Herald Tribune* (9 June 1994).
140. *Tenets of Polish Security Policy*, p. 14.
141. A. Sabbat-Swidlicka, 'Poland: Friendship Declarations Signed with Ukraine and Russia', *Report on Eastern Europe*, 1 (2 November 1990) pp. 25–7; and R. Boyes, 'Poland and Ukraine forging new links', *The Times* (16 October 1990).
142. 'Ukrainian Envoy Arrives', Weekly Record of Events, 21 November, *Report on Eastern Europe*, 2 (29 November 1991) p. 38.
143. 'Polish–Ukrainian Talks', Weekly Review, *RFE/RL Research Report*, 1 (7 February 1992) p. 65; and J.B. de Weydenthal, 'Polish–Ukrainian Rapprochement', *RFE/RL Research Report*, 1 (28 February 1992) p. 25.
144. I.J. Brzezinski, 'Polish–Ukrainian Relations: Europe's Neglected Strategic Axis', *Survival*, 35 (Autumn 1993) p. 29.
145. De Weydenthal, 'Polish–Ukrainian Rapprochement', p. 26.
146. De Weydenthal, 'Polish–Ukrainian Rapprochement', p. 25.
147. J.B. de Weydenthal, 'Economic Issues Dominate Poland's Eastern Policy', *RFE/RL Research Report*, 2 (5 March 1993) p. 24.
148. 'Ukraine, Poland on Regional Security System', *RFE/RL News Brief*, 2 (24–28 May 1993) p. 13.
149. Interview with Dr. Henryk Szlajfer, Deputy Director, Polish Institute of International Affairs, Warsaw, 9 November 1992.
150. Sabbat-Swidlicka, 'Poland: Friendship Declarations Signed with Ukraine and Russia', pp. 25–7.
151. S.R. Burant, 'Polish–Belarusian Relations', *RFE/RL Research Report*, 1 (18 September 1992) p. 42.
152. Burant, 'Polish–Belarusian Relations', p. 42.
153. 'Poland–Belarus Military Talks', *RFE/RL News Briefs*, 2 (10–23 December 1992) p. 17.
154. De Weydenthal, 'Economic Issues Dominate Poland's Eastern Policy', p. 24.
155. Interview with Dr. Henryk Szlajfer.
156. S.R. Burant, 'Polish–Lithuanian Relations: Past, Present and Future', *Problems of Communism*, XL (May–June 1991) pp. 68–9 and 83; and S. Girnius and A. Sabbat-Swidlicka, 'Current Issues in Polish–Lithuanian Relations', *Report on Eastern Europe*, 1 (12 January 1990) p. 40–2.
157. Girnius and Sabbat-Swidlicka, 'Current Issues in Polish–Lithuanian Relations', pp. 42–4; and Burant, 'Polish–Lithuanian Relations', p. 80.
158. Sabbat-Swidlicka, 'Poland: Senate Calls for Changes in Eastern Policy', p. 26.
159. Burant, 'Polish–Lithuanian Relations', p. 80.

160. J.B. de Weydenthal, 'The Polish–Lithuanian Dispute', *Report on Eastern Europe*, 2 (11 October 1991) pp. 20–1.
161. 'Polish–Lithuanian Declaration Signed', *RFE/RL Research Report*, 1 (24 January 1992) p. 75; and 'Poland Protest to Lithuania Over Minority Councils', *RFE/RL Research Report*, 1 (3 April 1992) p. 67.
162. 'Lithuanian Prime Minister in Warsaw', Weekly Review, *RFE/RL Research Report*, 1 (9 October 1992) p. 68; and de Weydenthal, 'Economic Issue Dominate in Poland's Eastern Policy', p. 25.
163. 'Polish–Lithuanian Treaty Completed', *RFE/RL News Briefs*, 3 (21–25 February 1994) p. 14.
164. Interview with Dr. Slawomir Dabrowa.
165. 'Cooperation Plans with Lithuania', Military and Security Notes, *RFE/RL Research Report*, 1 (9 October 1992) p. 56.
166. 'Poland, Lithuania sign Military Agreement', *RFE/RL News Briefs*, 2 (1993) p. 15.
167. S. Girnius, 'Lithuania's Foreign Policy', *RFE/RL Research Report*, 2 (3 September 1992) pp. 32–3.
168. The International Institute for Strategic Studies, *The Military Balance 1992–1993* (London: Brassey's for the IISS, 1992) pp. 99–100.
169. D.L. Clarke, 'Former Soviet Armed Forces in the Baltic States', *RFE/RL Research Report*, 1 (17 April 1992) pp. 44–8.
170. 'Official Support for Rifle Organization', Military and Security Notes, *RFE/RL Research Report*, 1 (13 March 1992) p. 56; and Clarke, 'Former Soviet Armed Forces in the Baltic States', p. 48 and fn 27.
171. 'Alarm Over Kaliningrad Buildup', Military and Security Notes, *RFE/RL Research Report*, 1 (13 March 1992) p. 56; and Interview with senior official, Polish delegation, CSCE Forum on Security Cooperation, Vienna, 7 October 1992.
172. Interview with Polish Defence Ministry official, 15 September 1992; and 'Russian threat turns Polish army east', *The Guardian* (21 November 1992).
173. Interview with Ministry of Foreign Affairs official, Warsaw, 12 November 1992.
174. Interview with senior official, Polish delegation, CSCE Forum on Security Cooperation, Vienna, 7 October 1992.
175. A.A. Michta, *East–Central Europe after the Warsaw Pact: Security Dilemmas in the 1990s* (New York: Greenwood Press, 1992) pp. 84–6; A. Hyman, 'Refugees and citizens: the case of the Volga Germans', *The World Today*, 48 (March 1992) p. 41; D. Moody, 'Germany: the return of diaspora', *The World Today*, 47 (February 1991) p. 24; and D. Gow, 'Soviet Germans win backing to rebuild homeland on the Volga', *The Guardian* (11 September 1991).
176. A. Tomforde, 'Volga home for ethnic Germans' *The Guardian* (23 November 1991); D. Hamilton, 'Germany After Unification', *Problems of Communism*, XLI (May–June 1992) pp. 13–14; and 'New Hope for Volga Germans', Weekly Review, *RFE/RL Research Report*, 1 (8 May 1992) p. 60.
177. O. Waever and P. Joenniemi, 'Region in the Making – A Blueprint for Baltic Sea Politics', in C. Wellmann (ed.), *The Baltic Sea Region: Conflict*

or Cooperation? (Munster: Lit Verlag, 1992) pp. 26–7.

178. E. Lucas, 'Kaliningrad seeks to emerge from Monster's shadow', *The Independent* (17 September 1990); F. Studemann, 'Russians haunted by the shadows of a German past', *The Guardian* (1 May 1991); H. Sietz, 'New Body Finds Its Old Heads', *The Guardian* (6 September 1991); C. Nevin, 'Lost Years in Kaliningrad', *The Guardian* (10 October 1992); and K. Gerner, *European Security After 1989; A New Iron Curtain?*, Paper presented at the Danish Foreign Policy Workshop on Soviet, Russian and Baltic Security, Svaneke (25–27 September 1991) pp. 5–6.

179. M. Smith, *The Soviet Faultline: Ethnic Insecurity and Territorial Dispute in the Former-USSR* (London: Royal United Services Institute, 1991) p. 17; and J. Rettie, 'Russians are told to leave Baltic enclave', *The Guardian* (17 February 1992).

180. Gerner, *European Security After 1989*, p. 6.

181. Interview with Dr. Slawomir Dabrowa.

182. J.B. de Weydenthal, 'Cross-border Diplomacy in East–Central Europe', *RFE/RL Research Report*, 1 (23 October 1992) pp. 22–3.

183. M. Sadykiewicz and D.L. Clarke, 'The New Polish Defence Doctrine: A Further Step Toward Sovereignty', *Report on Eastern Europe*, 1 (4 May 1990) p. 23, fn 1.

184. R. Boyes, 'Mazowiecki fearful over forces' loyalty', *The Times* (24 August 1989).

185. 'Defence hardliner survives Polish military reshuffle', *The Times* (6 September 1989); and M. Sadykiewicz and L. Vinton 'Politicization and the Polish Military', *Report on Eastern Europe*, 1 (30 March 1990) pp. 31–3.

186. 'Parties Banned from the Military', Weekly Record of Events, 2 February 1990, *Report on Eastern Europe*, 1 (9 February 1990) p. 49; and 'Depoliticizing the Military', Weekly Record on Events, 10 May, *Report on Eastern Europe*, 1 (18 May 1990) p. 51.

187. 'Civilians Appointed to Defense Ministry', Weekly Record of Events, 3 April, *Report on Eastern Europe*, 1 (13 April 1990) p. 52.

188. 'Sejm Rejects Prime Ministers Proposals', Weekly Record of Events, 6 July, *Report on Eastern Europe*, 1 (20 July 1990) p. 52.

189. T. Ripley, 'Poland shakes up forces structure', *Jane's Defence Weekly* (8 December 1990); and 'Changes in Armed Forces Announced', Weekly Record of Events, 15 November, *Report on Eastern Europe*, 1 (23 November 1990) p. 35.

190. 'A Civilian Minister of Defense', *RFE/RL Research Report*, 1 (10 January 1992) p. 48.

191. 'Reductions in Military Personnel', Military and Security Notes, *RFE/RL Research Report*, 1 (14 February 1992) p. 68.

192. J.B. de Weydenthal, 'Poland: Building a National Security System', *Report on Eastern Europe*, 2 (14 June 1991) p. 13; and J.B. de Weydenthal, 'Political Problems Affect Security Work in Poland', *RFE/RL Research Report*, 1 (17 April 1992) pp. 39–40.

193. L. Vinton, 'Conflict Erupts Over Polish Armed Forces', *RFE/RL Research Report*, 1 (17 January 1992) p. 55; 'No Purge For Armed Forces', Military and Security Notes, *RFE/RL Research Report*, 1 (24 January

1992) p. 64; and 'Old Guard Encouraged to Resign', Military and Security Notes, *RFE/RL Research Report*, 1 (28 February 1992) p. 52.

194. 'Defence Minister Warns Politicians', Military and Security Notes, *RFE/RL Research Report*, 1 (17 April 1992) p. 55; de Weydenthal, 'Political Problems Affect Security Work in Poland', p. 41; L. Vinton, 'Conflict Between President and Government over Defence Policy Rages On', *RFE/RL Research Report*, 1 (1 May 1992) p. 65; and 'Defence Minister Jolts Establishment', Military and Security Notes, *RFE/RL Research Report*, 1 (17 April 1992) pp. 55–6.

195. Vinton, 'Conflict Between President and Government', p. 65.

196. L. Vinton, 'Battle over Defence Prerogatives in Poland Continues', *RFE/RL Research Report*, 1 (15 May 1992) p. 29.

197. 'Defence Minister Resigns in Wake of Sejm Investigation', Military and Security Notes, *RFE/RL Research Report*, 1 (29 May 1992) p. 59; and 'Defence Minister on Reinforcing Links with NATO', Military and Security Notes, *RFE/RL Research Report*, 1 (19 June 1992) p. 71.

198. 'Poland Stages Military Exercises', Military and Security Notes, *RFE/RL Research Report*, 1 (10 July 1992) p. 68.

199. L. Vinton, 'Poland's "Little Constitution" Clarifies Walesa's Power', *RFE/RL Research Report*, 1 (4 September 1992) p. 24.

200. *Tenets of Polish Security Policy*, p. 20.

201. A. Korbonski, 'The Polish Military at a Time of Change', *RFE/RL Research Report*, 2 (29 July 1994) pp. 17–22.

202. 'Poland debates defense organization', *RFE/RL News Briefs*, 3 (24–27 May 1994) p. 10.

203. 'New National Security Council for Poland?', *RFE/RL News Briefs*, 2 (29 November–3 December 1993) p. 10; and 'Poland's Defense Reform delayed', *RFE/RL News Briefs*, 3 (6–10 June 1994) p. 15.

204. J. Borger, 'Polish MPs slam Walesa over Military and Media Ambitions', *The Guardian* (14 October 1994); and 'Rebel as anti-hero', *The Economist* (22 October 1994), p. 54.

205. J. Borger, 'Polish Minister Sacked after row with Walesa', *The Guardian* (11 November 1994).

206. T.S. Szayna, *The Military in a Postcommunist Poland*, N-2209-USDP (Santa Monica, Cal.: RAND, 1991) p. 43.

207. Sadykiewicz and Clarke, 'The New Polish Defence Doctrine'; and 'Poland: Force Level Details', *Jane's Defence Weekly* (3 February 1990).

208. Sadykiewicz and Clarke, 'The New Polish Defence Doctrine', p. 22.

209. J. Prystrom, *The Military–Strategic Emancipation of Poland*, PRIF Reports No. 25 (Frankfurt am Main: Peace Research Institute Frankfurt, January 1992) p. 3.

210. T. Ripley, 'Poland shakes up force structure', *Jane's Defence Weekly* (8 December 1990); T. Ripley, 'The Polish Armed Forces in the 1990s', *Defence Analysis*, 8 (April 1992) p. 89; and 'Changes in Armed Forces Announced', Weekly Record of Events, 15 November, *Report on Eastern Europe*, 1 (23 November 1990) p. 35.

211. De Weydenthal, 'Political Problems Affect Security Work in Poland', p. 41; and 'Prime Minister on the Military', Military and Security Notes, *RFE/RL Research Report*, 1 (14 February 1992) p. 68.

212. 'National Defence Council Meets', Military and Security Notes, *RFE/RL Research Report*, 1 (21 February 1992) p. 57; 'Defence Minister Rejects Army Cuts', Military and Security Notes, *RFE/RL Research Report*, 1 (21 February 1992) p. 57; and 'Polish Defence Minister Jan Parys Opposes Defence Cuts', *Periscope – Daily Defense News Capsules* (10 February 1992).

213. De Weydenthal, 'Political Problems Affect Security Work in Poland', p. 40; and Vinton, 'Battle over Defence Prerogatives in Poland Continues', p. 30.

214. 'Defence Minister Rejects Restructuring Plan', *RFE/RL Research Report*, 1 (10 April 1992) p. 46.

215. *Tenets of Polish Security Policy*, p. 16.

216. *Tenets of Polish Security Policy*, p. 18.

217. 'Defence Reforms to Continue', Military and Security Notes, *RFE/RL Research Report*, 1 (31 July 1992) p. 63; and *The Arms Control Reporter 1993* (Cambridge, Mass.: Institute for Defense and Disarmament Studies, 1993) p. 407. E-1.119.

218. Interview with Ministry of Defence official, Warsaw, 13 November 1992.

219. Korbonski, 'The Polish Military at a Time of Change', p. 21.

220. T. Ripley, 'Polish Defence Economics in the 1990s' *RUSI Journal*, 136 (Summer 1991) pp. 51–5.

221. 'Armed Forces Working With Reduced Budget', *Foreign Broadcast Information Service–Eastern Europe–91–217*, (8 November 1991) p. 27; and A. Karkoszka, 'Transition to Defence-Orientated Configurations', *Disarmament*, XV (1992) p. 111.

222. Interview with Dr. Janusz Prystrom.

223. 'Shifting Polish Forces', Military and Security Notes, *RFE/RL Research Report*, 1 (12 June 1992) p. 8.

224. Interview with Ministry of Defence official, Warsaw, 13 November 1992.

225. Interview with Dr. Henryk Szlajfer.

226. 'New defence minister "realistic" about NATO entry', *Summary of World Broadcasts – Eastern Europe*, 1831 (28 October 1993) A/10.

5 Czechoslovakia and After

1. T. Szayna, *The Military in a Postcommunist Czechoslovakia*, A RAND Note, N-3412-USDP (Santa Monica, Cal.: The RAND Corporation, 1992) pp. 19–20; and W.H. Luers, 'Czechoslovakia: Road to Revolution', *Foreign Affairs*, 69 (1990) pp. 96–7.

2. *The Arms Control Reporter 1989* (Cambridge, Mass.: Institute for Defense and Disarmament Studies, 1989) p. 407.B.288–9.

3. Interview with Prince Karel Schwarzenberg, Chancellor of the Office of the President of Czechoslovakia, London, 26 January 1992.

4. D.J. Schemo, 'Soviet troops to leave Czech soil', *The Baltimore Sun* (6 January 1990).

5. 'Moscow to begin troop pull-out', *The Times* (10 February 1990); E. Lucas, 'Prague rethink on Soviet troops', *The Independent* (14 February 1990); and 'Prague and Moscow Agree on Troops', *International Herald Tribune* (23 February 1990).

6. F.X. Clines, 'Havel and Gorbachev Agree on Mid-1991 Pullout', *International Herald Tribune* (27 February 1990).
7. P. Green, 'Tank men lead the way home to Russia', *The Times* (27 February 1990).
8. R. de Nevers, *The Soviet Union and Eastern Europe: The End of an Era*, Adelphi Paper 249 (London: Brassey's for the International Institute for Strategic Studies, March 1990) p. 48.
9. F. Harris, 'Prague starts negotiations over forces' withdrawal', *The Daily Telegraph* (16 January 1990); and Szayna, *The Military in a Postcommunist Czechoslovakia*, p. 23.
10. Speech by Jiri Dienstbier, Foreign Minister of the Czech and Slovak Republic, at the Warsaw Treaty Organization Meeting, Prague, 17 March 1990 in A.D. Rotfeld and W. Stutzel (eds), *Germany and Europe in Transition* (Oxford: Oxford University Press, 1991) p. 139.
11. '"We will not quit WP"', *Jane's Defence Weekly* (14 April 1990).
12. S. Clovely, 'Czech PM warns Pact to reform', *The Guardian* (4 July 1990).
13. 'Pact reform', *The Independent* (21 July 1990).
14. F. Harris, 'Prague pulls out of military exercises with Warsaw Pact', *The Daily Telegraph* (11 September 1990).
15. 'Pointless Pact', *The Independent* (22 October 1990).
16. 'Influx fear', *The Independent* (23 November 1990); 'Worries about Soviet refugees', 18 December, Weekly Review, *Report on Eastern Europe*, 2 (4 January 1991) p. 59; and P. Green, 'Czechoslovakia braces itself for invasion of Soviet migrants', *The Times* (24 December 1990).
17. J. Obrman, 'Czechoslovakia Reacts to Crackdown in the Baltic Republics', *Report on Eastern Europe*, 2 (8 February 1991), pp. 25–8.
18. 'No military threat', *The Guardian* (4 February 1991); M. Simmons, 'Prague fears wider Soviet crackdown', *The Guardian* (30 January 1991); and F. Harris, 'Czechs agree the need for anti-Kremlin military pact', *The Daily Telegraph* (7 February 1991).
19. 'Foreign Minister on USSR and Gulf', 12 February, Weekly Review, *Report on Eastern Europe*, 2 (22 February 1991) p. 47.
20. F. Harris, 'Czechs call for talks on quitting Warsaw Pact', *The Daily Telegraph* (14 January 1991).
21. Obrman, 'Czechoslovakia Reacts to Crackdown in the Baltic Republics', p. 27.
22. *The Independent* (30 April 1991).
23. J. Obrman, 'The Attempted Coup in the Soviet Union; East European Reactions – Czechoslovakia', *Report on Eastern Europe*, 2 (30 August 1991) pp. 5–8.
24. Szayna, *The Military in a Postcommunist Czechoslovakia*, p. 89.
25. 'Response to Soviet Developments', 21 August, Weekly Record of Events, *Report on Eastern Europe*, 2 (30 August 1991) p. 44.
26. 'NATO Membership?'. 23 August, Weekly Record of Events, *Report on Eastern Europe*, 2 (6 September 1991) p. 38.
27. J. Obrman, 'Czechoslovakia: Relations with Germany', *Report on Eastern Europe*, 2 (15 November 1991) pp. 13–15.
28. 'Havel supports unified Germany', *The Daily Telegraph* (20 February 1990).

29. L. Colitt, 'Havel endorses German unity', *Financial Times* (3 January 1990); and 'Havel Sets Conditions For German Unity', *International Herald Tribune* (3 January 1990).
30. B. Donovan, 'Eastern Europe and German Unity', *Report on Eastern Europe*, 1 (2 March 1990) p. 50.
31. L. Barber, 'Czech leader spells out to Baker price of Soviet troop withdrawal', *Financial Times* (7 February 1990); and *The Arms Control Reporter 1990* (Cambridge, Mass.: Institute for Defense and Disarmament Studies, 1990) p. 407.B.322.
32. Interview with Prince Karel Schwarzenberg.
33. 'Support for Poland in Two-Plus-Four Talks', 4 May, Weekly Record of Events, *Report on Eastern Europe*, 1 (18 May 1990) p. 47.
34. J. Palmer, 'Czechs back Poland's demand for inviolable frontier', *The Guardian* (3 March 1990).
35. 'President Welcomes United Germany', 3 October, Weekly Record of Events, *Report on Eastern Europe*, 1 (12 October 1990) p. 47.
36. The Speech of the President of the Czechoslovak Socialist Republic to the Polish Sejm and Senate (25 January 1990) pp. 3–4.
37. P. Moore, 'Bratislava and Bonn: Two Conferences on Europe's Future', *Report on Eastern Europe*, 1 (11 May 1990) pp. 43–4; and J. Obrman, 'Czechoslovakia – Foreign Policy: Sources, Concepts, Problems', *Report on Eastern Europe*, 1 (14 September 1990) p. 13.
38. The Speech of the President of the Czechoslovak Socialist Republic to the Polish Sejm and Senate, p. 4.
39. Address of the President of the Czechoslovak Republic to a joint Session of the United States Congress, Washington, DC, (21 February 1990) pp. 5–6.
40. E. Lucas, 'Havel returns from US as the conquering hero', *The Independent* (24 February 1990); and P. Martin, 'Czechoslovakia's New Foreign Policy', *Report on Eastern Europe*, 1 (9 March 1990) p. 19.
41. Both Havel and Dienstbier signed the March 1985 Prague Appeal, calling for the dissolution of the Warsaw Pact and NATO, the removal of all nuclear weapons from Europe and the withdrawal of all Soviet and American troops from foreign territory. See Obrman, 'Czechoslovakia – Foreign Policy: Sources, Concepts, Problems', pp. 8–9.
42. Address by His Excellency Mr. Jiri Dienstbier, Minister of Foreign Affairs of the Czechoslovak Federative Republic, at Chatham House, London (3 April 1990) p. 11.
43. Speech by Jiri Dienstbier, Foreign Minister of the Czech and Slovak Republic, at the Warsaw Treaty Organization Meeting, Prague, 17 March 1990, p. 139.
44. Memorandum on the European Security Commission issued on 6 April 1990 by the Federal Ministry of Foreign Affairs of the Federal Republic of Czechoslovakia, *Disarmament*, XIII (1990) pp. 193–6.
45. Address by His Excellency Mr. Jiri Dienstbier, Minister of Foreign Affairs of the Czechoslovak Federative Republic, at Chatham House, pp. 11–14.
46. Full text of speech by the President of the Czech and Slovak Federal Republic Vaclav Havel at the parliamentary assembly of the Council of

Europe, *Ceteka Daily News and Press Survey* (10 May 1990) pp. 10–11.

47. Z. Matejka, 'Building an All-European Security System: A Czechoslovak View', *Disarmament*, XIV (1991) p. 40.
48. Statement delivered by the President of the Czech and Slovak Federal Republic, His Excellency Mr. Vaclav Havel, CSCE Summit, Paris (19 November 1990) p. 3.
49. 'Relations with NATO', 5 February; and 'President Wants Closer Contacts with NATO', 6 February, Weekly Record of Events, *Report on Eastern Europe*, 2 (15 February 1991) p. 47.
50. 'No Security without NATO', 27 February, Weekly Record of Events, *Report on Eastern Europe*, 2 (8 March 1991) pp. 48–9.
51. Declaration of the Czech and Slovak Federal Republic, on the occasion of the visit of President Vaclav Havel to the Headquarters of the North Atlantic Treaty Organization, 21 March 1991, *NATO Review*, 39 (April 1991) pp. 31–5.
52. President Havel's address to the NATO Council, *NATO Review*, 39 (April 1991) pp. 30–1.
53. 'Security Conference in Prague', 25 April, Weekly Record of Events, *Report on Eastern Europe*, 2 (3 May 1991) p. 40.
54. J. Dienstbier, 'The future of European security: Prague conference confirms agreement on basic ideas', *NATO Review*, 39 (June 1991) p. 4.
55. 'Czechs host NATO', *Jane's Defence Weekly* (20 April 1991) p. 623.
56. 'Officials Discuss Defense Matters', 12 June; and 'Czechoslovakia Does Not Want to Join NATO', 13 June, Weekly Record of Events, *Report on Eastern Europe*, 2 (21 June 1991) pp. 36–7.
57. J. Hoagland, 'Vaclav Havel: A New Prison for the Poetic Rebel', *International Herald Tribune* (15–16 June 1991).
58. Interview with Ivan Busniak, Foreign Minister's Office, Czechoslovak Federal Ministry of Foreign Affairs, Prague, 20 November 1992.
59. Interview with Dr. Svatopluk Buchlovsky, Director, European Security Department, Federal Ministry of Foreign Affairs, Czechoslovakia, London, 11 March 1992.
60. 'Havel Fails to Move Bush on NATO', *International Herald Tribune* (23 October 1991).
61. 'Dienstbier on Role of NATO in Central Europe', *Foreign Broadcast Information Service–Eastern Europe 91–220* (14 November 1991) pp. 8–19.
62. Interview with Ivan Busniak.
63. G. Gerosa, 'The North Atlantic Cooperation Council', *European Security*, 1 (Autumn 1992) p. 273.
64. 'Czechoslovakia – Reactions to New Commonwealth', Weekly Record of Events, *RFE/RL Research Report*, 1 (10 January 1992) p. 65.
65. Interview with Ivan Busniak.
66. A. McElvoy, 'Sudeten Germans still live in hope of compensation', *The Times* (8 November 1990).
67. 'President Rejects Sudeten Reparation Demands', 2 December, Weekly Record of Events, *Report on Eastern Europe*, 1 (14 December 1991) p. 41.
68. J. Obrman, 'Czechoslovakia: Relations with Germany', *Report on Eastern Europe*, 2 (15 November 1991) p. 14.

69. 'Prague Urges Bonn to Act on Pact', *International Herald Tribune* (6 August 1991); and 'Diplomat Presses for German Treaty to Be Signed', 3 September, Weekly Record of Events, *Report on Eastern Europe*, 2 (13 September 1991) p. 44.
70. 'Treaties with USSR and Germany Concluded', 12 September, Weekly Record of Events, *Report on Eastern Europe*, 2 (20 September 1991) p. 49.
71. M. Hockaday, 'Sudeten question rankles in Prague', *The Independent* (9 October 1991).
72. D. Gow, 'SPD stiffens resistance to wider role for Bundeswehr', *The Guardian* (17 January 1992); 'German Treaty', Weekly Review, *RFE/ RL Research Report*, 1 (24 January 1992) p. 74; I. Traynor, 'Prague pact soured by old enmity', *The Guardian* (28 February 1992); and J. Obrman, 'Czechoslovak Assembly Affirms German Friendship Treaty', *RFE/RL Research Report*, 1 (22 May 1992) pp. 19–20.
73. Obrman, 'Czechoslovak Assembly Affirms German Friendship Treaty', pp. 20–4; 'Bundestag Ratifies Czechoslovak and Hungarian Treaties', Weekly Review, *RFE/RL Research Report*, 1 (5 June 1992) p. 68; 'Dienstbier Warns Bavaria About Sudeten Claims', Weekly Review, *RFE/ RL Research Report*, 1 (26 June 1992) p. 76; and 'Havel Regrets Bavarian Rejection of Czechoslovak–German Treaty', Weekly Review, *RFE/ RL Research Report*, 1 (10 July 1992) p. 75.
74. 'German Foreign Affairs Minister in Prague' and 'Foreign Affairs Minister Agree on "Prague Theses"', 11 April, Weekly Record of Events, *Report on Eastern Europe*, 2 (19 April 1991) pp. 25–6.
75. 'Army Chief of the General Staff in Germany', 6 November, Weekly Record of Events, *Report on Eastern Europe*, 2 (15 November 1991) p. 3.
76. I. Traynor, 'Prague pact soured by old enmity', *The Guardian* (28 February 1992).
77. F. Harris and R. Gedge, 'Czech fear of German economic offensive', *The Daily Telegraph* (5 February 1992).
78. M. Battiata, 'Czechs Seek US Investment to Balance German', *International Herald Tribune* (11 February 1992).
79. 'Czechoslovak–Russian Treaty', Weekly Review, *RFE/RL Research Report*, 1 (28 February 1992) p. 79.
80. J. Obrman, 'Russia and Czechoslovakia Sign Friendship Treaty', *RFE/ RL Research Report*, 1 (8 May 1992) pp. 17–21.
81. S. Greenberg, 'Czech invasion letter unveiled', *The Guardian* (17 July 1992); and 'CIS Troops to Transit Slovakia', Military and Security Notes, *RFE/RL Research Report*, 1 (30 October 1992) pp. 64–5.
82. A.A. Reisch, 'Transcarpathia and Its Neighbors', *RFE/RL Research Report*, 1 (14 February 1992) p. 45.
83. E. Lucas, 'Rebirth of Warhol's people', *The Independent* (9 May 1990).
84. I. Traynor '"14 dead" after Czechs and Soviets clash on border', *The Guardian* (25 January 1991).
85. Reisch, 'Transcarpathia and Its Neighbors', pp. 43–5.
86. Reisch, 'Transcarpathia and Its Neighbors', pp. 43–6; and 'Autonomists in Transcarpathia Appeal to Czechoslovakia', Weekly Review, *RFE/RL Research Report*, 1 (31 January 1992) p. 66.

87. 'Ukrainian–Czechoslovak Relations', Weekly Review, *RFE/RL Research Report*, 1 (14 February 1992) p. 71.
88. 'Czechoslovakia has no claims on Sub-Carpathian Rus', Weekly Review, *RFE/RL Research Report*, 1 (10 April 1992) p. 59.
89. 'Ukraine and Czechoslovakia Initial Friendship Treaty', Weekly Review, *RFE/RL Research Report*, 1 (5 June 1992) p. 68.
90. R. Bassett, 'Czech Army "will defend communism"', *The Times* (24 November 1989); and E. Lucas, 'Czechs fear of tanks no longer justified', *The Independent* (5 December 1989).
91. J. Obrman, 'Czechoslovakia: Civilian Appointed New Defense Minister', *Report on Eastern Europe*, 1 (9 November 1990) pp. 1–2; and Szayna, *The Military in a Postcommunist Czechoslovakia*, p. 21.
92. J. Obrman, 'Czechoslovakia: Changing Conditions for the Army and the Police', *Report on Eastern Europe*, 1 (26 January 1990) pp. 1–2.
93. P. Green, 'Troops out in Prague as rumours of coup spread', *The Times* (27 January 1990).
94. 'Rumors of Coup Dismissed', 26 January, Weekly Record of Events, *Report on Eastern Europe*, 1 (9 February 1990) p. 45; Green, 'Troops out in Prague'; 'Richard Sacher Reacts to Coup Rumors', 29 January, Weekly Record of Events, *Report on Eastern Europe*, 1 (16 February 1990) p. 45; and F. Harris, 'Czech army alert amid coup fears', *The Daily Telegraph* (30 January 1990).
95. J. Obrman, 'The Czechoslovak Armed Forces: The Reforms Continues', *RFE/RL Research Report*, 1 (7 February 1992) p. 48.
96. F. Harris, 'Thousands of Czech officers leave forces in "loyalty" protest', *The Daily Telegraph* (10 September 1990).
97. J. Obrman, 'Czechoslovakia: Changes in the Armed Forces', *Report on Eastern Europe*, 1 (6 April 1990) p. 12.
98. Obrman, 'Czechoslovakia: Civilian Appointed New Defense Minister', pp. 3–4.
99. Obrman, 'Czechoslovakia: Civilian Appointed New Defense Minister', pp. 1–2.
100. Szayna, *The Military in a Postcommunist Czechoslovakia*, p. 68.
101. Szayna, *The Military in a Postcommunist Czechoslovakia*, p. 59.
102. Obrman, 'The Czechoslovak Armed Forces: The Reform Continues', p. 52.
103. *The Arms Control Reporter 1990*, pp. 407.B.287–8.
104. 'New Defense Doctrine', 22 May, Weekly Record of Events, *Report on Eastern Europe*, 1 (1 June 1990) p. 52.
105. Obrman, 'Czechoslovakia: Civilian Appointed New Defense Minister', p. 3; and Szayna, *The Military in a Postcommunist Czechoslovakia*, pp. 35–6.
106. Obrman, 'The Czechoslovak Armed Forces: The Reforms Continues', p. 50; and Szayna, *The Military in a Postcommunist Czechoslovakia*, pp. 61–2.
107. Obrman, 'The Czechoslovak Armed Forces: The Reforms Continues', p. 50–1.
108. *The Arms Control Reporter 1991* (Cambridge, Mass.: Institute for Defence and Disarmament Studies, 1991) p. 407.E-1.31.

109. 'CSFR withdrawing troops from Western border', *International Defense Review*, 10 (1990).
110. Obrman, 'The Czechoslovak Armed Forces: The Reforms Continues', p. 51.
111. 'First fighter flies in', *Jane's Defence Weekly* (14 November 1992).
112. *The Arms Control Reporter 1991*, p. 407.E-1.51; and 'Czechoslovakia: Defense Minister Unhappy with Budget', Military and Security Notes, *RFE/RL Research Report*, 1 (17 January 1992) p. 54.
113. 'Czechoslovakia: Armed Forces to be Cut', Military and Security Notes, *RFE/RL Research Report*, 1 (15 May 1992) p. 31.
114. O. Ulc, 'The Bumpy Road of Czechoslovakia's Velvet Revolution', *Problems of Communism*, XLI (May–June 1992) pp. 19–33; S.L. Wolchik, 'The Politics of Ethnicity in Post-Communist Czechoslovakia', *East European Politics and Societies*, 8 (1994) pp. 153–88; and O. Pick, 'Eastern Europe: Czechoslovakia's Divisions', *The World Today*, 48 (1992) pp. 83–5.
115. Obrman, 'Czechoslovakia – Foreign Policy: Sources, Concepts, Problems', p. 8.
116. Szayna, *The Military in a Postcommunist Czechoslovakia*, pp 37–8.
117. Ulc, 'The Bumpy Road', p. 31.
118. Obrman, 'The Czechoslovak Armed Forces: The Reform Continues', pp. 53–4; and Szayna, *The Military in a Postcommunist Czechoslovakia*, pp. 72–9.
119. J. Obrman, 'Yugoslav Crisis Has Little Impact on Czechoslovak Domestic Policy', *Report on Eastern Europe*, 2 (9 August 1991) pp. 30–2.
120. J. Pehe, 'Czechoslovak Parliament Votes to Dissolve Federation', *RFE/RL Research Report*, 1 (4 December 1992) p. 2.
121. M.Z. Bookman, 'War and Peace: The Divergent Breakups of Yugoslavia and Czechoslovakia', *Journal of Peace Research*, 31 (1994) pp. 175–87.
122. S. Fisher, 'Czech–Slovak Relations Two Years after the Elections', *RFE/RL Research Report*, 3 (8 July 1994) pp. 9–17.
123. J. Obrman, 'After the Split: Challenges for Czech Foreign Policy', *RFE/RL Research Report*, 1 (13 November 1992) p. 28.
124. 'Czechs seek EC talks', *The Guardian* (2 December 1992).
125. 'New members', *The Independent* (30 June 1993); and 'Czech and Slovak Republics sign association agreements with EC', *Summary of World Broadcasts – Eastern Europe*, EE/1812 (6 October 1993) A/3.
126. 'Klaus on Czech Republic's EU Membership', *REF/RL News Briefs*, 3 (7–11 March 1994) p. 19; and 'Czech Republic to seek EU Membership before '96', *RFE/RL News Briefs*, 3 (20–24 June 1994) p. 12.
127. 'NATO Supreme Commander Meets Czech Leaders', *RFE/RL News Briefs*, p. 2 (21–25 June 1993) p. 19; and 'Klaus, however, is less bullish', *RFE/RL News Briefs*, 2 (30 August–3 September 1993) pp. 14–15.
128. 'President Havel addresses parliament on Czech membership of NATO', *Summary of World Broadcasts – Eastern Europe*, EE/1819 (14 October 1993) A/1–3.
129. 'Czech Officials on NATO', *RFE/RL News Briefs*, 2 (11–15 October 1993) p. 10.

130. 'Foreign Minister tells army officers why NATO membership remains goal', *Summary of World Broadcasts – Eastern Europe*, EE/1849 (18 November 1993) A/1.

131. 'Left Bloc deputy Ortman criticizes Havel's address to parliament on NATO', *Summary of World Broadcasts – Eastern Europe*, EE/1820 (15 October 1993) A/2.

132. 'Czech Officials Comments on NATO Announcement', *RFE/RL News Briefs*, 2 (18–22 October 1993) p. 18.

133. 'Premier Klaus says entry to NATO is a long-term question', *Summary of World Broadcasts – Eastern Europe*, EE/1831 (28 October 1993) A/1.

134. 'Klaus, Havel on NATO', *RFE/RL News Briefs*, 2 (25–29 October 1993) p. 9.

135. 'Prague MPs back NATO link', *The Guardian* (10 February 1994); and 'Czech Republic joins Partnership for Peace', *RFE/RL News Briefs*, 3 (7–11 March 1994) p. 19.

136. 'UK seeks closer ties with new republics', *Jane's Defence Weekly* (24 April 1993).

137. 'NATO Supreme Commander Meets Czech Leaders'.

138. 'US Air Force COS received by Czech Army CGS and air regiment', *Summary of World Broadcasts – Eastern Europe*, EE/1820 (15 October 1993) A/1; 'Defence Minister Baudys receives US Air Force COS: co-operation discussed', *Summary of World Broadcasts – Eastern Europe*, EE/1821 (16 October 1993) A/1; 'Czech drive for direct links with USAF', *Jane's Defence Weekly* (6 March 1993); J. Obrman, 'Military Reform in the Czech Republic', *RFE/RL Research Report*, 2 (15 October 1993) p. 42; and C. Covault, 'Czechs Modify Force, Seek NATO Acceptance', *Aviation Week & Space Technology* (14 March 1994).

139. 'Czech–French Military Exercises', *RFE/RL News Briefs*, 3 (30 May–3 June 1994) p. 10.

140. 'Canada signs defence memorandums with Czech and Slovak Republics', *RFE/RL News Briefs*, 3 (8–12 August 1994) p. 13.

141. 'CSFR Politicians Reportedly See No Future in Visegrad Three Cooperation', *Summary of World Broadcasts – Eastern Europe*, EE/1374 (7 May 1992) A2/2.

142. 'Czechs opt to Act Alone on NATO Issue', *International Herald Tribune* (7 January 1994).

143. 'Klaus on Czech Republic's EU Membership'.

144. J. Palmer, 'Slovenes and Czechs head long line to join EU', *The Guardian* (24 September 1994).

145. J. Obrman, 'Sudeten Germans Controversy in the Czech Republic', *RFE/RL Research Report*, 3/2 (14 January 1994) pp. 9–16.

146. 'Czech–German Cooperation', *RFE/RL News Briefs*, 2 (24–28 May 1993) p. 13; and 'Germans, Czechs Sign Pledge', *Current News*, 25 May 1993.

147. 'Czech, Polish, German Soldiers March Together', *RFE/RL News Briefs*, 3 (16–19 August 1994) p. 12.

148. 'President Havel discusses relations with Germany'. *Summary of World Broadcasts – Eastern Europe*, EE/1823 (19 October 1993) A/1.

149. Obrman, 'Military Reform in the Czech Republic', pp. 38–9.

150. Obrman, 'Military Reform in the Czech Republic', p. 39; P. Valpolini, 'Czech army casts aside Soviet structures', *International Defense Review*, 11 (1993) pp. 913–14; and B. Sauerwein, 'In Transition: The Army of the Czech Republic', *International Defense Review*, 4 (1994) pp. 69–71.

151. Obrman, 'Military Reform in the Czech Republic', pp. 40–1; and Sauerwein, 'In Transition', p. 71.

152. 'Meciar on Slovakia's Future', Weekly Review, *RFE/RL Research Report*, 1 (21 August 1992) p. 76. The formation of the CIS at the end of 1991 had also led to suggestions that Slovakia might seek association with it. See the Economist Intelligence Unit, *Czechoslovakia Country Report*, 2 (London: EIU, 1992) p. 11.

153. Interview with Dr. Svetoslav Bombik, Analytical Department, Slovak Ministry of Foreign Affairs, Bratislava, 25 November 1992.

154. 'Disagreement over Slovakia's Foreign Policy', *RFE/RL News Briefs*, 2 (10–23 December 1992) p. 23; and S. Fisher, 'Slovakia's Foreign Policy since Independence', *RFE/RL Research Report*, 2 (10 December 1993) pp. 28–9.

155. Fisher, 'Slovakia's Foreign Policy since Independence', pp. 28–9.

156. 'Slovakia, Austria Sign Military Agreement', *RFE/RL News Briefs*, 2 (9–13 August 1993) p. 17.

157. 'Priorities in Slovak Foreign and Defense Policy', *RFE/RL News Briefs*, 2 (20–24 September 1993) pp. 14–15.

158. 'UK seeks closer ties with new republics', *Jane's Defence Weekly* (24 April 1993); 'US Air Force COS holds talks with Defence Minister', *Summary of World Broadcasts – Eastern Europe*, EE/1822 (18 October 1993) A/6; and 'Shalikashvili visits Slovakia', *RFE/RL News Briefs*, 2 (21–25 June 1993) p. 14.

159. 'Slovakia signs Partnership for Peace', *RFE/RL News Briefs*, 3 (7–11 February 1994) p. 18.

160. J. Obrman, 'Slovakia Forges a Foreign Policy – Uncertain Prospects for Independent Slovakia', *RFE/RL Research Report*, 1 (11 December 1992) p. 45.

161. 'Slovak Premier: Treaty with Russia could herald a new type of cooperation', *Summary of World Broadcasts – Eastern Europe*, EE/1775 (24 August 1993) A2/5; and Fisher, 'Slovakia's Foreign Policy since Independence', p. 33.

162. 'Slovak Defense Minister in Russia', *RFE/RL News Briefs*, 2 (22–26 November 1993) p. 19.

163. Fisher, 'Slovakia's Foreign Policy since Independence', p. 33.

164. 'Slovak and Romanian Presidents sign cooperation treaty, give press conference', *Summary of World Broadcasts – Eastern Europe*, EE/1804 (27 September 1993) A/4; and 'Illiescu meets Meciar, addresses Slovak parliament', *Summary of World Broadcasts – Eastern Europe*, EE/1804 (27 September 1993) A/3.

165. Fisher, 'Slovakia's Foreign Policy since Independence', p. 33.

166. Fisher, 'Slovakia's Foreign Policy since Independence', pp. 33–4.

167. Interview with Ivan Busniak.

168. 'Slovak President Visits Ukraine', *RFE/RL News Briefs*, 2 (28 June–2

July 1993) p. 14; and 'Slovak–Ukrainian Military Agreement Signed', *RFE/RL News Briefs*, 2 (25–29 October 1993) p. 20.

169. J. Obrman, 'Slovakia Forges a Foreign Policy', p. 45.

170. 'IMF Approves Stand-by Loan for Slovakia', *RFE/RL News Briefs*, 3 (25–29 July and 1–5 August 1994) p. 13.

171. I. Traynor, 'Fears for Slovak stability as Meciar triumphs in poll', *The Guardian* (3 October 1994); I. Traynor, 'Slovakia's populist victor lies low and keeps friends and foe guessing', *The Guardian* (5 October 1994); and I. Traynor, 'Feuds and deadlock dog ex-communist', *The Guardian* (7 November 1994).

172. 'Slovakia No Threat to Hungary', Military and Security Notes, 'Slovak Prime Minister Warns Hungary', and 'Hungarian–Slovak Discussions', Weekly Review, *RFE/RL Research Report* 1 (14 August 1992) pp. 49–73.

173. A.A. Reisch, 'Slovakia's Minority Policy under International Scrutiny', *RFE/RL Research Report*, 2 (10 December 1993) pp. 35–42.

174. S. Fisher, 'Meeting of Slovakia's Hungarians Causes Stir', *RFE/RL Research Report*, 3 (28 January 1994) pp. 42–7; and I. Traynor, 'Jittery Slovakia hears echoes of Bosnia', *The Guardian* (10 January 1994).

175. A.A. Reisch, 'Hungarian–Slovak Relations: A Difficult First Year', *RFE/RL Research Report*, 2 (17 December 1993) pp. 18–20.

176. Reisch, 'Hungarian–Slovak Relations: A Difficult First Year', pp. 16–18; and V. Rich, 'The Murky Politics of the Danube', *The World Today*, 49 (August–September 1993) pp. 151–2.

177. Reisch, 'Hungarian–Slovak Relations: A Difficult First Year', pp. 22–3.

178. 'Slovak Parliament approves Law on Names', *RFE/RL News Briefs*, 3 (30 May–3 June 1994) p. 10.

179. 'Slovak Parliament creates Army and Defense Ministry', *RFE/RL News Briefs*, 2 (10–23 December 1992) p. 8.

180. 'Meeting between Meciar and army chiefs cancelled to avoid "misinterpretation"', *Summary of World Broadcasts – Eastern Europe*, EE/1803 (25 September 1993) A/3–4.

181. 'Army association approves of MFDS/SNP coalition', *Summary of World Broadcasts – Eastern Europe*, EE/1830 (27 October 1993) A/3.

182. 'Reorganization of Slovak Defense Ministry', *RFE/RL News Briefs*, 3 (16–19 August 1994) p. 15.

183. 'Slovak Parliament creates Army and Defense Ministry'.

184. N. Ball *et al.*, 'World Military Expenditure', Chapter 12 in Stockholm International Peace Research Institute, *SIPRI Yearbook 1994* (Oxford: Oxford University Press, 1994) p. 434.

185. 'Slovakia receives extra Fulcrums', *Flight International* (12 January 1994).

6 Hungary

1. A. Reisch, 'Hungary's Wish Comes True: Some Soviet Troops to Leave', *RAD Background Report/52* (Radio Free Europe Research, Radio Free Europe/Radio Liberty, 21 March 1989) pp. 1–2.

2. The Economist Intelligence Unit, *Hungary Country Report*, 3 (London: EIU, 1989) pp. 10–11.

3. V. Sobell, 'Hungary's Response to Western Initiative on Economic Aid', *RAD Background Report/147* (Radio Free Europe Research, Radio Free Europe/Radio Liberty, 11 August 1989) p. 2.

4. K. Devlin, 'Hungary's New Defense Doctrine: "Enemy Not the West but Romania"', *RAD Background Report/101* (Radio Free Europe Research, Radio Free Europe/Radio Liberty, 16 June 1989) pp. 1–4; and D. Clarke, 'Hungary Proposes Border Security Zones', *RAD Background Report/181* (Radio Free Europe Research, Radio Free Europe/Radio Liberty, 27 September 1989) pp. 1–7.

5. V. Sobell, 'Austria, Hungary and the Question of Neutrality', *RAD Background Report/156* (Radio Free Europe Research, Radio Free Europe/Radio Liberty, 24 August 1989) p. 3.

6. 'Call for Hungary to leave Pact', *The Independent* (17 April 1989).

7. '"Neutral" Hungary', *The Daily Telegraph* (20 September 1989).

8. 'Kremlin says Hungary "is free to leave Pact"', *The Independent* (30 October 1989).

9. A. Reisch, 'Hungarian Neutrality: Hopes and Realities', *Report on Eastern Europe*, 1 (30 March 1990) pp. 14–15.

10. *The Arms Control Reporter 1990* (Cambridge, Mass.: Institute for Defense and Disarmament Studies, 1990) p. 407.E-1.4.

11. Z.D. Barany and A. Reisch, 'Hungary: Withdrawal of All Soviet Troops by End of 1990 Demanded', *Report on Eastern Europe*, 1 (9 February 1990) p. 24.

12. Z.D. Barany, 'A Hungarian Dream Comes True: Soviet Troops to Leave After 45 Years', *Report on Eastern Europe*, 1 (30 March 1990) pp. 23–8.

13. Reisch, 'Hungarian Neutrality', pp. 19–20.

14. A. Reisch, 'The Hungarian Dilemma: After the Warsaw Pact, Neutrality or NATO?', *Report on Eastern Europe*, 1 (13 April 1990) pp. 17–21.

15. A. Reisch, 'Hungary: Government Wants Negotiated Withdrawal from the Warsaw Pact', *Report on Eastern Europe*, 1 (8 June 1990) pp. 24–34.

16. B. Sauerwein, 'Hungary's National Defense', *International Defense Review* 11 (November 1990) p. 1220.

17. A. Reisch, 'Hungary to Leave Military Arm of Warsaw Pact', *Report on Eastern Europe*, 1 (29 June 1990) pp. 20–5.

18. 'Premier Jozsef Antall Presents Governments Programme', *Summary of World Broadcasts – Eastern Europe*, EE/0773 (25 May 1990) C1/3–9.

19. A. Reisch, 'Hungary: Interview with Foreign Minister Geza Jeszenszky', *Report on Eastern Europe*, 1 (27 July 1990) pp. 17–18.

20. Interview with Csaba Kiss, Head of Defence Policy Planning Department, Ministry of Defence, Budapest, 2 December 1992.

21. 'Hungarian Premier in Brussels', *Summary of World Broadcasts – Eastern Europe*, EE/0821 (20 July 1990) A1/1–2.

22. 'Hungarian Premier on his proposal for a Central–East European Union', *Summary of World Broadcasts – Eastern Europe*, EE/0862 (6 November 1990) A1/1.

23. The Economist Intelligence Unit, *Hungary Country Report*, 4 (London: EIU, 1990) pp. 8–9.

24. 'NATO Secretary-General in Hungary', *Summary of World Broadcasts – Eastern Europe*, EE/0933 (28 November 1990) A1/3.

25. 'Hungarian MPs vote for NATO', *The Independent* (30 January 1991).
26. 'Interest in Western Organization', 23 April, Weekly Record of Events, *Report on Eastern Europe*, 2, (3 May 1991) p. 41; 'German–Hungarian Forum Opens in Budapest', 4 June, Weekly Record of Events, *Report on Eastern Europe*, 2 (14 June 1991) pp. 42–3; and *The Arms Control Reporter 1991* (Cambridge, Mass.: Institute for Defense and Disarmament Studies, 1991) p. 407.E-1.36.
27. A. Reisch, 'Hungary: The Hard Task of Setting Relations with the USSR on a New Footing', *Report on Eastern Europe*, 2 (24 May 1991) pp. 12–18.
28. J. Warr, 'Three nations set deadline to quit the Warsaw Pact', *The Daily Telegraph* (23 January 1991).
29. Reisch, 'Hungary: The Hard Task', pp. 10–17.
30. K. Okolicsanyi, 'The Attempted Coup in the Soviet Union: East European Reactions – Hungary', *Report on Eastern Europe*, 2 (30 August 1991) pp. 8–9.
31. 'Hungarian Premier in USA: Proposes Sovereign Yugoslav Republics – Role for NATO', *Summary of World Broadcasts – Eastern Europe*, EE/1198 (9 October 1991) A1/1.
32. 'Hungarian Premier in Brussels: Visits EC and NATO Headquarters', *Summary of World Broadcasts – Eastern Europe*, EE/1219 (2 November 1991) A1/1–2.
33. 'Call for New Security Guarantees', Military and Security Notes, *RFE/RL Research Report*, 1 (8 May 1992) p. 53.
34. A. LeBor, 'Budapest calls for EC help on border', *The Independent* (20 September 1991).
35. 'Hungarian Premier in Brussels: Visits EC and NATO Headquarters', *Summary of World Broadcasts – Eastern Europe*, EE/1219 (2 November 1991) A1/2; and 'Antall Discusses SFRY Situation with Vance', *Foreign Broadcast Information Service – Eastern Europe 91–217* (8 November 1991) p. 19.
36. 'Foreign Ministry Welcomes NATO Summit Results', *Foreign Broadcast Information Service – Eastern Europe 91–219* (13 November 1991) p. 17.
37. A.A. Reisch, 'Hungary Pursues Integration with the West', *RFE/RL Research Report*, 2 (26 March 1993) p. 34.
38. 'USA to help modernize Hungarian Armed Forces', Military and Security Notes, *RFE/RL Research Report*, 1 (31 January 1992) p. 63.
39. Gyorgy Csoti, Vice-President of the Committee of Foreign Affairs of the Hungarian National Assembly, 'Hungary, NATO and the Conflicts in Europe', Speech to the North Atlantic Assembly, n/d.
40. 'Gyula Horn Addresses Parliament on Socialist Party Backing for Security Policy', *Summary of World Broadcasts – Eastern Europe*, EE/1617 (19 February 1993) B/10.
41. 'Foreign Minister Jeszenszky concludes debate on security policy principles', *Summary of World Broadcasts – Eastern Europe*, EE/1629 (5 March 1993) B/1.
42. A. Marshall, 'Hungary seeks NATO protection from its foes', *The Independent* (18 May 1993).

43. S. Markotich, 'Former Communist States Respond to NATO Ultimatum', *RFE/RL Research Report*. 3 (25 February 1994) pp. 8–9.
44. L. Bruce, 'Hungarian Tells of Meeting With Kohl on Opening Border', *International Herald Tribune* (24 September 1990).
45. A.A. Reisch, 'Hungarian–German Treaty Cements Close Relations', *RFE/RL Research Report*, 1 (6 March 1992) pp. 26–31.
46. Reisch, 'The Hungarian Army in Transition', *RFE/RL Research Report*, 2 (5 March 1993) p. 47.
47. Reisch, 'Hungarian–Russian Relations Enter a New Era', *RFE/RL Research Report*, 2 (8 January 1993) pp. 5–8.
48. Reisch, 'Hungarian–Russian Relations Enter a New Era', pp. 5–8.
49. Reisch, 'Hungary Acquires MiG-29s from Russia', *RFE/RL Research Report*, 2 (20 August 1993) pp. 49–56.
50. Reisch, 'Hungarian–Russian Relations Enter a New Era', p. 8.
51. Interview with Dr. Laszlo Lang, Central European Research Centre, Budapest, 27 November 1992. Similar views were also expressed in an interview with the author by Miklos Derer, Deputy Director, and Col. Janos Gombos, Military Adviser, Centre for Defence and Security Studies, Budapest, 4 December 1992.
52. 'Jeszenszky rejects NATO–Russian guarantee of Central Europe Security', *Summary of World Broadcasts – Eastern Europe*, EE/1820 (15 October 1993) A/4.
53. 'Hungary, Ukraine, sign Partnership for Peace', *RFE/RL News Briefs*, 3 (7–11 February 1994) p. 15.
54. A.A. Reisch, 'Hungarian Parties' Foreign–Policy Electoral Platforms', *RFE/RL Research Report*, 3 (13 May 1994) pp. 14–21; and A.A. Reisch, 'Consensus on Hungary's Foreign Policy Frayed by Elections', *RFE/RL Research Report*, 3 (20 May 1994) pp. 42–8.
55. A.A. Reisch, 'The New Hungarian Government's Foreign', *RFE/RL Research Report*, 3 (26 August 1994) pp. 46–57.
56. 'Premier Jozsef Antall Presents Government Programme', *Summary of World Broadcasts – Eastern Europe*, EE/0773 (25 May 1990) C1/3–9.
57. E. Oltay, 'Hungary: Minorities as Stumbling Block in Relations with Neighbors', *RFE/RL Research Report*, 1 (8 May 1992) p. 28.
58. Oltay, 'Hungary: Minorities as Stumbling Block in Relations with Neighbors', p. 27.
59. Interview with Dr. Istvan Gyarmati, Director, Department of Security Policy and European Cooperation, Ministry of Foreign Affairs, Budapest, 2 December 1992.
60. Reisch, 'The Hungarian Army in Transition', p. 45.
61. 'NATO Secretary-General in Hungary', *Summary of World Broadcasts – Eastern Europe*, EE/0933 (28 November 1990) A1/4.
62. Interview with Dr. Istvan Gyarmati.
63. Interview with Dr. Pal Dunay, Associate Professor, International Law Department, Eotvos University, Budapest, 1st December 1992; and Interview with Dr. Laszlo Lang.
64. A.A. Reisch, 'The New Hungarian Government's Foreign Policy', *RFE/RL Research Report*, 3 (26 August 1994) pp. 46–57.
65. D. Ionescu, 'Chronology of Hungarian Protests at Romanian Resettle-

ment Plans', *RAD Background Report/129* (Radio Free Europe Research, Radio Free Europe/Radio Liberty, 9 July 1988) pp. 3–4.

66. V. Socor, 'Summit Meeting Between Hungarian and Romanian Leaders', *Romania Situation Report/11* (Radio Free Europe Research, Radio Free Europe/Radio Liberty, 16 September 1988) pp. 21–6.

67. 'Hungary Asks UN Probe of Romania', *International Herald Tribune* (28 February 1989).

68. M. Shafir, '"Revisionism" under Romanian General's Fire: Ceausescu's Brother attacks Hungarian Positions', *RAD Background Report/86* (Radio Free Europe Research, Radio Free Europe/Radio Liberty, 17 May 1989) pp. 2–10.

69. E. Oltay, 'Hungarian–Romanian Relations reach New Low Point', *Hungary Situation Report/12* (Radio Free Europe Research, Radio Free Europe/ Radio Liberty, 27 July 1989) p. 40.

70. L. Colitt, 'East bloc seeks to hide cracks', *Financial Times* (7 July 1989); P. Millar, 'Satellite states in anti-glasnost pact', *The Sunday Times* (16 July 1989); R. Taylor, E. Tessieri, C. Bobinski and J. Lloyd, 'Warsaw Pact to face calls for looser structure', *Financial Times* (26 October 1989); and 'Hungary rejects interference', *The Independent* (3 October 1989).

71. Devlin, 'Hungary's New Defense Doctrine', p. 1.

72. D. Clarke, 'The Romanian Military Threat to Hungary', *RAD Background Report/130* (Radio Free Europe Research, Radio Free Europe/ Radio Liberty, 27 July 1989) pp. 1–8.

73. J. Pataki, 'Free Hungarians in a Free Romania: Dream or Reality?', *Report on Eastern Europe*, 1 (23 February 1990) pp. 18–22.

74. Pataki, 'Free Hungarians in a Free Romania: Dream or Reality?', pp. 22–5; and 'Ethnic Conflicts Reported', 26 January, Weekly Record of Events, *Report on Eastern Europe*, 1 (9 February 1990) p. 51.

75. 'Hungarian Fears of Renewed Nationalism', 21 February, Weekly Record of Events, *Report on Eastern Europe*, 1 (9 March 1990) p. 63.

76. V. Socor, 'Forces of Old Resurface in Romania: The Ethnic Clashes in Tirgu-Mures', *Report on Eastern Europe*, 1 (13 April 1990) pp. 36–9.

77. M. Shafir, 'The Romanian Authorities' Reactions to the Violence in Tirgu-Mures', *Report on Eastern Europe*, 1 (13 April 1990) pp. 43–7.

78. J. Pataki, 'The Hungarian Authorities' Reactions to the Violence in Tirgu-Mures', *Report on Eastern Europe*, 1 (13 April 1990) pp. 23–5.

79. M. Binyon, 'Alarm grows over fate of Hungarians in Romania', *The Times* (22 March 1990).

80. A.A. Reisch, 'Hungarian Parties Seek to Reassure Romania on Border Issue', *Report on Eastern Europe*, 1 (15 June 1990) p. 28.

81. 'Prime Minister on Ethnic Hungarians in Romania', 21 May, Weekly Record of Events, *Report on Eastern Europe*, 1 (1 June 1990) p. 53.

82. 'Hungarian–Romanian Talks', Weekly Review, *RFE/RL Research Report*, 1 (15 May 1992) p. 614.

83. A. Reich, 'Hungary: New Bilateral Military Agreements', *Report on Eastern Europe*, 2 (8 November 1991) p. 5.

84. Reich, 'Hungary: New Bilateral Military Agreements', pp. 5–6.

85. Reich, 'Hungary: New Bilateral Military Agreements', p. 6.

86. Reich, 'Hungary: New Bilateral Military Agreements', p. 6.
87. Reich, 'Hungary: New Bilateral Military Agreements', pp. 6–7.
88. 'Claims of Hungarians Troop Movements Denied', Military and Security Notes, *RFE/RL Research Report*, 1 (9 October 1992) p. 56.
89. 'Hungary No Military Threat to Romania', Military and Security Notes, *RFE/RL Research Report*, 1 (18 December 1992) p. 69.
90. D. Ionescu and A.A. Reisch, 'Still No Breakthrough in Romanian–Hungarian Relations', *RFE/RL Research Report*, 2 (22 October 1993) pp. 26–32.
91. Reisch, 'The New Hungarian Government's Foreign Policy', pp. 54–6.
92. M. Shafir, 'Ethnic Tension Runs High in Romania', *RFE/RL Research Report*, 3 (19 August 1994) pp. 24–32.
93. 'Hungarian, Romanian Defense Ministers Meet', *RFE/RL News Briefs*, 3 (26–29 July and 1–5 August 1994) pp. 17–8.
94. Interview with Dr. Istvan Gyarmati.
95. Reisch, 'Hungary: Interview with Foreign Minister Geza Jeszenszky', pp. 18–19.
96. J. Pataki 'Hungary: Relations with Yugoslavia Troubled by Weapons Sale', *Report on Eastern Europe*, 2 (22 February 1991) pp. 15–19.
97. A.A. Reisch, 'Hungary's Policy on the Yugoslav Conflict: A Delicate Balance', *Report on Eastern Europe*, 2 (9 August 1991) pp. 36–7.
98. J. Gow, 'Deconstructing Yugoslavia', *Survival*, XXXIII (July/August 1991) p. 296.
99. M. Andrejevich, 'Yugoslavia: Vojvodina Hungarian Group to Seek Cultural Autonomy', *Report on Eastern Europe* 1 (12 October 1990) pp. 43–4; and E. Oltay, 'Hungarians in Yugoslavia Seek Guarantees for Minority Rights', *Report on Eastern Europe*, 2 (20 September 1991) pp. 39–46.
100. Reisch, 'Hungary's Policy on the Yugoslav Conflict', pp. 37–9.
101. Reisch, 'Hungary's Policy on the Yugoslav Conflict', pp. 37–9.
102. Reisch, 'Hungary: New Bilateral Military Agreements', p. 8.
103. A. LeBor, 'Hungary ready "to use force on the border"', *The Independent* (30 August 1991).
104. 'Concern over Yugoslavia', 18 October, Weekly Record of Events, *Report on Eastern Europe*, 2 (1 November 1991) p. 27; J. Pataki, 'Hungary: Refugee Wave from Croatia Puts Strain on Relief Efforts', *Report on Eastern Europe*, 2 (27 September 1991) pp. 12–13; and A. LeBor, 'Budapest calls for EC help on border', *The Independent* (20 September 1991).
105. Interview with Csaba Kiss.
106. A. LeBor, 'Hungary protests over air attack', *The Independent* (30 October 1991); and 'Defense Ministry Summons SFRY Ambassador, Says Bombing "Deliberate"', and 'Spokesman Briefs Media', *Foreign Broadcast Information Service – Eastern Europe 91–217*, (8 November 1991) p. 18.
107. 'Border Violations Protested', 18 October, Weekly Record of Events, *Report on Eastern Europe*, 2 (8 November 1991) p. 38.
108. 'Military Readiness Increased; Troops Sent to Border', *Foreign Broadcast Information Service – Eastern Europe 91–217*, (8 November 1991) pp. 18–19.
109. 'Neutral Airspace Zone Established on SFRY Border', *Foreign Broad-*

cast Information Service – Eastern Europe 91–219, (3 November 1991) p. 16.

110. Interview with Csaba Kiss.
111. Reisch, 'Hungary's Policy on the Yugoslav Conflict', p. 40; P. Moore, 'Yugoslavia: The Minorities' Plight amid Civil War', *Report on Eastern Europe*, 2 (13 December 1991) pp. 31–2.
112. Moore, 'Yugoslavia: The Minorities' Plight amid Civil War', pp. 31–2.
113. H. Poulton, 'Rising Ethnic Tension in Vojvodina', *RFE/RL Research Report*, 1 (18 December 1992); S. Markotich, 'Vojvodina: A Potential Powder Keg', *RFE/RL Research Report*, 2 (19 November 1993) pp. 13–18; and E. Oltay, 'Hungarians under Political Pressure in Vojvodina', *RFE/RL Research Report*, 2 (3 December 1993) pp. 42–8.
114. '"Arkan" Starts Election Campaign in Vojvodina' *RFE/RL News Briefs*, 2 (22–26 November 1993) p. 15.
115. 'Autonomy for Vojvodina Hungarians', *RFE/RL News Briefs*, 3 (31 January–4 February 1994) pp. 9–10; and I. Traynor, 'Neighbours bring Serbs in from cold', *The Guardian* (14 February 1994).
116. 'Yugoslav, Hungarian Foreign Minister Meet', *RFE/RL News Briefs*, 3 (18–22 July 1994) p. 13.
117. Traynor, 'Neighbours bring Serbs in from cold'.
118. 'Hungary Concerned about New Croat–Serb War', *RFE/RL News Briefs*, 2 (19–23 July 1993) p. 18.
119. Oltay, 'Hungarians in Yugoslavia Seek Guarantees for Minority Rights', p. 43; and 'Federation of Hungarians in Croatia discuss autonomy endeavours', *Summary of World Broadcasts – Eastern Europe*, EE/1798 (20 September 1993) C/15.
120. Oltay, 'Hungarians in Yugoslavia Seek Guarantees for Minority Rights', p. 31; 'Hungary and Slovenia Sign Treaty', Weekly Review, *RFE/RL Research Report*, 1 (11 December 1992) p. 67; and 'Hungarian Parliament approves treaty with Croatia and Slovenia', *RFE/RL News Briefs*, 2 (1–5 November 1993) p. 13.
121. A. Reisch, 'Transcarpathia's Hungarian Minority and the Autonomy Issue', *RFE/RL Research Report*, 1 (7 February 1992) pp. 17–18.
122. A. Reisch, 'Hungary and Ukraine Agree to Upgrade Bilateral Relations', *Report on Eastern Europe*, 1 (2 November 1990) pp. 6–12.
123. A. Reisch, 'Hungary: Agreement Signed with Ukraine to Upgrade Bilateral Relations', *Report on Eastern Europe*, 2 (21 June 1991) p. 16.
124. A. Reisch, 'Transcarpathia and Its Neighbours', *RFE/RL Research Report*, 1 (14 February 1992) pp. 44–5.
125. Reisch, 'Transcarpathia's Hungarian Minority and the Autonomy Issue', p. 17.
126. A. Reisch, 'Hungarian–Ukrainian Relations Continue to Develop', *RFE/RL Research Report*, 2 (16 April 1993) pp. 22–3.
127. Reisch, 'Hungarian–Ukrainian Relations Continue to Develop', pp. 22–5.
128. 'Hungarian–Ukrainian Summit in Transcarpathia', *RFE/RL News Briefs*, 2 (3–7 May 1993) pp. 10–11.
129. 'Hungarian–Ukrainian Treaty Ratified', *RFE/RL News Briefs*, 2 (10–14 May 1993) p. 15.
130. Reisch, 'Hungarian–Ukrainian Relations Continue to Develop', p. 22.

131. 'Tractors for Ukrainian Arms?', Military and Security Notes, *RFE/RL Research Report*, 1 (28 February 1992) p. 52.
132. 'Cooperation Agreement with Ukraine', Military and Security Notes, *RFE/RL Research Report*, 1 (13 March 1992) p. 55.
133. 'Ukrainian Defense Minister visits Budapest', *RFE/RL News Briefs*, 3 (7–11 February 1994) p. 16.
134. 'Hungarian Defense Minister meets Ukrainian, Yugoslav Counterparts', *RFE/RL News Briefs*, 3 (16–19 August 1994) p. 10.
135. 'Hungarian–Ukrainian Relations Reviewed', Weekly Review, *RFE/RL Research Report*, 1 (8 May 1992) p. 61.
136. 'Ukrainian–Hungarian Commission on Minorities', Weekly Review, *RFE/RL Research Report*, 1 (14 August 1992) p. 71.
137. 'Hungarian–Ukrainian Joint Committee Meets', *RFE/RL News Briefs*, 2 (28 June–2 July 1993) pp. 10–11.
138. Reisch, 'Hungarian–Ukrainian Relations Continue to Develop', pp. 24–5; 'Transcarpathian Economic Free Zone Rejected', *RFE/RL News Briefs*, 2 (8–12 November 1993) p. 17; and 'Strife Among Transcarpathia's Ethnic Magyars', *RFE/RL News Briefs*, 3 (16–19 August 1994) p. 10.
139. E. Oltay, 'Hungarian Minority in Slovakia Sets Up Independent Organization', *Report on Eastern Europe*, 1 (16 March 1990) pp. 18–22; and E. Oltay, 'Hungarians in Slovakia Organize to Press for Ethnic Rights', *Report on Eastern Europe*, 1 (1 June 1990) pp. 21–7.
140. J. Obrman, 'Language Law Stirs Controversy in Slovakia', *Report on Eastern Europe*, 1 (16 November 1990) pp. 13–17; and A.A. Reisch, 'Hungarian Ethnic Parties Prepare for Czechoslovak Elections', *RFE/RL Research Report*, 1 (1 May 1992) p. 30.
141. A.A. Reisch, 'Hungarian Coalition Succeeds in Czechoslovak Elections', *RFE/RL Research Report*, 1 (26 June 1992) pp. 20–2; and A.A. Reisch, 'Meciar and Slovakia's Hungarian Minority', *RFE/RL Research Report*, 1 (30 October 1992) pp. 13–20.
142. A.A. Reisch, 'The Gabcikovo–Nagymaros Project: A Wasteland Awaiting the Fruits of Political Change', *Report on Eastern Europe*, 1 (26 January 1990) pp. 25–9.
143. P. Martin, 'The Gabcikovo–Nagymaros Dam Dilemma', *Report on Eastern Europe*, 2 (16 August 1991) pp. 6–11.
144. K. Okolicsanyi, 'Hungary Cancels Treaty on Danube Dam Construction', *RFE/RL Research Report*, 1 (26 June 1992) pp. 46–50.
145. K. Okolicsanyi, 'Slovak–Hungarian Tension: Bratislava Diverts the Danube', *RFE/RL Research Report*, 1 (11 December 1992) pp. 49–54.
146. 'End in sight to Danube dam row', *Financial Times* (30 October 1992); Okolicsanyi, 'Slovak–Hungarian Tension: Bratislava Diverts the Danube', p. 53; and T. Barber, 'Danube divides nations', *The Independent* (9 January 1993).
147. T. Szayna, *The Military in a Postcommunist Czechoslovakia*, A RAND Note, N-3412-USDP (Santa Monica, Cal.: The RAND Corporation, 1992) pp. 37–8.
148. A.A. Reisch, 'The Difficult Search for Hungarian–Slovak Accord', *RFE/RL Research Report*, 1 (23 October 1992) pp. 26–7.
149. Interview with Csaba Kiss.

150. Devlin, 'Hungary's New Defense Doctrine', p. 3.
151. Z.D. Barany, *Soldiers and Politics in Eastern Europe, 1945–90: The Case of Hungary* (Houndmills: Macmillan, 1993) p. 119.
152. Z.D. Barany, 'Major Reorganization of Hungary's Military Establishment', *RAD Background Report/230* (Radio Free Europe Research, Radio Free Europe/Radio Liberty, 28 December 1989) p. 3; and 'Apolitical role of Hungarian Guard', *Jane's Defence Weekly* (14 October 1980) pp. 80–5.
153. Barany, *Soldiers and Politics in Eastern Europe*, p. 129.
154. Sauerwein, 'Hungary's National Defense', p. 1219.
155. Interview with Dr. Istvan Gyarmati, Similar views were also expressed in an interview with the author by Imre Fulop and Andras Balogh, Institute for Strategic and Defence Studies, Ministry of Defence, Budapest, 30 November 1992.
156. 'Hungarian Parliament adopts New Defense Law', *RFE/RL News Briefs*, 2 (6–10 December 1993) p. 15; and R. Tutak, 'Hungarians to appoint single defence chief', *Jane's Defence Weekly* (5 March 1994).
157. 'Hungary to Cut Arms', *International Herald Tribune* (31 January 1989).
158. Devlin, 'Hungary's New Defense Doctrine', p. 3; and Clarke, 'Hungary Proposes Border Security Zones'.
159. 'The Military Doctrine of the Hungarian Republic', Lt-Gen, Laszlo Borsitcs, Chief of Staff of the Hungarian Army, to the Military Doctrine Seminar of the Talks on Confidence- and Security-Building Measures, Vienna, 19 January 1990, Documentation, *Survival* XXXII (March/April 1990) p. 178.
160. 'Premier Jozsef Antall Presents Government Programme', C1/10.
161. I. Volgyes and Z. Barany, 'Hungarian Defenders of the Homeland', Chapter 12 in J. Simon (ed.), *European Security Policy After the Revolutions of 1989* (Washington, DC: The National Defense University Press, 1991) p. 361.
162. *Hungarian Defence Policy: Basic Principles and Tasks*, Draft (Budapest: Ministry of Defence, 1992).
163. A.A. Reisch, 'The Hungarian Army in Transition', *RFE/RL Research Report*, 2 (5 March 1993) p. 44; and Interview with Csaba Kiss.
164. 'Defence Secretary Raffay Views Army Reforms Needs', *Foreign Broadcast Information Service – Eastern Europe 91–219*, (13 November 1991) p. 19.
165. Reisch, 'The Hungarian Army in Transition', pp. 44–5.
166. Interview with Csaba Kiss.
167. P. Dunay, *After the System Change: Hungary in the new European Security System* (Budapest: Department of International Law, Eotvos University, 1992) p. 13.
168. Reisch, 'The Hungarian Army in Transition', pp. 45–6.
169. Sauerwein, 'Hungary's National Defense', p. 1222.
170. Interview with Csaba Kiss.
171. Reisch, 'Hungary: Armed Forces Reorganized and 1991 Defence Budget Passed', pp. 18–19.
172. 'Defence Secretary Raffay Views Army Reform Needs', p. 19.

173. Reisch, 'The Hungarian Army in Transition', p. 47.
174. Reisch, 'The Hungarian Army in Transition', pp. 47–8; and Reisch, 'Hungary Acquires MiG-29s from Russia'.
175. 'MiGs for Budapest', *RFE/RL News Briefs*, 2 (1–4 June 1993) p. 15; and 'MiGs to Arrive in Hungary in Autumn', *RFE/RL News Briefs*, 2 (9–13 August 1993) p. 10.
176. Reisch, 'The Hungarian Army in Transition', pp. 48–9.
177. 'Foreign Minister Jeszenszky Presents Security Policy Report to Parliament', *Summary of World Broadcasts – Eastern Europe*, EE/1616 (18 February 1993) B/2.

7 East–Central Europe and the New European Security Order

1. P. Moore, 'Bratislava and Bonn: Two Conferences on Europe's Future', *Report on Eastern Europe*, 1 (11 May 1990) pp. 43–4; and J. Obrman, 'Czechoslovakia – Foreign Policy: Sources, Concepts, Problems', *Report on Eastern Europe*, 1 (14 September 1990) p. 13.
2. Hungary joined the Council of Europe in November 1990, Czechoslovakia in January 1991 and Poland in November 1991.
3. R.L. Tokes, 'From Visegrad to Krakow: Cooperation, Competition, and Coexistence in Central Europe', *Problems of Communism*, XL (Nov.– Dec. 1991) p. 104.
4. Tokes, 'From Visegrad to Krakow', p. 104; and J.B. Spero, *The Warsaw– Prague–Budapest Triangle: Central European Security After the Visegrad Summit*, Occasional Papers No. 31 (Warsaw: Polish Institute of International Affairs, 1992) p. 7.
5. J. Obrman, 'Czechoslovakia: Putting the Country Back on the Map', *Report on Eastern Europe*, 1 (28 December 1990) p. 13.
6. A. Reisch, 'Hungary: The Hard Task of Setting Relations with the USSR on a New Footing', *Report on Eastern Europe*, 2 (24 May 1991), pp. 9–11.
7. Text of the Visegrad Summit Declaration, *Report on Eastern Europe*, 2 (1 March 1991) pp. 31–2.
8. Tokes, 'From Visegrad to Krakow', p. 111.
9. Partnership with the Countries of Central and Eastern Europe, Statement issued by the North Atlantic Council meeting in Ministerial Session in Copenhagen on 6 and 7 June 1991, *NATO Review*, 39 (June 1991) p. 28.
10. 'NATO tells Moscow not to interfere', *The Times* (4 July 1991).
11. 'Weapons Ban Lifted on Czechs, Hungarians and Poles', *Periscope – Daily Defense News Capsules* (6 August 1991).
12. Tokes, 'From Visegrad to Krakow', p. 112; D.M. Perry, 'The Attempted Coup in the USSR: East European Reactions', *Report on Eastern Europe*, 2 (30 August 1991) p. 2; 'Poland, Czechoslovakia, and Hungary Discuss Crisis', Weekly Record of Events, 20 August, *Report on Eastern Europe*, 2 (30 August 1991) p. 46; L. Vinton, 'The Attempted Coup in the Soviet Union: East European Reactions – Poland', *Report on Eastern Europe*, 2 (30 August 1991) p. 12; and 'President Urges Faster EC Association', Weekly Record of Events, 25 August, *Report on Eastern Europe*, 2 (6 September 1991) p. 40.

13. 'The Situation in the Soviet Union', Statement issued by the North Atlantic Council meeting in Ministerial Session at NATO Headquarters, Brussels, on 21 August 1991, *NATO Review*, 39 (August 1991) p. 9. (The emphasis is added.)

14. I. Traynor, 'Fledgling market economies look to EC to end trade curbs', *The Guardian* (21 August 1991).

15. 'The Cracow Declaration', *European Security*, 1 (Spring 1992) pp. 104–6.

16. 'Visegrad Triangle Foreign Ministers Meet EC Counterparts Before Prague Summit' and 'Conclusions of Visegrad Triangle Summit: Joint Application to Join EC', *Summary of World Broadcasts – Eastern Europe*, EE/1375 (8 May 1992) A2/1–2.

17. K. Okolicsanyi, 'The Visegrad Triangle's Free-Trade Zone', *RFE/RL Research Report*, 1 (15 January 1993) p. 19.

18. M.A. Vachudova, 'The Visegrad Four: No Alternative to Cooperation?', *RFE/RL Research Report*, 2 (27 August 1993) p. 41.

19. D.J. Bartyzel, 'Knocking on the EC Door', *Warsaw Voice* (8 November 1992).

20. Okolicsanyi, 'The Visegrad Triangle's Free-Trade Zone', pp. 19–22.

21. Tokes, 'From Visegrad to Krakow'.

22. Text of the Visegrad Summit Declaration, pp. 31–2.

23. J.B. de Weydenthal, 'The Cracow Summit', *Report on Eastern Europe*, 2 (25 October 1991) p. 29.

24. 'Poland, Hungary, CSFR To Sign Treaty With EEC', *Foreign Broadcast Information Service – Eastern Europe 91-218* (12 November 1991) p. 1.

25. '"Triangle" Countries Seek Faster NATO Links', Military and Security Notes, *RFE/RL Research Report*, 1 (10 April 1992) p. 46.

26. Vachudova, 'The Visegrad Four: No Alternative to Cooperation?', p. 41.

27. D.L. Clarke, 'Central Europe: Military Cooperation in the Triangle', *RFE/RL Research Report*, 1 (10 January 1992) pp. 42–3.

28. Clarke, 'Central Europe: Military Cooperation in the Triangle', pp. 44–5; and '"State of Military Readiness" Maintained during Soviet Coup', Weekly Record of Events, 28 August, *Report on Eastern Europe*, 2 (6 September 1991) p. 41.

29. '"Triangle" Defense Ministers Meet', Military and Security Notes, *RFE/RL Research Report*, 1 (20 March 1992) pp. 49–50; and 'Hungary/Poland/Czechoslovakia: Cooperation in Defence', *Atlantic News*, No. 2404 (11 March 1992) p. 2.

30. Clarke, 'Central Europe: Military Cooperation in the Triangle', p. 44.

31. Vachudova, 'The Visegrad Four: No Alternative to Cooperation?', pp. 41–2.

32. 'Visegrad Group Appeals for EC Membership', *RFE/RL News Briefs*, 2 (7–11 June 1993) p. 13.

33. 'Visegrad Defense Officials Meet in Poland', *RFE/RL News Briefs*, 2 (6–10 September 1993) pp. 13–14.

34. G. Kolankiewicz, 'Consensus and Competition in the Eastern Enlargement of the European Union', *International Affairs*, 70 (July 1994) p. 484.

35. I. Traynor, J. Borger and S. Tisdall, 'East European quartet out of synch over NATO', *The Guardian* (7 January 1994).

36. A. LeBor, 'Poles accuse Czechs of hijacking prestige visit', *The Times* (12 January 1994).
37. Kolankiewicz, 'Consensus and Competition in the Eastern Enlargement of the European Union', p. 480.
38. J. Palmer, 'EU decides on East Europe's favoured few for early entry', *The Guardian* (5 October 1994).
39. J. Palmer, 'Six ex-communist states take big step towards EU', *The Guardian* (1 November 1994).
40. J. Palmer, 'Slovenes and Czechs head long line to join EU,' *The Guardian* (24 September 1994).
41. Z. Brzezinski, 'Security is a warm embrace', *The Guardian* (5 May 1994); and I. Black, 'Six must wait for EU date', *The Guardian* (5 November 1994).
42. 'Visegrad Countries to speed up Free Trade Timetable', *RFE/RL News Briefs*, 3 (7–11 February 1994).
43. 'Havel on Visegrad', *RFE/RL News Briefs*, 2 (6–10 September 1993) p. 19.
44. 'The Cracow Declaration', pp. 104–5.
45. J. Pinder, *The European Community and Eastern Europe* (London: Pinter Publishers/The Royal Institute of International Affairs, 1991) p. 70.
46. H. Kramer, 'The EC and the Stabilisation of Eastern Europe', *Aussenpolitik*, 43 (1992) p. 17.
47. J.B. de Weydenthal, 'Czechoslovakia, Hungary, and Poland Gain Associate Membership in the EC', *RFE/RL Research Report*, 1 (7 February 1992) p. 24.
48. 'Visegrad Triangle Foreign Ministers Meet EC Counterparts before Prague Summit', *Summary of World Broadcasts – Eastern Europe*, EE/1375 (8 May 1992) A2/1.
49. A. Podraza, *The Western European Union and Central Europe: A New Relationship*, RIIA Discussion Papers No. 41 (London: The Royal Institute of International Affairs, 1992) p. 21.
50. '"Visegrad Three"-EC Meeting', Weekly Review, *RFE/RL Research Report*, 1 (15 May 1992) p. 61.
51. L. Barber, 'EC to seek pacts with ex-Soviet republics', *Financial Times* (6 October 1992).
52. 'Visegrad Three–EC Talks in London: Readiness for "intensification of Dialogue"', *Summary of World Broadcasts – Eastern Europe*, EE/1526 (31 October 1992) A1/2; and J.B. de Weydenthal, 'EC Keeps Central Europe at Arm's Length', *RFE/RL Research Report*, 2 (29 January 1993) p. 29.
53. A. Marshall, 'EC to improve links with East Europe', *The Independent* (29 October 1992).
54. P. Webster, 'Summit opens door to former Soviet states', *The Times* (23 June 1993).
55. J.B. de Weydenthal, 'East–Central Europe and the EU: Forging Political Ties', *RFE/RL Research Report*, 3 (22 July 1994) p. 17; and M. Jopp, *The Strategic Implications of European Integration*, Adelphi Paper 290 (London: Brassey's for the International Institute for Strategic Studies, July 1994) pp. 55–6.
56. J. Palmer, 'EU decides on East Europe's favoured few for early entry',

The Guardian (5 October 1994); and Palmer, 'Six ex-communist states take big step towards EU'.

57. D. Gardner, 'EU to draw up plan for admitting six eastern members', *Financial Times* (5 October 1994).

58. 'French Proposal for a Pact on Stability in Europe', in Stockholm International Peace Research Institute, *SIPRI Yearbook 1994* (Oxford: Oxford University Press, 1994) pp. 247–9.

59. 'Europeans' Security Talks Expose Broad Differences', *International Herald Tribune* (27 May 1994).

60. Jopp, *The Strategic Implications of European Integration*, pp. 52–4; and A.D. Rotfeld, 'Europe: Towards a New Regional Security Regime', Chapter 7 in Stockholm International Peace Research Institute, *SIPRI Yearbook 1994* (Oxford: Oxford University Press, 1994) pp. 220–2.

61. Podraza, *The Western European Union and Central Europe*, p. 28.

62. Communiqué, WEU Council of Ministers, Bonn, 18 November 1991, (London: Peace Through NATO, Text 026, 1991) pp. 1–2.

63. Podraza, *The Western European Union and Central Europe*, p. 29–30.

64. Jopp, *The Strategic Implications of European Integration*, pp. 51–2.

65. 'Special Status for East Europeans in WEU', *RFE/RL News Briefs*, 2 (29 November–3 December 1993) p. 14.

66. De Weydenthal, 'East–Central Europe and the EU: Forging Political Ties', p. 17.

67. J. Palmer, 'EU defence arm embraces the east', *The Guardian* (11 November 1994).

68. Jopp, *The Strategic Implications of European Integration*, pp. 51–2.

69. 'Declaration of the Member States of the Western European Union issued on the occasion of the 46th European Council meeting on 9 and 10 December 1991 at Maastricht', Annexe D in N. Gantz and J. Roper (eds), *Towards a New Partnership: US–European relations in the post-Cold War era* (Paris: The Institute for Security Studies, Western European Union, 1993) p. 228.

70. 'WEU signs Danube Blockade Accord', *RFE/RL News Briefs*, 2 (14–21 May 1993) p. 19.

71. 'London Declaration on a Transformed North Atlantic Alliance', Documentation, *NATO Review*, 38 (August 1990) p. 32.

72. M. Walker, 'Links to NATO for Eastern Europe', *The Guardian* (4 October 1991).

73. 'The Cracow Declaration', p. 105.

74. 'Statement made at Cracow on 5 October 1991 by the three Ministers for Foreign Affairs Concerning Cooperation with the North Atlantic Treaty Organization', Annex II to UN General Assembly Document A/C.1/46/7 (United Nations, 1991).

75. 'Havel rebuffed on NATO links', *The Times* (24 October 1991); and 'Hungary's Leader Seeks Closer Ties to NATO', *International Herald Tribune* (29 October 1991).

76. 'NATO plans forum with former enemies in East', *The Independent* (1 November 1991).

77. 'Rome Declaration on Peace and Cooperation', Documentation, *NATO Review*, 39 (December 1991) pp. 20–1.

78. 'North Atlantic Cooperation Council Statement on Dialogue, Partnership and Cooperation', Documentation, *NATO Review*, 40 (February 1992) pp. 29–30.
79. D. Gow and H. Pick, 'Germany pushes NATO further East', *The Guardian* (8 January 1992); and 'Work Plan for Dialogue, Partnership and Cooperation', Documentation, *NATO Review*, 40 (April 1992) pp. 34–5.
80. 'Statement Issued at the Meeting of Defence Ministers at NATO Headquarters, Brussels on 1st April, 1992', Documentation, *NATO Review*, 40 (April 1992) pp. 31–3.
81. 'NATO's Woerner Discusses East European Security', *Foreign Broadcast Information Service – Eastern Europe 91-218* (12 November 1991) p. 21.
82. 'Work Plan for Dialogue, Partnership and Cooperation', p. 34.
83. 'Statement Issued at the Meeting of Defence Ministers at NATO Headquarters, Brussels on 1st April, 1992', p. 32.
84. Interviews in Poland, November 1992. NATO defence ministers noted in 1992 that 'a considerable proportion of our defence-related cooperation effort involves the provision of specific practical expertise to individual partners, both by NATO and by individual Allies'. 'Defence Planning Committee Communiqué', Documentation, *NATO Review*, 40 (December 1992) p. 32.
85. J. Palmer, 'NATO and CIS plan treaty to cut conventional forces in Europe', *The Guardian* (11 March 1992).
86. 'Communiqué issued by the Ministerial Meeting of the North Atlantic Council, Brussels, 17 December 1992', Documentation, *NATO Review*, 40 (December 1992) p. 30.
87. 'Communiqué of the Ministerial meeting of the North Atlantic Council in Oslo, 4th June 1992', Documentation, *NATO Review*, 40 (June 1992) p. 31; and 'Communiqué issued by the Ministerial Meeting of the North Atlantic Council, Brussels, 17 December 1992', Documentation, *NATO Review*, 40 (December 1992) pp. 28–9.
88. 'Statement issued at the Meeting of the North Atlantic Cooperation Council, Brussels, 18 December 1992', Documentation, *NATO Review*, 41 (February 1993) p. 28.
89. 'Work Plan for Dialogue, Partnership and Cooperation 1993, Issued at the Meeting of the North Atlantic Cooperation Council held at NATO Headquarters, Brussels on 18 December 1992', Documentation, *NATO Review*, 41 (February 1993) p. 30.
90. 'Meeting of the North Atlantic Cooperation Council, Athens, Greece, 11 June 1993, Report to Ministers by the NACC Ad Hoc Group on Cooperation in Peacekeeping', Documentation, *NATO Review*, 41 (August 1993).
91. Interview with Dr. Slawomir Dabrowa, Deputy Director, Department of European Institutions, Ministry of Foreign Affairs, Warsaw, 12 November 1992.
92. 'Secret talks', *The Daily Telegraph* (17 June 1992).
93. Interview with Dr. Janusz Prystrom, Polish Institute of International Affairs, Warsaw, 9 November 1992.
94. '"Triangle" Countries seek faster NATO links', Military and Security Notes, *RFE/RL Research Report*, 1 (10 April 1992) p. 46.

95. 'Visegrad Triangle Foreign Ministers Meet EC Counterparts Before Prague Summit' and 'Conclusions of Visegrad Triangle Summit' A2/1–2.
96. A.A. Reisch, 'Central and Eastern Europe's Quest for NATO Membership', *RFE/RL Research Report*, 2 (9 July 1993) pp. 44–6.
97. 'Woerner: East Europeans might join NATO', Military and Security Notes, *RFE/RL Research Report*, 1 (20 March 1992) p. 50.
98. 'US Secretary of Defense Recommends NATO Membership for Central Europe', Military and Security Notes, *RFE/RL Research Report*, 1 (13 November 1992) p. 63.
99. V. Ruhe, 'Shaping Euro-Atlantic Policies', *Survival*, 35 (Summer 1993) p. 135.
100. Reisch, 'Central and Eastern Europe's Quest for NATO Membership', p. 45.
101. 'Russian President Boris Yeltsin's letter to US President Bill Clinton, 15 September 1993', in Stockholm International Peace Research Institute, *SIPRI Yearbook 1994* (Oxford: Oxford University Press, 1994) pp. 249–50.
102. 'Meeting of NATO Defence Ministers, Travemunde, 20–21 October 1993', *NATO Review*, 41 (December 1993) p. 24; and Rotfeld, 'Europe: towards a New Regional Security Regime', pp. 215–16.
103. 'Partnership for Peace: Invitation'; 'Partnership for Peace Framework Document', and 'Declaration of Heads of State and Government participating in the meeting of the North Atlantic Council held at NATO Headquarters, Brussels, on 10–11 January 1994', *NATO Review*, 42 (February 1994) pp. 28–33.
104. 'Declaration of Heads of State and Government participating in the meeting of the North Atlantic Council held at NATO Headquarters, Brussels, on 10–11 January 1994', pp. 30–1.
105. 'NATO and Russia to work together for European security', *NATO Review*, 42 (August 1994) p. 5.
106. 'Declaration of Heads of State and Government participating in the meeting of the North Atlantic Council held at NATO Headquarters, Brussels, on 10–11 January 1994, p. 32.
107. Address by Willy Claes, Secretary-General of NATO, at the 40th Assembly of the Atlantic Treaty Association, The Hague, Netherlands, 28 October 1994 (Brussels: NATO Press Service, 1994) p. 3.
108. J. Freedland, 'US spurs NATO's Eastward Growth', *The Guardian* (28 October 1994).
109. *Charter of Paris for a New Europe, 16 November 1990*, pp. 1–6 and pp. 17–18.
110. Interview with Dr. Istvan Gyarmati, Director, Department of Security Policy and European Cooperation, Ministry of Foreign Affairs, Budapest, 1 December 1992.
111. Interview with Prince Karel Schwarzenberg, Chancellor of the Office of the President, Czechoslovakia, London, 26 January 1992.
112. R. Kionka, 'The CSCE and the Baltic States', *Report on the USSR*, 2 (23 November 1990); and S.R. Burant, 'Polish–Lithuanian Relations: Past, Present, and Future', *Problems of Communism*, XL (May–June 1991) pp. 4 and 6.

113. *The Arms Control Report 1991* (Cambridge, Mass.: Institute for Defense and Disarmament Studies, 1991) pp. 402.B.280.3–4 and p. 402.B.280.11; and M. Fisher, 'Security Talks Settle on a Compromise', *International Herald Tribune* (21 June 1991).

114. Interview with Ambassador Nils Eliasson, Director, CSCE Secretariat, Prague, 20 November 1992.

115. *CSCE Helsinki Document 1992: The Challenges of Change*, pp. 7–24.

116. 'Shaping a New Europe – The Role of the CSCE, Summary and Conclusions of the Stockholm Council Meeting, Stockholm, 15 December 1992', in Stockholm International Peace Research Institute, *SIPRI Yearbook 1993: World Armaments and Disarmament* (Oxford: Oxford University Press, 1993) pp. 212–18.

117. 'Decisions of the Rome CSCE Council Meeting, Fourth Meeting of the CSCE Council, Rome, 1 December 1992', in Stockholm International Peace Research Institute, *SIPRI Yearbook 1994* (Oxford: Oxford University Press, 1994) pp. 257–64.

118. As noted above it was a Czechoslovak initiative which led to the 'consensus-minus-one' rule agreed at the June 1991 Berlin CSCE Council meeting. See also 'New Hungarian Proposal on Expanded Role for CSCE in Conflict Prevention and Crisis Management', *European Security*, 1 (Summer 1992) pp. 239–47.

119. Interview with Ambassador Miroslav Polreich, Head of Delegation, and Pavol Hamzik, Councillor, Czechoslovak Delegation to the CSCE Forum on Security Cooperation, Vienna, 6 October 1992.

120. D. Shorr, 'CSCE Tries Preventive Diplomacy in Several Hot Spots', *Basic Reports*, 26 (9 November 1992) pp. 1–4; and D. Shorr, 'Progress Reported for One of Two Conflicts in Georgia' and 'CSCE Action on Moldova Awaits Envoy's Meeting with Yeltsin', *BASIC Reports*, 27 (23 December 1992) p. 1.

121. Rotfeld, 'Europe: Towards a New Regional Security Regime', p. 228.

122. 'The Cracow Declaration', p. 106.

123. Interview with Csaba Kiss, Head of Defence Policy Planning Department, Ministry of Defence, Budapest, 2 December 1992.

124. J.M.O. Sharp, 'Conventional Arms Control in Europe', Chapter 13 in Stockholm International Peace Research Institute, *SIPRI Yearbook 1991: World Armaments and Disarmament* (Oxford: Oxford University Press, 1991) pp. 410–11 and p. 420.

125. Sharp, 'Conventional Arms Control in Europe', pp. 455–6; J. MacIntosh, 'Confidence-Building Measures in Europe: 1975 to the Present', in R.D. Burns (ed.), *Encyclopedia of Arms Control and Disarmament*, Volume II (New York: Charles Scribner's and Sons, 1993) pp. 941–3; and P.M. Lewis, 'The Treaty on Open Skies', *Bulletin of Arms Control*, 10 (May 1993) pp. 13–15.

126. Z. Lachowski, 'Implementation of the Vienna Document 1990 in 1991', Appendix 12A in Stockholm International Peace Research Institute, *SIPRI Yearbook 1992: World Armaments and Disarmament* (Oxford: Oxford University Press, 1992) p. 486; and Interview with senior official, CSCE Conflict Prevention Centre, Vienna, 6 October 1992.

127. *The Arms Control Report 1992* (Cambridge, Mass.: Institute for Defense

and Disarmament Studies, 1992) p. 402.B.310; and interview with Mr. Deszo Horvath, Deputy Head, Hungarian Delegation, CSCE Forum on Security Cooperation, 5 October 1992.

128. Interview with senior official, Polish delegation, CSCE Forum on Security Cooperation, Vienna, 7 October 1992.
129. Z. Lachowski, 'Conventional Arms Control and Security Cooperation in Europe', Chapter 14 in Stockholm International Peace Research Institute, *SIPRI Yearbook 1994* (Oxford: Oxford University Press, 1994) pp. 583–93.
130. Interview with senior official, United States delegation, CSCE Forum on Security Cooperation, Vienna, 5 October 1992.
131. D. Hearst, 'Russia seeks European security deal', *The Guardian* (7 May 1994).

Index